THE CRAIGHILLS OF CHINA

Marian G. Craighill

MARIAN G. CRAIGHILL

TRINITY PRESS

708 BETHLEHEM PIKE, AMBLER, PA. 19002

I am greatly indebted to Mr. I-Hsiung Ju of the Art Department of Washington and Lee University for designing the cover of this book.

Marian G. Craighill

THE CRAIGHILLS OF CHINA

© 1972 BY

TRINITY PRESS

708 BETHLEHEM PIKE, AMBLER, PA. 19002

ISBN 0-912046-08-2

Printed in the United States of America

Rt. Rev. Lloyd R. Craighill, 1940.

This book is dedicated to the memory of my husband Rt. Rev. Lloyd R. Craighill, Retired, Bishop of the Episcopal Diocese of Anking, China.

TABLE OF CONTENTS

FOREWORD

This is not a formal history or biography nor was it the author's intention that it be so. We are given the privilege of seeing in detail the intimate life of two missionaries who had the good fortune to live for nineteen years in the old Chinese city of Nanchang where life moved in ancient patterns, an unsophisticated life that involved them in a truly oriental environment. We have the day by day experience of two westerners who knew the joy of Chinese friendships.

Nanchang became the crossroads of military activities as Chiang Kai Shek made his headquarters there; and the city was surrounded by gangs of marauding bandits. Thus the situation became always more dangerous, and the book gives a vivid account of history in the making.

Mrs. Craighill is a born raconteuse; the pages are vibrant with activities great and small and her letters home sparkle with humor. Here is the authentic flavor of the countryside: its color, beauty, smells, and the sturdy character of the Chinese peasant.

In the latter years Mr. Craighill was the only western clergyman in the vast Diocese of Anking and consequently bore heavy responsibilities. Thus, at Bishop Huntington's retirement in 1940 when Lloyd Craighill was elected second Bishop of the Diocese, he brought a rich experience, won through many difficulties, to this broader work. Indeed the whole book speaks of dangerous opportunity met with imagination and courage.

This is not only a glimpse into history in the making. It is also a love story on two levels; one the personal and private life, the other a warm relationship with the Chinese people, the humble, the official class, the students and the Church members.

The singularly harmonious personal life moved in an outreach of concern where people and events of an oriental culture met the western one in a rich interchange.

In the words of Antoine de Saint Exupery, life had taught them "that love does not consist in looking at each other but in looking outward together in the same direction."

Virginia H. Huntington
Cambridge, Mass. October 1971

PREFACE

Three days before my husband died suddenly on March 13, 1971, we attended a Lenten Lecture at the R. E. Lee Memorial Church, conducted by Bishop Marmion. The subject was the loss of a sense of value of the individual in this present age, and of his alienation from society. After the lecture there was a good deal of discussion about the effect of technology on the life of today, but almost nothing about the effect wrought on individuals by sociological change. I noticed that Lloyd's hand went up and he evidently had something he wanted to say, but as we sat far to the right of the leader he went unnoticed. Later I asked him what he would have said if he had had an opportunity. He answered, as nearly as I can remember: "I wanted to say that we are losing a sense of God and His direct relationship with each individual. It is the belief that God cares for each one of us which makes for a sense of a man's value as a human being and frees him from a feeling of isolation from others." This was the underlying faith of Bishop Craighill and that is what his life expressed.

*   *   *   *   *   *   *

We ended our story with our farewell to China in 1948 and 1949 as the Communists were taking over. After that time we lived full happy lives together for twenty-two years, and while we remained very much "The Craighills of China" in our hearts, we also became deeply involved in life in this country. For the first six years, from 1950 on, Lloyd was rector of a very old parish in Maryland, founded in 1692. The present church of St. James was built in 1767, and many of the parishioners traced their ancestry to the early days of the settlement there. We loved the old church building, surrounded by trees which overhung the churchyard. We were glad the rectory was modern and very comfortable, and also that we were near Virginia Seminary where our sons were studying for the priesthood. Before we left our relationship with the parish was one of mutual trust and affection.

At the end of those years in Maryland we moved to Lexington, Virginia where we had built a brown shingled house with a red door to signify "Welcome" in the Chinese manner. Here we "dropped anchor" as the Chinese say, after our turbulent years in China, and here Lloyd found again many old friends, some of them those with whom he had gone camping while he was in college. How thankful we have been that we had chosen this place for our retirement, where we found such a welcome and made a very easy adjustment. We were near Lynchburg, too, where Lloyd's sister and her husband, the Rev. and Mrs. William Marshall are living, as well as many other relatives whom we see there and at camp.

We were able to fulfill the desire of our hearts and travel in Europe together, which we had never done before. In 1959 we had two wonderful months in England, Scotland and on the continent. It added a new dimension to our lives and we lived those days over as we read my journal together in later years.

We went around the world twice, too, largely because our family was so scattered. Both our sons followed their father's vocation as missionaries under the Episcopal Church, and both are working on their doctorates. All our three have married the children of missionaries. A family reunion in 1969 brought all our children, grandchildren and even one great-grandchild together at Mountain Rest, a summer home for missionaries in Massachusetts, so Lloyd saw them all in a wonderfully happy and memorable week.

I can't look at the mountains without thinking of his joy in them, and his thankfulness that we had a view of them from our porch where he loved to sit in the years since 1967 after a stroke had crippled him. He never let himself become an invalid, and in spite of the difficulties involved in walking he went to church each Sunday. His courage and sheer determination in these last years bore a triumphant witness to his faith and made him a tower of strength for others.

He wanted me to include these verses I wrote for him on his 83rd birthday because he said it showed the spirit in which we both were accepting the limitations of these years, the final ones of his life.

"To have to learn the limits of affliction
And keep your spirits cheerful as before;
To have to lay aside your many duties
And still not find your days are just a bore;
To keep abreast of what the world is doing
As well as what is happening at home
And still have faith and courage for the future,
Remembering we do not stand alone.
To feel response to every sight of beauty;
To find a bit of good in every man;
To find your friends a constant source of pleasure;
To be the Elder Statesman of the Clan;
Thankful each day for all your many blessings,
Though never blind to tragedy and fear;
Still keeping for your wife your heart's devotion,
That's you at eighty-three, my very dear."

ACKNOWLEDGEMENT

This book would not have been written if it hadn't been for the urging of the Historian of the Diocese of Southwest Virginia, Dr. Brewster Ford, of the English Faculty of Virginia Military Institute who wished to add the story of Bishop Craighill's life in China to the "Living History" series of the diocese. Since it was impossible for Bishop Craighill to undertake it at this time, I have tried to do this, making use of the many letters I wrote my family for a period of twenty-five years, from 1915-1940. Dr. Ford came each week throughout the winter to tape the script and the letters, and Mrs. Ford typed the whole manuscript as a labor of love. I can't adequately express my gratitude for the help they have given me, nor my thankfulness that Bishop Craighill heard all of it and contributed to it before his death.

My sons and daughters-in-law have been of the greatest assistance in their suggestions and editing. Dr. William A. Jenks, head of the History Department at Washington and Lee University has also read the script and encouraged me to think our story would be of interest to people outside the family. Mrs. D. T. Huntington, wife of the Bishop of Anking who preceded my husband, has written the introduction as only she could do it, with her knowledge of the diocese and the people and her great literary ability. Maryly Craighill the wife of our older son, Lloyd, Jr., has read the proof. Betty Brewbaker has given the manuscript its second typing, for which I am most grateful.

Much of this book was a family enterprise and I hope it will prove a fitting memorial to the head of the family, who inspired all of it.

Marian G. Craighill
Lexington, Va.
October, 1971

SECTION I

BEGINNINGS IN AMERICA AND CHINA

1886-1925

I

Lloyd Rutherford Craighill was born in 1886 in Lynchburg, Virginia—the fourth child in a family of five: three brothers and two sisters. It was a very warm, demonstratively loving family circle in which he was fortunate to belong. He remembers that each member of the family greeted every other member with a good morning kiss, something which must sound apocryphal to modernday youngsters. His father, George P. Craighill was one of nine brothers and sisters. The first of the Craighill family to come from Scotland lived in Westmoreland County in the Northern Neck, but two generations later, William Price Craighill, who was incidentally a close friend and neighbor of Pres. Monroe as well as of the Washingtons, evidently impressed by the beautiful greenness and fertility of the northern end of the Valley of Virginia, settled in Charles Town, which became a part of West Virginia after the Civil War. There the family lived and intermarried with members of that locality for three generations. His grandfather, William Nathaniel Craighill, married Sarah Elizabeth Brown and through her mother they became descendants of Robert Rutherford, a friend of Washington and a leading citizen of that area.

His father, born in 1851, was too young to join the army of the Confederacy, but he often told the family of pressing through the crowd to see John Brown hanged after the raid on Harper's Ferry. The Civil War had a great impact on this family, as it did on everyone of that era in Virginia. Three of the brothers enlisted in the Confederate army, but the oldest son, a West Point graduate who was second in his class and who

1

subsequently had a distinguished career stayed with the Union army. It must have been a heartbreaking decision for him to have made, and they have always understood that he arranged never to go into combat duty with the danger that he would be in an engagement fighting one of his own brothers. This same Uncle Willie became Chief of U.S. Engineers after the war, and eventually retired to Charles Town, where he was a very respected citizen and active member of Zion Church. A large window there is dedicated to his memory. Zion Church might be called the ancestral temple of the Craighill family, for here generations have found their final resting place in the church yard.

Three of the Craighill brothers moved to Lynchburg after the war. Possibly the fact that Charles Town became a part of West Virginia had something to do with that. The older sons had had a chance for a formal education before the war. One was a doctor and one a lawyer, but Lloyd's father had no such opportunity. He managed, however, to study chemistry under a doctor in Cincinnati and became chief chemist in the tanning extract factory of his brother-in-law.

Chemistry was his vocation, but reading was his avocation. His house was full of books, and these were constantly having additions. He not only bought books but read them, so that at his untimely death at the age of 51 the library numbered over 3,000 volumes. There was little else in the way of assets.

Lloyd's mother, Lydia Eliza Langhorne, was from a well known family in that part of Virginia. His grandfather Maurice Langhorne had wooed and won a member of the distinguished Morris family of Philadelphia, Elizabeth Giles Morris, when he was visiting his brother, a medical student at the University of Pennsylvania. His mother kept her close relationship with her family even though separated by many miles, and eventually by the Mason Dixon line. It was right after the Civil War that she

2

sent three of her younger children by packet boat and train to Philadelphia to be cared for by her parents. Lloyd has a photograph of that trio, decked out in the finery which that city could offer even at the end of the war, when people in the South were fashioning costumes of window draperies—if they had them.

Lloyd's father and mother were active members of Grace Church, Lynchburg, and it was there that he came under the influence of Dr. John Lloyd. It was through Dr. Lloyd and his wonderful saintly life that he saw clearly what it meant to be a Christian and probably had the inspiration which later led him to study for the ministry. His father's death came while he was in his senior year at high school at a time when both his older brothers were away from home, one finishing at V.M.I., the other a clergyman about to be married. It meant that he had to put aside all thought of college at that time and undertake, as best he could, to help out the family income. He worked in a real estate office in Lynchburg and there learned how to keep books, which was a most valuable asset in his years in China. He also may have learned something about patience, and he certainly learned how to live economically and still happily. The family had to eke out their scant income in every possible way. His mother and sisters even organized a lending library of their books. Through it all, in spite of financial difficulties, they had a happy home life with much simple entertaining and a great deal of companionship. Grandpa Langhorne had given each daughter, as she married, a piece of property, on which they built their homes, so they were surrounded by kin folk of all ages, many of whom were helpful to them. Lloyd used to go to dances given by the first class at Sweet Briar and since there was no passenger service to Lynchburg at the hour the dances were over, the men would board a freight train and arrive in the city in their tuxedos at an early hour in the morning, a rather startling sight.

3

It seemed at times as though this state of affairs might continue indefinitely—but after six years the break came. The Rev. Cosby Bell had married a sister of his brother Peyton's wife, and they were interested and sympathetic with his desire for further study. About this time they had moved to Lexington where Mr. Bell was rector of R. E. Lee Memorial Church. There it was that they offered to take him into their home at the rectory to board at such a nominal fee that the family were able to swing it. In 1909 he entered Washington and Lee and began the career which would eventually lead him to the China mission. That year with Cosby and Nancy Bell was one of the truly formative experiences of his life. He was in daily contact with minds deeply informed, responsive to beauty in nature and art and poetry, interested in world movements, and with convictions which enabled them to meet every experience as mature Christians. Cosby's influence in the Virginia Seminary is well known and needs no enlargement here. Lloyd felt that he was greatly blessed in having been a member of that household for his first year in college, and when he went to Virginia Seminary two years later, where Cosby had become Professor of Theology, the strength and lucidity of his teaching influenced Lloyd's thinking throughout his life. "As Cosby Bell used to say" came naturally to his lips in meeting any theological problem.

During his next two years at college he lived in another of Lexington's beautiful old houses, Stono, which was owned jointly by Dr. John Campbell and his sister-in-law, Miss Bertha Howell. Dr. Campbell was a Virginia gentleman of the best of that tradition, and Miss Bertha a most interesting character—of Philadelphia background, well read, and very eccentric. These older people who were close to him in his college years have been mentioned but he also made friends with the younger crowd in Lexington, and because he never lived on campus, this group of town men and girls became closer friends than did his classmates. One very pleasant aspect of that was that on his return to Lexington for retirement in 1956, he found many dear friends of his college years still living here, making it very easy for the Craighills to become a part of the Lexington community.

Lloyd R. Craighill on graduation, 1912.

Because of his eagerness to get ahead with his education he was able to finish college in three years, with a Phi Beta Kappa key dangling at his watch fob. He entered Virginia Seminary in the class of 1915. The physical aspect of the Seminary hadn't changed much since Civil War days. They had little wood stoves in their rooms, and brought up the wood for them from the basement. Their bath house was a building detached from the dormitory, where all the plumbing appliances were installed. At the time he entered seminary he used to recall that he wheeled his trunk to Aspinwall Hall in a wheelbarrow.

These details, which sound so primitive to modern ears, were by no means what he remembered most about his Seminary life, where he found great mental and spiritual stimulation, as well as a close fellowship with faculty and students. Among his intimate friends were William Marshall who later married his sister Wistar, Herbert Tucker, William Byrd Lee, Jr., Jeff Allfriend, and Norman Binstead, who became a Bishop in Japan and after that the Bishop of the Philippines.

At that time, as well as in the years preceding and after his time there, the Seminary was one of the greatest seed beds for

5

the Overseas Missions of the Church. All the Overseas Mission Fields in the Episcopal Church were started by alumni of Virginia Seminary. In Prayer Hall in his day the walls were hung with photographs of every man who had gone from the Seminary to missions overseas, and they were prayed for by name in succession. During his final year at Seminary they had a visit from the Rev. Edmund Lee who was a missionary from Anking, China. He stayed at the Seminary for several days. After his presentation of the work in the Missionary District of Anking and his call for volunteers, Lloyd decided that he would apply for appointment as a missionary in that district. In due time, he was appointed, said farewell to his family and friends gathered at his brother's camp at Rockbridge Baths near Lexington in the summer of 1915, and started out on his long trip to China.

As a requirement for his canonical examination he had been asked by the Seminary to write a paper about the graduates of Virginia Seminary who had been members of the China Mission, starting with Bishop William J. Boone, who was among the first group of Episcopalians to arrive in Shanghai in 1859. That marked the beginning of the mission to China of the Episcopal Church. It made a most interesting and instructive study for me and I absorbed it the hard way, by typing this paper for Lloyd to send back to the Seminary in 1918. Evidently there had not been a requirement that it be finished before he was ordained to the priesthood in 1916.

He learned during the study for this paper some of the fundamental facts about our mission in China of which he would be a member. The first missionary district, that of Shanghai at the mouth of the Yangtze River, had been expanded through the years into the three districts which were there on our arrival in China. The Shanghai District with St. John's University and Medical School, St. Elizabeth's Hospital and St. Mary's School, as well as many parishes throughout the

6

city of Shanghai, extended up river to include Nanking, as well as several other large cities. The District of Anking which was west of that, was the one to which Lloyd had been assigned, and where the most important city was that of Anking though the cities of Wuhu and Nanchang were both larger. Up river from Anking was the District of Hankow, where a great deal of work both institutional and evangelistic had developed in the cities of Hankow and Wuchang, across the river from each other. Hankow was five hundred miles up the Yangtze, and it took three or four days to reach it by river boat.

The District of Anking was the latest to have been created since that area had first been included in the Hankow District. The Episcopal Church never developed a university or college in our district. Our several boarding schools had to depend for our highly trained personnel on graduates of St. John's in Shanghai or Boone in Wuchang. The city of Anking was not a treaty port but was the center of a great area in which no work had been established. It was difficult of access since none of the English river boats had a wharf there, but stopped in midstream to land their passengers onto a huge sampan, or scow, sometimes a dangerous performance. We heard that Anking had been chosen for the See City rather than Wuhu, a treaty port, because the term "the Bishop of Wuhu" never failed to strike an American audience as a Gilbert and Sullivan designation, and produced a gale of laughter. I always wondered if the story was true or apocryphal:

The rest of China had been divided into dioceses under the Anglican and Canadian Church. I believe there were eight dioceses in our early days all under English bishops, and one under the Canadian Church. All of these dioceses, including the three American districts, had been united into one overall Church, designated the Chung Hua Sheng Kung Hui (or Chinese Holy Catholic Church), which met together at stated intervals. Toward the end of our life in China Chinese bishops had been

7

consecrated for many of these dioceses, and one diocese in the far west was supported entirely by funds raised in China by the Chinese Church.

All this was as yet in the realm of 'book learning,' but it whetted his appetite for the experience of travel and encounter which lay ahead. Later, after our marriage, Lloyd and I were assigned to a pioneer work in the city of Nanchang, the capital of Kiangsi Province, a city of approximately 500,000 people, and the largest in the District of Anking, but almost unknown to the Episcopal Church in the U.S.A. A small beginning had been made there under our mission, but, as I will tell, it was a hopelessly inadequate plant for any real growth.

II

It was a very provincial young man who started out for China in July 1915. (Only once had Lloyd ever left his native state before this, and that was when he decided to visit Boston, going on a coastal ship which started out from Norfolk. Two of his friends in Lynchburg had gone to Wellesley, and from them he had heard a good deal about that area, which he decided to see for himself. Boston made an undoubted impression, but the most outstanding one was made by a fellow traveler on his trip North, Dr. Howe, the Professor of Chemistry at Washington and Lee, who was well known to generations of students as a remarkable teacher and also for his accomplishments during his years of retirement. He showed to him here the friendliness and wisdom which made that professor admired as one of the outstanding people he had known, in a friendship which lasted during the remaining years of Dr. Howe's life.) Duvall Gwathmey, a clergyman and distant cousin, accompanied him across the continent, and taught him among other things, how good a cup of tea could be. How many thousands he was to drink in the years to come!

It was the year of the Pan American Exposition in San Francisco. After traveling through the wonders of the Rocky Mountains on the Canadian Pacific Railroad with a stop-over at Banff to give him a never-to-be-forgotten impression of the towering majesty of those snow-capped peaks, he had the excitement and interest of visiting his first World's Fair.

The Mongolia, on which as it happened, both Mr. Craighill and Miss Gardner (the author of this book) sailed on August 25th, was noteworthy in many respects. It was built to transport cattle, we were told, and had been converted into a passenger vessel. This would be its last trip as a trans-Pacific liner, for it was to be converted into a troop ship for use in the First World War, then ending its first year. The result of the

9

conversion, as far as we were concerned, was that we were traveling on a remarkably steady vessel, and one in which every nook and cranny was filled by passengers, the larger majority missionaries like ourselves—I believe there were 130 of them, more or less, not counting the large families of children. It was the gayest and liveliest and friendliest of all my ten subsequent voyages across the Pacific. We were many of us young people just out of college or Seminary, starting on this great adventure and wondering just where it would lead us. We had Y.M.C.A. secretaries aboard, and old seasoned missionaries who seized the opportunity for morning sessions to tell us something about what we would find and how we should behave. For the first and last time in all my travels we had daily conferences. When we discovered that we crossed the date line. on Sunday, and so went directly from Saturday to Monday, it was something of a poser for the missionaries. We solved it by going to church Monday morning and having athletic events in the afternoon.

Among the many single women aboard the Mongolia was a certain Miss Gardner who was introduced to Lloyd by a mutual friend. We soon found that we would be in Language School in Nanking together, which made us realize this might be more than a temporary acquaintance. We sang the good old songs together leaning on the rail as we rode through the Inland Sea, a magic trip by moonlight. We went on a shopping expedition together in Kobe, and then by ricksha over a mountain pass to some scenic temple. I found that he was good company in all these experiences and he was inclined to forgive the fact that I had lived in New Jersey and had gone to Smith College in Massachusetts. I admitted without any apologies that I had never been south of New York City, but he remembered at this point that one of his grandmothers was a Yankee.

After three weeks of travel, including a stopover of a night in Honolulu, we arrived in Shanghai at the unusual hour of 2 a.m. Due to the conditions of the tides and the need of the Captain to hurry on with his cargo, he made his decision to land us at that hour. I will never forget that disembarking on the wharf at that time of night, surrounded by a crowd of ricksha coolies shouting for us to get into their vehicles, by Sikh policemen, their scornful faces topped by red turbans, trying to maintain control of the mob with rattan switches, and the weary, somewhat tense faces of our fellow travelers.

Lloyd was met by our mission treasurer, who conducted him by ricksha through narrow streets, the shops alongside hung with huge signs in gold and lacquer, covered with odd Chinese characters; more exotic in the faint street lights than he ever saw them afterwards. Everything seemed odd and unfamiliar, and he tried in vain to think that this could ever seem like home.

The arrival at the home of the Smalleys was reassuring in its welcome, and he tumbled into bed and sank into an exhausted slumber. The next morning he was awakened by a rap at the door, and a cup of hot English tea was deposited by his bedside. Life began to seem more hopeful. This was followed by the entrance of a coolie trotting in on his bare feet, carrying a pole on his shoulder, from each end of which dangled a large bucket of steaming hot water which he poured into a container in the bathroom that looked to Lloyd like a huge flower pot. Thus was he introduced to the famous Soochow tub.

All the days after that contained a succession of sights and sounds full of interest as he was shown the mission buildings in Shanghai, met a host of people who were members of the mission, and then took a trip up the Yangtze to Anking, which he thought was to be his eventual location. There he met again the Rev. Edmund Lee and his charming wife, Bishop Huntington, and Dr. Harry Taylor—all destined to become his very close friends, as well as many other members of the mission. But he was headed for Language School, so after a short visit he took

The Language School gives a play. Mr. Craighill in pith helmet; Miss Gardner in Chinese cap and beads.

the boat again, this time down river to Nanking. The language school was in one of the buildings of Nanking University. He was to board with a couple who taught in the Middle (or High) School of the University.

The Language School was supported by various missions and business firms who sent their new arrivals there to have a year spent in studying the language by what was then known as the "direct method." All of the teachers except the dean of the school spoke Chinese to us, and were never allowed to use English even if they knew some. The first hour or so in the morning was spent in listening to the "new words," given to us by a most remarkable Chinese teacher, Mr. Gia, who was an excellent actor and mimic and managed to get the meaning across in Chinese without having the dean come to our assistance with a word of English. We, of course, repeated his words after him. We patted ourselves that first day and used the word "I" in the proper tone, for there were five tones in the Nanking dialect, and if you pronounced the word in the wrong "tone" or "pitch" it would have an entirely different meaning. We also pointed to our neighbors and said "you" and across the room and said "he."

Mr. Gia was adept at seizing any class room happening as material for his remarks to us—all in Chinese, of course. The language school class rooms were unheated, except one, where Mr. Gia gave us our new words and our review of the ones we had learned. The temperature in winter was frequently below freezing and we put on an increasing number of garments, but nothing seemed to warm my feet. One day I obeyed an impulse and pulled the wrists of my gauntlet gloves over my shoes leaving the fingers spread out on the floor making me markedly resemble my Simian relatives. I hoped no one would notice, but that hope was vain. Mr. Gia had good eyesight and I sat on the front row. Suddenly I heard, "Miss Gardner's feet are incorrect. Why are they incorrect? Because she has gloves on her feet. Why

13

does she put her gloves on her feet and not on her hands?" "Because they are cold," I shouted in chorus with the rest of the class. It must have been a good way to learn the language for I never forgot that incident. I will also insert the fact, amazing to me, that he never used a new word in speaking to us which wasn't a part of the lesson for that day.

Lloyd never was a good linguist and many times that first year, he told me, he felt like turning in his Phi Beta Kappa key, as he struggled not only with the sounds, but trying to learn to make the strokes for the characters in the proper sequence and arrangement. However, no matter how difficult this was for him he never felt like calling it quits. Somehow he would be able to get through this stage of the language study and get to work.

In the meantime the intensity of our concentration on language study was broken by excursions of various kinds on Saturdays, to the Ming Tombs outside the city, to the Confucian Temple on a hill inside the great wall over twenty miles long, which surrounded the city, and once to an old Buddhist monastery near Chinkiang where we saw hundreds of monks in training, listened to their chanting, heard the solemn notes of the great bell, and began to realize what a dominating influence this religion had in the country. There were about seventy of us in our class and as we became better acquainted we developed a group loyalty and interest in each other. We also learned about Chinese geography as we learned where each of our classmates was to be located. Chinese history, language, customs, geography, food—we were surrounded by this country and at night we dreamt of it.

As for "Mr. Craighill"—we were both so aware of the job we had been sent out to do, and the amount of time it would take to fit ourselves for this, that there was little time for romance. A walk on the wall, a supper party or two, a daily greeting—but continuing certainty that we were enjoying our brief times

14

together.

That year I really learned my tones along with my sounds, but when I went to my station north of Nanking it was overwhelming to find that the words were pronounced differently and in different tones. I spent my two years in Nan Hsu Chow trying to change to the dialect of that city, as Lloyd was doing in Anking with the dialect there. And then—we both moved, by that time a married couple—to Nanchang, seventy miles south of the river, and the process began all over again. Only the written characters remained the same. Lloyd kept his Anking dialect but my northern sounds were too odd there. I tried to change and the result was that I never had any consistency either in tones or sounds. I spoke rapidly and was always able to convey my meaning if I didn't try to indulge in abstract ideas. I learned from the children years later that the servants had said that I spoke "Mrs. Craighill's Chinese."

Lloyd's first summer was to be at the mountain resort of Kuling, a valley on the top of the Lushan Range in central China, on the Yangtze River. Most of the classmates would be there too—including myself. The trip up the mountain was long and tiring for ourselves, but especially for the coolies who carried us. That first year there was no bus as there was later, to take us from the river port of Kiukiang to the foot of the mountain, so we rode for four hours through the plains in the blazing sun in chairs made of rattan with long poles inserted in each side which were carried by four coolies, one at each end. We were shaken and tossed about in the process, but went forward at a lively gait until we began to ascend the steep mountain. Then the coolies ceased their chatter and spent all their effort in carrying this load up, up, up—at one place a thousand continuous steps, with magnificent views nearly all the way. Then on up and up along winding paths until at last we reached the summit at over 3,000 feet above the river valley, an eight hour trip in all. There we breathed the fresh mountain air,

15

Above. *The mountain resort of Kuling. Union Church in foreground.*

Left. *The Goddess of Mercy Bridge at the foot of the Lee Shan Range.*

16

felt the cool breezes blowing away the heat and humidity of the Yangtze Valley, and felt renewed in body and spirit.

Stone bungalows were scattered about through the valley with no walls surrounding them. Mountain streams rushed along beside many of the paths. We felt exhilarated. To bring us down to earth again we began our language study at once, but this time interspersed with so much gaiety in the way of picnics, dinners, hikes over the mountains and performances in the auditorium that the study was a very small item in the general picture.

This mountain vacation became a regular part of our lives there in our years in China, so I have given this description to let you know how much it meant to us to have this beautiful resort as a place for rest and recreation. It also was, we knew, a lifesaver for Western children, who had built up no resistance to the diseases which surrounded us in a Chinese city, and who were particularly susceptible to germs in a long, hot summer.

After this summer Lloyd went to Anking for a few more months of study until he was asked by Mr. Lee to take over the principalship of the Kuling American School. He was never fitted by temperament or training for such a position and he never felt happy at the way he carried out that assignment, but in the first days of the following summer an event occurred which wiped out the memory of those difficult days—Lloyd and I became engaged. We still had to wait—I felt I must give a year to the Presbyterian mission to find my replacement—but Lloyd agreed to that without question. We would have a lifetime together to forget that year of separation. Incidentally he found out later that the Episcopal Board had had to pay over $200 to the Presbyterian Board for his bride as an adjustment on my travel and outfit allowance. At least he knew how much his wife was worth!

He had his next year in Wuhu, helping in the boys' school there under Mr. Lund, who spent his final years in Lexington. We were married at Hwai Yuan on June 13, 1918, with the Rev. Munzie Gill and the Rev. DuBois Morris officiating. The service took place in one of the gardens under three lovely trees, with only a few guests present. I couldn't stay in Nan Hsu Chow for this great event in our lives for there was no room in the two small Western-style houses on the compound to entertain our out-of-town guests. If it had been possible for me to stay there we would of course have had our wedding in the church—with a large crowd of onlookers as well as the congregation, who would have regarded this as the best of entertainments. I was glad for the simplicity that Hwai Yuan made possible for us. Lloyd's first cousin, Jean Herald of Lynchburg, was one of my two bridesmaids, and Edmund Lee was best man. Among the ushers was Lossing Buck, and Pearl Buck wrote an account of the wedding for the newspaper in Shanghai. At that time the Bucks were members of the mission at Nan Hsu Chow. Mother had my trousseau made in America, and a friend of my sister's made my wedding cake. These were all mailed out to me and, wonder of wonders for those war days, arrived in time. They even sent me a picture hat with a wreath of pink roses around it. I had my wedding dress made in Shanghai in February and I remember being disturbed at how quaint it looked when I tried it on over woolen underwear and hightopped shoes.

I can't find the newspaper account of the wedding, but I did find among the papers Mother left for me a letter Pearl wrote my mother to tell her about the wedding, which I will quote here.

Nan Hsu Chow, An.
June 23, 1918

My Dear Mrs. Gardner:

Doubtless you have received many letters in regard to Marian's wedding, and they have told you in detail everything.

June 13, 1918
The Lloyd R. Craighills

But I had the honor of arranging Marian's bouquet and of pinning on her veil, and so that gives me a special privilege, I think.

Marian looked as sweet as a picture as a bride. The princess lace and the little fillet you sent were vastly becoming with her veil. I put a few real leaves from the orange tree with the wax flowers and they looked like living flowers. Marian made such an adorable bride-y little bride. She was feeling quite rested and well, and lacked the tired look that so many brides have.

I went up to her room just before she dressed, and helped her into her pretty things. I have never seen such a happy girl, I think—surely none ever was happier. She just radiated quiet absolute happiness.

I wish I could give you the picture I have of her as she sat before the mirror and we arranged the veil and thought of your share in it all. I don't think she forgot you for an instant all day.

I like to think of her, too, as she walked across the green lawn under the shadow of the three great trees, where Mr. Craighill was waiting for her. She looked so dainty and sweet, in her white dress with the green, green background, and the radiance on her face.

It was very hard for me to give her up, for Marian has been so much to me this year, and I miss her everywhere. This station is a lonely and difficult one, and I am glad for Marian that she has gone elsewhere, but I think we shall not soon find one so fitted with a sweet and cheerful spirit to cope with the situation here.

I suppose "the Craighills" are in Japan now. I am hoping to visit them next autumn. I know Marian will have a sweet home.

How proud of her you must be! . . . And the wedding cake

was delicious!

Very cordially yours,

Pearl S. Buck
(Mrs. J. Lossing Buck)

It was a rare group of missionaries at Hwai Yuan, both in their culture and depth of commitment. We shall never be thankful enough for the wonderful memories we have of the way they planned and carried out that great event for us, as if we were in truth members of their own families. The DuBois Morrises gave a beautiful dinner for the wedding party the night before the wedding. The Ladies' House entertained us for breakfast next day, and the three Murdoch sisters of Baltimore gave us our lunch in their Chinese house, full of their antique mahogany furniture and family portraits which they had brought to China when they decided to make this country their home. (Later all of it was looted.) The whole group had saved the mission ice for the affair so there was enough to make delicious fresh apricot ice cream for a dessert which was practically unknown in upcountry mission circles.

We had two months in Japan for a wedding trip which the most wealthy might have envied, and all achieved on a mission salary of a little over a thousand dollars a year. We slept in Japanese inns beside murmuring streams, we climbed up into the Kamikochi Valley, a part of the Japanese Alps, and even up to the top of Hodake, snowcapped, over 14,000 feet high. When we reached the top the guides told me that I was only the second woman to have reached the top of that mountain. I always said I climbed it by mistake, since I was too tired when I reached the top to look at the view. I lay on the ground with my eyes closed, hearing the others talk about seeing Fuji, until we started back. It took me days before I could sit down without considerable agony, compounded by the fact that we had only cushions to sit on.

Later we visited Unzen with its bubbling hot springs and its sulphurous smell, and finally we came back to China in September, 1918 to take up an assignment in Nanchang, the capital of Kiangsi Province, a city of approximately 500,000, right in the center of China. It was a conservative old city, seventy miles south of Kiukiang, the southernmost point on the Yangtze, and was the terminus of a railroad which ran due south from Kiukiang.

III

(Marian Craighill tells her story—up to 1918)

After one of my talks to an Auxiliary about China, an old lady came up to me and said: "My dear, do you mean to tell me that you actually went out to China by yourself as a missionary at the age of 24! Why at that age all I ever thought about was beaux and dancing!"

It was fortunate for me and my future happiness that my horizon had no such limits, and quite in keeping with my upbringing that I should have been setting out on such an adventure at that comparatively early age. My father was a Presbyterian minister—years older than my mother, but because he was a very warmhearted outgoing man, with a love for children, he adapted himself remarkably well after his years as a bachelor, to the achievement in due course of time of a family of five children. I was the youngest of the five, alternately teased and petted by my brothers and sisters. My first thirteen years were spent in Chatham, New Jersey, a suburb of New York, but very much of a village in those days. It was quite a delightful place for our family to grow up in, small and friendly but easily accessible to New York. Mother frequently organized trips to take us there to see museums. Father had graduated from Amherst College in 1858 and at one time before his marriage had spent two years traveling in Europe. Our house was filled with the oil paintings he had bought in Florence, some beautiful alabaster vases from Italy, and many other souvenirs. But I was much more impressed by his stories of his travels. Ninety years after his trip Lloyd and I toured Europe, and at every turn I would find myself seeing something father had told us of which he had seen—so many years ago. I may have gathered subconsciously in my childhood an idea that travel and life in a country other than my own was nothing to be feared.

23

But the best lessons of that home came from the deep Christian faith and devotion of both my parents. My mother had come from a small town in Western New York. My father met her when he went there to hold Evangelistic services and stayed with her parents, as all the guests of the Congregational Church there seemed to do. She was beautiful and winning and to the delight and surprise of my father's family he succumbed to her charms. Those parents of ours were the inspiration and guiding light for all their children. We learned our Bible, reading verses sitting around in a circle at family prayers. The church activities were constant and we were a part of most of them—not always willingly, I must admit.

As father grew older he moved to a smaller town where the demands were less exacting, and I was sent to Blair Academy, then a coeducational school with good scholarships for minister's children as well as excellent preparation for college. I entered Smith in 1909, again on a partial scholarship, and had the usual experiences of a student in those days when we accepted the academic plan without a question and found our lectures tremendously rewarding. We never had our marks sent us unless we failed, so I was truly surprised to find my name on the Phi Beta Kappa list my Senior year.

The Student Volunteer Movement was sweeping the colleges in my day, and as a person who had always been involved with the Christian Association, I found myself considering the fact that mission teachers were much needed—probably in China more than any other country. I had met many missionaries, who frequently stayed at our home when they had a speaking engagement in our church, and I had found them interesting people. Mother had formed a missionary society among the women, and I had read many missionary biographies. I had taken the education courses which fitted me to teach, and I kept hearing an insistent voice: "Wouldn't your life mean more as a teacher in a Mission School, perhaps China, than in the

United States?" I considered it for several months, but when I found that my dearest friends at Blair—one then at Wellesley and one at Mt. Holyoke—had become Student Volunteers, that, I think helped me decide that I would join also.

After graduation and a year of teaching at my old prep school, I had a year at Teachers College and Union Seminary, which gave me a Masters degree from Columbia. At this point I received an urgent summons from the Presbyterian Board to come down and talk over a need which had arisen in a very new work, a small city in northern Anhwei named Nan Hsu Chow where the entire expense of personnel, building, etc., had been undertaken by the Madison Avenue Church in New York, whose minister was the Rev. Henry Sloan Coffin, a great churchman, scholar, and a most delightful and humorous gentleman—later widely known for the many years when he was President of Union Seminary in New York.

It seemed to me an interesting assignment, and the fact that the whole church would feel a personal interest in the development of the work at Nan Hsu Chow was a distinct advantage. It was a relationship which would be helpful to me as well as stirring up interest in overseas missions in that church. I accepted, and sailed for China on the Mongolia—with a certain Mr. Craighill.

I was met in Shanghai by the Rev. George Hood and his wife from my new station, who escorted me in time to the train which took me over storybook landscape up to this city of about 30,000 in Anhwei. It is an interesting comment on the quality of the small American group in that station, that at one time, of the seven missionaries there, four became authors of note, including Pearl Buck and Thomas Carter, who wrote the definitive work on the invention of printing in China, later becoming the Head of the Far Eastern Department at Columbia University.

It was a rather depressing area for the soil was poor, the people many of them poverty stricken, and there was none of the glamour of the larger cities of Shanghai and Nanking in such surroundings. But here I was to find the job of being head of the first school in that whole region which had opened for girls, of giving the students an opportunity to learn about Christ and the love which brought Him to this earth to live and die for them as well as for Americans, of the fact that they were of as great value as any boys, that they had minds which they could use to learn anything they tried—including English—and that if they didn't bind their feet we would have a grand time playing games in the big open space outside the school. They were the first girls in town who didn't bind their feet, and the fact that we had such fun with relay races and basketball may have had something to do with it.

There were calls in homes where no American had ever been seen before, trips to the country to try to teach very ragged, very earnest women to read a few Chinese characters so they could "learn our religion," and a constant stream of callers who loved to see how Westerners lived.

It was all very interesting and absorbing, and I was glad that Mr. Craighill was willing to wait a bit. Perhaps after all I was meant to stay at that job until I had seen it through.

But somehow in spite of all my hesitation and uncertainty, the sight of Lloyd Craighill waiting for me in Kuling that summer of 1917 settled everything, and not in the direction of Nan Hsu Chow.

The women and girls of that town were sad at the news that I was to leave them, but they were not surprised. "It is the will of Heaven," they said. Practically every girl in China is married. The thing they questioned and really had to know was how I had managed this affair with no family as a go-between. Such matters, of course, can't ever be settled by the two most involved. They gave me a wonderful farewell party and a great banner with characters saying, "Your marriage was made in Heaven." After all these years I am more certain than ever that it was.

I waved goodbye to that crowd of women and girls from the rear platform of the train with a lump in my throat. I left them still puzzled as to how that engagement had ever been brought about.

IV

After a few days in Shanghai, following our return to China from Japan we started up river on our new assignment, stopping off in Wuhu to collect our furniture. A couple in our mission who had returned to the U.S. were willing to sell us everything they had left behind, and my aunt's wedding present of $500 paid for all of it—a real bonanza. I told in a family letter of the long procession of coolies which were required to move all these new possessions of ours. It took 117 trips from the house to the river, and the confusion and excitement can be easily pictured by anyone familiar with the Orient. I'll quote a few sentences with which my letter closed. "That wonderful man of mine certainly does show himself more remarkable to me all the time. It isn't very easy, packing all that immense amount of stuff in such hot weather, but he did it all with a calm spirit and never forgetting a thing, and always so cheerful and serene. I couldn't help thinking how rare such a spirit is, and what a sure proof he would last in China. That procession of coolies alone was enough to wreck most people's nerves."

The train trip from Kiukiang to Nanchang on that August day in 1918 was quite an indication of the life which lay ahead of us. We found, when we purchased our tickets, that the soldiers of the war lord then in charge of that area had commandeered all the passenger cars, so we were to travel the seventy miles on a freight car, sitting on most uncomfortable straight-backed wooden benches. Fortunately we were young and strong and undaunted by the leap into the freight car, open at the sides only, and by the ensuing seven or more hours as we loitered along on our way south.

Also, fortunately, there was a great deal to claim our attention. The countryside was beautiful, as the train slowly puffed its way along the foot of the Lu Shan Range, where we had spent two summers and where now we were looking up at the lofty peaks which we had climbed from our Kuling Valley. We caught glimpses of ancient temples with their red tiled roofs, perched on apparently inaccessible cliffs, of waterfalls plunging down the side of the mountain in a cloud of spray, and of flights of steps winding up paths unseen by us before.

Then came the carefully tended rice fields, so small compared to fields in our country, and terraced so they could be irrigated in times of drought. The harvest was ready to be cut and the fields were golden with the ripening grain.

Our fellow travelers interested us also. Train travel in China is very sociable and uninhibited. At every station flocks of food venders thronged the platforms, selling their wares through the open doors of the cars. Watermelon seeds, lotus pods, eggs hardboiled in salted tea and very delicious, fried crullers of various kinds and shapes, fried rice—any of the delicacies vended on the city streets were obtainable here, and bargaining for them and their purchase took up some of those seemingly interminable hours.

At last we began to approach our destination. In the distance we could see a high wall, very strong and well built, at least 50 feet high in some places. It was across the river from the station where we landed, and we could view this great structure well from that distance. It was inside this wall that we were to live the next ten years of our lives until even that great "fortress" was torn down to make way for progress.

We were met at the station by our deacon, as the struggling new church in Nanchang hadn't yet achieved the status of having a Chinese priest. He assisted us in the preliminaries of such an arrival—getting baggage coolies to carry our belongings dangling from the ends of carrying poles, down the slippery river bank to walk aboard a narrow plank into a waiting sampan. The price of everything had to be bargained for, so our

One of the lakes in Nanchang.

The main business street in Nanchang.

Decorating china, Nanchang.

progress was anything but rapid, especially as we were sur-rounded by crowds of fellow travelers, many of them curious to see this foreign couple.

Finally we were on our way, rowed across the river by our expert boatman, and deposited on the opposite bank, another slope slippery with the mud of a recent rainfall. Before us opened the great black entrance through the city wall, one of the seven gates of the city. A six inch high stone lintel was raised across the threshold, over which our ricksha coolie had to step, and over which every ricksha had to be pulled to bump down on the other side—a means we heard later of keeping evil spirits from entering the city.

As we rode along through the narrow streets we looked with the greatest interest at our surroundings. On each side were open shops in which we could see the handicrafts, little changed since the days the wall was built in the time of Marco Polo. It was a city renowned for certain products. We saw a whole street full of shops selling the blue and white cloth, stenciled with delightful patterns which had been handed down for genera-tions. Another street was given over to the selling of baskets, another full of silver shops, where artisans hammered out designs to be sewn on children's caps, or dangled on chains around their necks, again to ward off evil spirits. We had a short ride on the main street of the city, where we saw the great shops full of silks, brocade, and grass cloth or linen which was one of the city's chief products.

At last we pulled up in front of our own wall and a wizened little gateman came out to greet us. We stepped through the gate house and looked up at our home in which we were to spend the next 19 years of our lives, though we had little knowledge of this then.

It was rather a bleak-looking gray brick house at which we

Our house in 1919.

were gazing, with the first floor a story above the surrounding "lawn," as the house had been built on a basement which was all above ground and went under the whole edifice. We climbed a high flight of steps to the front porch and began to roam through the seemingly endless succession of rooms within. Such a big house! Most mission houses were large to accommodate the constant flow of guests coming and going, but this seemed and was larger than most.

What kind of a mission station was this we had come to? I came across a leaflet which we had printed two years later on our first furlough, when we were directing all our efforts to raising money for adequate buildings in this great city of over half a million people. This may cover it.

1. A congregation of over a hundred members which worships in a dingy damp guest room of an old Chinese residence, with narrow backless benches for pews.

2. A boys' school of sixty pupils, housed in a decayed Chinese building over 200 years old. No playground.

3. A girls' elementary school of 35 scholars crowded into one tiny room, two to a seat. No playground.

4. A Chinese clergyman and staff of workers housed in crowded unsanitary quarters.

There it was. We had seen the spacious compounds of our missions in Shanghai and Anking, full of Western style buildings and with adequate staffs of foreign and Chinese workers. This was not to be our lot—we were to be pioneers, and there was a challenge in the thought.

We were sure that what we needed even before we achieved adequate buildings was a Chinese priest, well-educated in both English and Chinese, who could command the respect of the educated class and understand the needs of the poverty stricken. The bishop found just the right man for us, the Rev. Kimber Den and his wife, a trained nurse, both from Anking. Kimber was a graduate of St. John's University and Divinity School, a most friendly and winning personality, a man of action and of compassion. He stayed in Nanchang from 1919 to 1938. During the early days of the war with Japan he moved into Free China, south of our city, to organize a rural reconstruction project which lasted till he was able to return to his work in the city at the war's end. Later he was consecrated Bishop of Chekiang Province, but was arrested by the communists, kept a prisoner for years, and finally released. We do not know now if he is alive or dead, but we know that in whatever state he was forced to live, he remained true to the Lord he served so faithfully. Perhaps I should explain here that in China at that time it was the custom for students in a missionary school to adopt Western names, partly because it was easier for their Western teachers to remember them, so "Kimber" Den, "Ida" Kahn, "Grace and Quentin" Hwang and others I mention got these names as a result.

The Western community of Nanchang should be described, for they became of great importance to us. We were the only Westerners in the Episcopal Mission for practically all our years in Nanchang, but we had many missionary friends in the city and knew the few business people connected with the salt gabelle, post office and British-American Tobacco Company.

There was a large group of Methodists who lived in compounds outside the north wall of the city, with the Baldwin School, a boarding school for girls, Nanchang Academy for boys, and a hospital, all of which were a great help to our mission.

A hospital for women and children under the supervision of Dr. Kahn of the Methodist Mission was near us and had most beautiful grounds around it, like a park. It was the beauty spot for the whole city. The Y.M.C.A. had started work in Nanchang before our arrival. We became devoted friends of the Secretary, Arthur Allen and his wife Netta.

There were English missionaries in Nanchang, too, in the China Inland Mission, and the Plymouth Brethren, very fundamentalist groups, but they all became our good friends. The ecumenical way of life was a part of our very existence. We shared our Thanksgiving dinners and our Christmas festivities. We had Sunday afternoon services in oh! so welcome English language at the "ladies house" of the Baldwin School for girls. A Methodist lady and I ran a Mothers Club together. The work was too pressing and the need too great for us to let any difference in churchmanship disturb our friendships.

Now a bit about our home, that little oasis of peace and happiness in the midst of those crowded city streets. I have described the house in my first view of it, as bleak in appearance. There was land around the house which had formerly been a vegetable garden, now full of tall weeds. This was surrounded by the high gray brick walls of the neighboring house, but at the rear the wall was low and gave a glimpse of the little lake or large pond on which we were located. It gave a certain unusual quality to Nanchang to have a series of three artificial lakes in the center of the city, to bring relief from the crowded narrow streets and high walls. Lotus grew on our lake, and occasionally a fisherman would set out on a raft with a huge net, which he could let down to scoop up the fish, not

Right.
Rev. Kimber Den and his oldest son.

Below.
Guests for tea in the summer house.

Our home in Nanchang a few years later.

The living room in Nanchang, 1919.

sporting but very efficient.

Our house was full of rooms and had many casement windows which let in the sun, and, alas, the wind in winter. There were no conveniences, no electricity or running water, no telephone or central heating, no refrigerator, not even a sink or a pump. Water was brought from a well on the street in buckets by a coolie, to be boiled and filtered before it was drunk. The coolie also carried our notes, in lieu of a telephone, and in due time created a beautiful flower garden.

I was determined to have a flower garden, having seen in my former compounds what a joy and refreshment they gave not only to the owners but to the guests. Chinese love flowers, and it was a universal language when our speech halted. As luck would have it, a temporary teacher at the Methodist Baldwin School had been a former president of the Garden Club of Baltimore, and as a good Episcopalian she was eager to help us get started on our project. At her suggestion we built a round summer house thatched with straw. A grassy walk led from it arched over by three arbors. In no time those arbors were covered with climbing roses, and the series of beds leading from them were full of beautiful rose bushes.

By the time my mother and sisters came to visit us in 1920 we had a real garden to show them, the surrounding walls of our shoebox shaped compound were partially covered with ivy, trees were flourishing. We had even planted a euonymous hedge on each side of the walk, from clippings, which had thrived miraculously in that hot, damp climate. It was a wonderful joy to have such a visit and from that time on my letters are full of references to the months we had had together in Nanchang and Kuling.

Our housekeeping would have been impossible if we hadn't achieved in course of time a staff of faithful servants who cared for us as if we were their kin, eating their own food, and all four of them paid less than half the salary of a maid in the United States. They helped explain our oddities to the world outside our walls, and their loyalty was our greatest asset in this old city where we were so different and so foreign.

As for our finances, we always seemed to have enough to get along, though never enough to "lay by us in store." Our stipend in U.S. currency should have been changed at three Chinese dollars for one U.S., but it was war time in our country and exchange dwindled so we received less in Chinese than in U.S. currency. The tailor turned Lloyd's suits when they became too shiny, ripping them apart, and sewing them together again. I turned the cuffs and collars on his shirts, and set the style for the community by wearing my sister's hand-me-down dresses. We had enough to eat and a job to do and were completely happy in each other. Financial difficulties simply didn't exist for us, aided, no doubt, by the fact that all the other missionaries were on just the same economic status as ourselves. Small as our income was the Chinese staff always lived on a lower economic level than ourselves, which was a continuing problem for which we never found a solution. Westerners could not live and educate their children for life in America on the basis of Chinese salaries, and if we tried to raise the payments of the Chinese staff to the Western level, it would have made a very heavy economic burden on the limited resources of the mission, and put them out of step with their fellow Christians.

We have often been asked about our routine as Evangelistic missionaries in Nanchang. With the exception of services in the church each Sunday at which Lloyd preached every other week, Bible classes, and an English class in the boys' school, I would have to say that there was nothing which fitted that word as a description of his activities. Life in China had little of the routine about it. Callers would arrive at any hour of the day, and must always be welcomed and served a cup of tea, with the accompaniment of peanuts and watermelon seeds. The latter have been dried in the sun and salted, and when eaten are cracked open and the center removed by a dexterous twist of the tongue. Minutes are consumed in that manner while the caller gradually arrives at his objective—if this is a call with a motive—in asking for help in educating his son, or influence in recommending him for a position in the post office—or telling of some crisis in his home life. Frequently the calls were merely friendly—a response to having been to church and become an Inquirer, as the earliest stage of Christian preparation was called—or having moved to Nanchang from other of the Episcopal missions. There were always accounts to be attended to, as Lloyd was treasurer of the station and in time became treasurer for no less than five organizations, including the Kuling Estate, the mountain area in which Westerners were allowed to live, and the American School located there for missionary children.

In those early days much effort was spent in learning to know our city of Nanchang, its localities, its customs, its history, its potentialities, and along with that calling on the church members and on others who, through contact with friends, with our schools, or the work established in our larger centers, wished to know more about us.

No report of our "work" would be adequate if we didn't mention the long hours spent at feasts, frequently in restaurants which might look drab externally but whose menu was utterly delicious and, since each separate bowl was served as a course by itself, and there might be as many as twelve or fifteen, hours passed in the whole process. We would spend as much as half an hour or more as a preliminary to the feast, drinking tea and eating peanuts, before we were ushered to the table where we sat on backless stools and rapidly became oblivious to anything except the excellence of each bowl as it was tasted. Others have reported on what these dishes were. I can only say that you ate and ate and since the meal was largely protein with no rice served until the end, and then in a semi-liquid state, you didn't put on weight as a result—what bliss!

The development of our work also required much time spent in buying land, and later in supervising the buildings to take the place of our inadequate church and schools—but that account will come in a later story.

The church was growing, and the work for women and girls developing with the arrival of a teacher from Anking and a trained woman worker to help with teaching the women and calling on them with me in their homes.

In the fall of 1920 we had been in China five years and were ready for the adventure of our first furlough. We knew that it would involve a great deal of speaking to try to create an interest in this new work in the largest city of the diocese and the least known to the Church. And how we hoped we would return with the promise of funds for our new church and schools.

V

The following letters, which I wrote my family during the years before our first furlough give an idea of what life was like for a newly-married American missionary couple in an "up-country" station, quite unchanged in any fundamental way by Western influence, and where a very new mission work had been begun.

Sept. 27, 1918. "I'm almost settling into a schedule. We have breakfast at 7:30 every morning, right on the dot, Lloyd being a punctual soul and having a good influence on me. Right after breakfast we come into the living room, which is flooded with sun from the East bay window, and have prayers. I guess I told you we were reading Fosdick's 'Meaning of Faith.' We always read the prayer that is in the daily reading, and then one or the other of us prays, too. That starts the day off right. Just a few minutes for Lloyd to scratch some notes or collect his thoughts in Chinese before he starts off for school. I've been fussing around, cutting flowers and putting away papers and straightening magazines in the meantime, and just about the time he goes, in comes the cook, with a wrinkle on his brow and an account book in his hands, ready to take accounts. A garbled discourse in Chinese and English follows [he was the only cook I ever had who knew English, and he didn't last long]. I know more scriptural passages than names for food, and occasionally write down 'chicken' instead of 'eggs'—and usually have more trouble catching his meaning when it's clothed in English than when he comes out with it in Chinese. But after awhile that's disposed of, and I can tell how much I've spent for vegetables and how much for meat and fruit with an occasional huge amount for pails or tubs.

"Then, having disposed of accounts, I proceed to plan meals. How I loathe green boiled vegetables, but there isn't anything else to be had, so I resign myself to my fate and let the cook do his own collecting. [I would have liked fresh vegetables but of course didn't dare eat anything uncooked]. I try to vary a straight chicken diet, and the meat grinder is wonderful. We've eaten all sorts of impossible cuts of beef and pork already thanks to it. Made a meat loaf the other day. The cook is a faithful old soul, and I've caught the birth of a smile on his face twice already. Finally we've wrestled out a couple of meals, he picks up his basket and departs, and about that time I'm told that the teacher has come. He is Lloyd's teacher and I often don't recognize old familiar Chinese characters under his pronunciation, so that job is a little taxing. I study about 3 quarters of an hour, going through the Prayer Book now, trying to learn the Lord's Prayer as the Episcopalians say it. The only thing I really know is the Prayer of Confession which we had every Sunday at Nan Hsu Chow.

"Then about a quarter past ten I'm through with him, and begin to really work—hanging pictures, putting up books, arranging the store rooms, sorting over clothes, mending, piecing out curtains. There has been a lot to do these first weeks, and I expect with this big house and yard I'll find I can always housekeep my mornings away.

"My afternoons haven't had a schedule yet, though I established one yesterday when I had the twelve little school girls come over to play games in the yard. They were so cute, and so happy to come. We played 'last couple out' and bean bags and blind man's buff, and I showed them Hilda. [This was a doll Mother had dressed for me when I was at Nan Hsu Chow]. They were rapturous over her—had never seen a foreign doll before. But a new complication arose when I found they thought it was my real child! Very good and not talkative because she hadn't learned Chinese yet. I begin to wonder how many at Nan Hsu Chow held the same notion! Anyway I took pains to dispel it at once.

42

"That wasn't my first entertaining of the Chinese. Last Saturday I asked the women of the church in for tea. Only six came, but they all had a good time—of that I have ample proof. One of them had never been in a foreign house before and it quite went to her head. She wandered about as though she were in a museum, and then finally asked to see the second floor. I led them up and let them gaze. Then I fed them tea and cakes, which they partook of heartily. Suddenly this same female saw that our neighbors by the lake were her old friends. Up she sprang to the window sill and established vociferous communication at once. 'Come on over. There's an upstairs. They've got a victrola in there that plays Chinese music. Better come while you've got a chance,' etc. And come they did, but were so impressed by the mansion and by my formal politeness, which I can adopt upon occasion, that they were very tractable."

October 20, 1918. "I'm quite firmly of the opinion that the Episcopal form of government is the best for mission purposes, where there is a head who decides, from a broad knowledge of all the comparative needs which he gets by his journeys around. We are pretty apt to get narrow and selfish and everyone seeing just his or her needs otherwise. This isn't a sudden conversion, and there are lots of good Presbyterians who think it too.

"And now let's advance to the great and wonderful news which has been flooding in on us these last days. The newspaper doesn't come till 9 p.m. but there is no dozing while it's read to us, these days. The news today was the rumor that the Kaiser had abdicated. Anyway—Germany has undoubtedly followed out Wilson's terms in making unconditional surrender, seeing nothing but disaster ahead if the war keeps on. Can you believe it! We're just prancing over here, and can't read the newspapers without falling on each other's necks. I expect the real tug of war may follow, in coming to peace terms, and yet this unconditional surrender sounds pretty humble. How we're thinking of you these days, and how we wish we could see you

43

and talk it all over and see the flags and hear the excitement. I think of the train of commuters, and the way newspapers are being brandished about—and of New York streets, and of the drug store steps in Chester. Every tiny hamlet the world over is thrilling with excitement—except China, which hardly knows what is happening. A new President has been elected here and there were hopes of bringing about unison and peace, but they were vain, judging from this morning's paper. The Secretary of the Treasury, a thoroughly beastly fellow, keeps on negotiating Japanese loans, pledging all China's natural resources as security. That's because the taxes are being quite openly and avowedly stuffed into the official pockets. Government schools are closing through lack of funds. The younger element is thoroughly discouraged and hopeless. Who wouldn't be when they hear, as we did last night from Mr. Coudron [He was the Post Office commissioner, a Frenchman] that the Military Governor had left the city, having made two million taels clear, considerably over two million dollars, by his nine months stay here. Officialdom is very profitable business, and any amount is paid in bribes for a chance to get a job. The old examination system was better, methinks."

October 28, 1918. "Yesterday we had a 'how wang'—as a trip to the country and general jubilation is termed. The little school boys have just achieved their khaki suits, patterned after Lloyd's and nothing would do but to take them through the city to spend the day in the country, quite especially to show them off. I decided to go too, tho' I would be the only female. I've hankered to get out into the country all fall, and we are having perfect weather.

"Naturally the kids were all agog, and they did look as cute as pins with their brown skins and eyes and little foreign suits. They got the whole rig—coat, trousers, hats, and puttees—for a bit over two dollars. The puttees were mere strips of khaki and gave them endless trouble—but what cared they. They lined up with the tallest in front carrying the huge school banner, and at the end I came in my ricksha, looking like the family idol being dragged along to the temple—or perhaps the wild woman from Borneo in the circus procession would be an illustration you'd comprehend better. Of course all the busiest streets were chosen, and you should have seen the shop keepers flock to their doors to see us pass. I don't wonder, for the infants did look most unusual—just like Brownies.

"After we got outside the city wall our first stop was at the Agricultural Gardens and School, where I trailed into a mammoth guest room with all the men, and they didn't know what should be the order of my going any more than I did. They always try to pass Lloyd in first, through the door, and he being the soul of politeness refused to leave me behind. They didn't know what caused the delay and it would usually result in one of the teachers coming to the rescue and hopping over the door sill—very humorous! [There was no chivalry in China—the man always went first, and always sat in the highest place; 'ladies first' was just unheard of—it was an entirely different set of customs.]

"They showed us around the buildings, and one room in which the farm tools were stored was especially noteworthy and typical, for all the good imported plows and harrows were covered with dust and rust, evidently never used. Moreover, outside, two women were working away picking seeds out of cotton by some curious slow native contrivance, while in this room were two good foreign cotton gins—'broken' they said, but I imagine it was because they didn't know how to use them.

"We went on from there about three miles farther to a pretty old temple, surrounded by trees. We ate under a tree on a low mound which had been described to us as a mountain. All the way I had been tremendously impressed by the farm houses—great brick structures, solid and fine looking. Now some of the inhabitants one by one came running out to see the foreigners eat their food. They stood silent and attentive till the last crumb had disappeared, then they put forward the leading lady of the village to speak to me. She was so nice looking and wore clothes which only the most elite of Nan Hsu Chow could have donned. They all beamed upon us as only country women can, and were so interested in talking to us that I suspected what I afterwards found to be true, we were the first foreigners they had seen. I never will forget the delighted look in one old lady's face when I asked her her age, and the way she patted my hand. It makes me wild to do country work. That's where you get most of your real satisfaction, I believe."

November 3, 1918. "We went to a dinner one evening. Dr. Kahn was there, the splendid Chinese woman doctor who was adopted, with Dr. Stone of Kiukiang, by Miss Howe, one of the first Methodist missionaries to come to Nanchang, when they were tiny children. And now they are each doing more good than ten ordinary foreigners. Miss Howe was there too, the sweet fragile little old lady I must have written you about. Dr. Kahn is very fat, very jolly, very frank. She hates Japan with a deadly hatred, and has been writing articles for Millards Review, expressing her feelings, and I guess vituperating Japan. Of course you know how Japan has been making huge loans to China, mortgaging her resources, and all the money goes into the pockets of officialdom and on to the various armies of the rival military leaders. Things are in an appalling state here, and every thinking Chinese knows it. Dr. Kahn says that the time has come for intervention by the powers, but dreads an intervention by Japan, as would we all. She and Lloyd got into an argument and talk waxed eloquent.

November 21–22, 1918. "So much has to be personally supervised in China. Take yesterday, for example, when they brought the coal. They pled with me to go out and see them weigh it, but I knew their wiles and refused. Imagine not having time to wait for the gentleman of the house, in China! When Lloyd did come he found plenty of reasons why they wanted me to boss the job. First the coolie reads the wrong number of pounds—one more than there really is—from the scales, which is a long pole held by two coolies, with a hook on one end and numbers on the other. He is foiled in that by the clever Lloyd, and their next wile is to weigh the pole on which the baskets are carted, every time, as well as the coal itself. Last time they tried to weigh the baskets each time, and not have their weight subtracted. Eternal vigilance, you perceive. Thus it is to buy a supply of coal in this land. Do you wonder we have to spend a bit of time?"

November 16, 1918. (Part of a letter to a group of old friends in the U.S.)

"The thought of housekeeping had given me some qualms before I started in. You have to know so many queer things in China, like how much butter you eat in a year, and the amount of soap which is used up in the laundry per week. Then all the canned goods from America or Shanghai have to be kept under lock and key in a peculiar spot called the store room—and the key always is upstairs when you are down. It was terrifying to contemplate, as I said, but now I've started at it and it seems like a kind of game. Lloyd has turned all his bookkeeping faculties on starting me a system of household accounts which beats the Dutch, and is my chief hope of gaining distinction in this foreign part. I never can remember figures, but if I look it up I can tell you the exact cost of every mouthful you eat. Pleasant thought! Do come and visit me! At present it is like a game, though I suppose by the time I have had ten years of trying not to let my cook squeeze more than do those at the Methodist compound, I'll get tired of it."

February 23, 1919. " Bishop Huntington, Mr. John W. Wood, the General Secretary of the Department of Overseas Missions, and his secretary, Mr. Ford, paid us a visit in February to look over our situation and make recommendations to the Church in the U.S.A. "Lloyd said he felt sure they were impressed with the importance of Nanchang and its needs, and said Mr. Wood told him to be on the look-out for land and when he found a suitable piece to let the Board know. That sounds encouraging, as does also the fact that Mr. Wood is going to give the church an organ. There is a sort of one over there but luckily it behaved worse than usual last Sunday. It is a hand-me-down from Kiukiang, and is manipulated by a blind organist. He comes from a school in Wuchang, and is able to play any of the hymns in the Episcopal or Methodist hymnal simply by hearing the number given out, and I do marvel at him whenever I think about it. It's a great deal more wonderful than remembering your friends' telephone numbers, even. He doesn't know just how many verses there are to each hymn, but that is the only place he slips up, and we manage that by simply howling out the 'amens' at the top of our lungs till he doesn't have a chance to go ahead. The worst part about the organ, however, is that regularly half the keys stick. You can imagine the strange medley of sound which that produces, and I saw our visitors, who hadn't had a thorough introduction to Chinese voices before this, twisting around on their seats the way you do when you hear a slate pencil misbehaving itself. It really isn't fair to ask a blind organist not only to press down the keys but to pick them up again as well, and that is what he attempts. So—we are to have a new organ!"

Nanchang, February 23, 1919.

". . . There was quite an abrupt termination to our peaceful afternoon ahead of us, for no sooner did we get settled in the living room than in burst the cook, looking wild as I have never seen him look before, made us each deep bows, bellowed forth that he wished us peace, and then proceeded to remove all possibility of it by pouring out a tale which he was too excited to make in the least coherent. But at last we found out the truth of the matter which was that while we were away the devil had got into the little gateman and he had gone into the cellar and stolen some wood. As that wood is 'on the cooks body' as the Chinese put it, he was on its trail as soon as he came back from the market, and discovered it in the gateman's house. When that same little gentleman was summoned in he confessed that it was true! It was so surprising to have him own up to it that it almost bust up the family. The fact is I like him better than all the rest of them, and to think of having him leave and no more hop on his little lame leg up the steps bringing us the mail, nor hear his long orations on the subject of how to raise flowers and how to make our grounds beautiful— why it moved me to tears at once. But he will have to go, of course, and the first of the month has been set for his departure. In the meantime his zeal, his energy, his complete devotion to our wishes, are most noteworthy and pathetic. I am having him help me plant the garden and he talks so proudly about what 'our' house will look like in the fall after the vines grow up, and how I better wait and have him plant the asters 'later.' It is quite too bad." [As a matter of fact the other servants left, for one reason or another, and the little gateman was the only one who stayed!]

The means of traveling in our area was by wheelbarrow, but since a Chinese wheelbarrow is very different from a Western one, I should say a bit about it. The Chinese wheelbarrow had one very large wheel with wide platforms on each side, slightly above the axle. The loads were adjusted as evenly as possible on each side of the wheel, a long strap extended from one handle to the other, and this strap rested on the neck of the pusher, thus lessening the weight on his arms. (Letter dated May 25) "Tuesday was eventful because I had my first wheelbarrow ride. The purpose of the trip was to visit the wife of a church member out in the country. One of our nicest church member women was going to take Mrs. Dong and myself. They came at nine and we started out, they on their wheelbarrow and I on mine. I've seen as many as five people on one of them, but we

49

The Craighill's and Towser on a wheel barrow.

didn't try that. It was a hot morning so I carried a palm leaf fan and an umbrella just as the others did.

"You don't know how funny it is to ride on a wheelbarrow till you've tried it. I kept expecting bumps where two wheels would have made them, and never expected the ones that came. You have to trust yourself utterly to the wheelbarrow man and luckily he is rather skillful for he trundles you along the narrowest little paths with an unspeakable pool on one side and stone pavings on the other. I learned to appreciate all the ridges worn in the stones by years of wheelbarrowing for they always meant less jolting.

"We went through a whole new set of suburbs that day, outside a different gate from any I had been—there are seven in the city—on and on till we came to the real country and the poor men began to quarrel with us about the amount of fare we had agreed on. We had said a certain street and it appeared that that street had no termination! Finally we turned into rice fields with such narrow little tracks that I got out and walked, and at last arrived at the farm house. It was one of the stucco and beamed variety which look just like a Queen Anne cottage, and was very comfortable and substantial in comparison with the mud houses of the north. The lady we had come to see with all the ramifications, which meant three daughters-in-law and all their families, came out to meet us. They were expecting us, and had the tea and cakes all ready. When I found out how far away the house was I was sorry I hadn't brought a tract, but our nice old Mrs. Yang produced from her pocket the one I had given her the week before and we began the preaching. That just consisted in reading over and over and explaining the few characters to the effect that, aside from Jesus no one could save people from their sins. They understood pretty well when Mrs. Yang read to them, though they couldn't get it from Mrs. Dong because she speaks Kiukiang dialect and that is a city 60 miles away! It's a marvel to me they ever get anything of our teaching when aside from the barrier of words there is the difficulty of handing out ideas to these minds which have had so little experience with anything outside of their narrow environment. But they do all of them seem to understand the idea of God, and sometimes you see their wonder over the first idea that God is love. The people in that farmhouse understood pretty well, and I was delighted to find the same characters on a big sheet fastened up at some previous time by the church member husband. Then I began to teach these characters. They recognized at least four before we left, and had memorized most of the words. So I foresee where in days to come the neighbors will be treated to a rendition of it, and the 'dowli' (the Word) will be spread. I go thus into detail because that is typical of one kind of call, and I judge I shall have a good deal of that kind to do for the people are so scattered here they can't come to many meetings."

May 18, 1919. "One day last week I found every servant out on the back porch staring their eyes out, and I joined and stared, too. There winding along the side of the lake was an apparently endless procession of school-boys with banners. We kept expecting the end—but it was certainly 'long in coming,' as we used to sing in college about the end of Professor Tyler's prayers. Not being totally ignorant of the political situation, I knew what it meant. This was a procession of some thousands of students from almost every school in the city, going to protest to the Provincial Assembly at the cession of Tsingtau to

Japan. There is an outburst of indignation now all over China at the action of the Peace Congress in letting Japan have her way. For the time being the indignation and fear and hatred are finding expression in these processions of students and boycott of Japanese goods. But as Egbert Hayes [the Y.M.C.A. Secretary at that time] was saying, none of that gets at the root of the evil. Last time there was such a boycott, Japan forced a large indemnity out of China to pay up, and of course she will again. We read that the 'Japanese aren't worried by the situation.' Of course the real movement should be against the utterly worthless leaders in Peking, trained by the Germans in military schools, who are selling the country to Japan. Their corruption and treachery are unbelievable, and the fearful tragedy is that the good elements in China seem powerless. The soldiers are controlled by these vile leaders, and where the military is, there is the power. If only this danger from Japan would be sufficient to draw the good elements in to common action, but just on the trail of this comes the news of the final dissolution of the attempted Peace Conference between North and South, in Shanghai. There was a fine editorial in the Press the other day saying that before long China's situation would be that of Korea. I'm beginning to believe it and it makes me shudder. Think of Japanese ideals and methods—which are purely and simply Prussian—penetrating this great country. And think of how the root of future wars and revolutions are being laid."

May 25, 1919. "Dr. Kahn is a most interesting person—She's so fat she can hardly move, but she gets around everywhere just the same and is a very fine physician, I hear. She is intensely patriotic, and how sorry I do feel for her now and the thousands of others like her. She told of the lengths to which the anti-Japanese agitation had gone here in Nanchang. One girl in the normal school had cut off her finger and written some characters with the blood. I saw another girl at the hospital who had started a case of melancholia just thinking over the conditions. The city is placarded, begging people not to buy Japanese goods, but there is so much Japanese influence in the city that we are rather skeptical. Just one instance—there are some hundreds of Japanese women in the city dressed as Chinese, who are concubines in the official homes and who act as spies! Many of the leading politicians have been educated in Japan, and their influence is for rather than against that country, though of course they can't do much now. We distrust and fear Japan more than anything else, thinking of how Korea's condition today is just a prophecy of the China of tomorrow unless something is done. Lloyd doesn't think Japan would allow an administration by a joint group of the Allies—particularly since we read that astounding revelation that the Allies had signed an agreement giving over Shantung to Japan if she would allow China to enter the war! Do you get it, and isn't it unbelievable? And when you hear, as we did the other day, that the coolies in Foochow refused to coal a Japanese ship though offered big sums of money, and the chair coolies won't tote a Japanese up the mountain no matter what the fare they'd get, then you realize that there is a lot of spirit in China which isn't expressed by the militarists of the north. That fine young Mr. Liu of the YMCA, whom Lloyd teaches every Sunday night, is another example of the kind of men in whom China can take hope. He asks *such* penetrating questions that Lloyd is on his mettle to answer them, and last Sunday they sat up till twelve discussing the political situation."

November 23, 1919. "The real event of the week came last Friday. Miss Loggin [one of the English missionaries] told me about a birthday celebration of an official she had just been to see. It was an ex-official who was celebrating his eightieth birthday in the utmost magnificence. The more I heard about it the more I wanted to go, and after a while we succeeded in getting up a party. It was being held in a big provincial club house near the Hopkins, and while of course it wasn't open to the general public it seemed that foreigners could march in as they wished. The entrance wasn't especially imposing, but after we had stepped through one or two entrance courts, such a vista opened up before us! We were at the entrance to the main court, at the back of which opened the guest room magnificently hung with silks and shimmering with brilliance from quantities of great red candles. The effect was all red and gold. You felt as though you were looking into some cave straight out of Arabian Nights. We walked right on into this inner sanctum, being privileged foreigners, and looked at the decorations more in detail. The court and entrance to the guest room was hung with tremendous lanterns of oiled silk, with long hanging tassels of red. Hanging down from the ceiling were red satin draperies and the chairs were covered with red satin beautifully embroidered with medallions of cranes. We had heard that the decorations cost a hundred thousand dollars, and we were almost ready to believe it. On all sides of this guest room and of every other one we went into were hung the great presentation scrolls, on almost every one of them the characters written on solid gold leaf which covered the paper. Of course each one of them was terribly expensive, and there were 3000! Think of having that many loving friends. At the back of the guest room was the shrine to old age. The figure of the god was embroidered on a huge red banner hung on the wall, and in front stood the ceremonial table covered with incense burners, the smaller ones in front, increasing in number to the huge ones at the back. All about on the table stood the red candles, two or three feet in height, with little colored figures moulded in the wax projecting out from the sides. There were great piles of rolls on this table too, and figures on them—and are you tired of my saying that they were red? because even they were that color."

VI

No one can well report on the excitement of a first furlough who hasn't experienced it. For five years we had been absorbing the sights and sounds, the language and customs of our area in China, learning to know our constituency and trying to understand something of their needs and their desires. Suddenly the time arrives to pull away from all that and go from this great city, so medieval in its culture, back to our homeland and our families. It is well that in those early days a long ocean voyage intervened to prepare us mentally and physically for this great change, so that by the time we reached the Eastern Shore of Maryland, where our first visit was made to Lloyd's sister and her husband, we were more ready for the adjustment back to the life we had lived of old.

The months of visiting and traveling which followed were far too full and varied to be described here. This was my first visit to the South, and to Lloyd's very large and welcoming family. I liked them all and made my way with them. In the fall of 1921 we went to my mother's home, located in Englewood, New Jersey, a suburb very close to New York and most convenient to our task of interesting both the Department of Missions and the Church at home in this new work. An effort at enlisting the Church more actively in the Overseas Program, called the "Nation-wide Campaign," was then in progress, and our needs in Nanchang were included in the list of objectives, which made our efforts at fund-raising much easier. During the following year both Lloyd and I became acquainted with the process of "Speaking about China"—trying in some way, during the few moments allowed us, to leap the chasm of distance, widely differing cultures, and abysmal ignorance of what our Overseas Mission really was trying to accomplish, and make a positive impression. In the process we may have made enemies we didn't know of, but we know we made many friends.

On the 27th of December 1921 we started back on our journey of nearly a month and a half, from Englewood to Nanchang. I wondered how this return from the comforts of life in the U.S.A. and all the interest we had had in being with old friends and relatives would seem to us, but I reported in a letter that we settled into the slow-moving ways of China as though we had never been away.

"After a stop-over first at Wuhu, and then Anking where there were large groups of workers, we were afraid that Nanchang might seem like quite a come-down, but the warmth of the welcome given us there at the station by our friends set any such fears at rest.

"It took a long six hours to cover the distance from Kiukiang to Nanchang and how glad we were to see the great gray wall of 'Our City', looming in the distance you can imagine. And then the next thing there was our Chinese clergyman beaming in at us at one window, and a faithful servant chuckling with joy at another. Then a sound of 'foreign' voices, and Mr. Gowen of our mission, and our Y.M.C.A. friends appeared to pull us bodily out of the car and into the midst of the church members and school children gathered to greet us. A great string of firecrackers hanging from a pole began to explode as we stepped off the train, in a manner that had terrified me six years before, but which I now knew was merely a very polite way of expressing a welcome. Then an order was given and the school 'band' of three instruments began to quaver and add to the melee.

"It was all very Chinesey and heart warming, and we found we were even happier to get back than they apparently were to have us. We bowed and smiled and shook our own hands as though we had been greeting our friends in America in that fashion, and finally managed to move ourselves along the platform to the river bank. Here an improvement greeted us, for

56

instead of a slippery scramble down a steep mud bank we found a real inclined roadway paved with stone in a manner which might have seemed crude to you but to us was the height of civilization. However there had been no change in the little narrow wobbly board along which we edged our way to the big flatbottomed scow in which we were to be rowed across the river, while the church members scrambled as best they could into a similar one beside us. The same variety of patched and tattered sail fluttered above our heads. We had the same kind of a two-inch wide plank for a seat. In fact it was the same old China!

"The first week or two was a whirl, so much of unpacking interspersed with receiving callers, going to feasts (two, plus a reception, on the day after we arrived), acknowledging presents of all kinds. Seventy-two eggs and five chickens had been given us, our coolie told us proudly. I didn't have time to count them myself.

"Now we are really settled down into our schedule, and I find something to do with every minute. A class of beginning English in the girl's school; games for the school girls on our lawn twice a week; an English class three times a week for the three delightful children of a high official here; a Sunday School class for the school girls; women's meetings and calls—all keep me more than busy. I mean to study Chinese in the crevices, but so far I haven't found any."

Lloyd continues this "Nanchang Letter", sent to many friends in the U.S.A. by telling of the growth of the schools, and the increasing size of the congregation. He reports that our girls' school teacher had forty-two girls of five classes in one small room. Part of the growth had come from the Wednesday night meetings for prayer and discussion, when the group brought up such topics as "The Right of Free Betrothal", "Ancestor Worship", "Foot Binding", "Home Relationships", and the like.

The buildings for the Boys' School were completed while we were on furlough, and since the money we had been hoping for had been allotted to us, we began the building of the church, parish hall and girls' school.

Lloyd wrote of the plan for the new Church building with much enthusiasm, "The carved window frames and doors; the round door-way opening into the pebbled court yard with its raised flower bed; the dark red of the woodwork with some black for contrast; the gray tiled roof; and crowning all the little square bell tower with its up-curving roof—all these distinctly Chinese features combined with the convenience and airiness of Western architecture make us feel that we have a combination which will appeal to Chinese and Westerners alike."

March 26, 1922. "We were so sorry we forgot the camera yesterday when we all went on the big trip of the year, to take the school boys over to the peach village. It was a good day, with the sun somewhat clouded so it didn't dazzle our eyes as much as usual on the water. We all started out from the school about ten, 'all' including the Dens, two amahs, their baby in a Chinese go-cart, the school cook, about seventy school boys, Netta and her infants, and the Craighills! Some procession. We filled four boats. I wish you could have heard the reviling that went up when we had to leave the small boat we started to sit down in and change to a larger one. It is something that just about can't be done. Anyway if I could have had a phonograph record of the cursing it entailed I could have made my fortune.

"We paddled along the Fuchow creek for about half an hour having a splendid chance to see all the crowded shipping and the big rafts of bamboo and wood, and the great enormous high sampans. We realize what a city we are when we get out like that and look at us from the outside. I'm so glad we're on a

58

river. Then the shores on the opposite side began to look prettier and prettier and finally we stopped at a big sandy beach. The boys were all there waiting for us, and they just fell upon the Allen children with utter joy. It was the first time the small Allens had ever had such close contact with big boys, but they all, including Netta, were perfect sports. The infants allowed their hands to be held by each boy in turn, and even submitted to being carried. Sometimes they rode in the Den baby carriage. I never knew Chinese school boys or any others could be so nice as they were. They came up and took our baskets and coats and carried them, they were perfectly sweet to those little Allens, and never grumbled or fussed or were anything but nice all day. They had whistles and horns and a basket ball. We truly were a procession as we straggled along the shores of the river toward the peach villages, and it seemed as though a large part of Nanchang had turned out to join us. It seems that it's quite the thing to do at this time of the year, and I must say that my respect for the citizens of Nanchang has gone up since I knew it. For words fail me to describe how lovely those villages are at this time of year. The houses are all of the Kiangsi village type, white plastered with big brown beams, looking just like Shakespeare's birthplace. They were surrounded by all sorts of bushes and trees, but quite particularly and above all by glorious peach trees covered with blooms. You have never in your lives seen such blossoms and when you get them in quantities, overhanging those village houses, the effect is ravishing. I was so all eyes for the peach trees that I never noticed for a long time that the great tall bushes with dark green foliage were holly trees. They really are trees in size, and were covered with tiny green berries, so we knew they were the right kind. We had some dug up for the garden, and I made a date with Netta on the spot for the 22nd of December which is their wedding anniversary and will be the day for us to trip it to the peach village and pick our holly. [We did it, too.]

"It was a real spree. When Lloyd got home he had to gobble supper and get over to the YMCA to teach his class of government school teachers in Economics. One of the secretaries translates for those who don't understand English, and it really is a most interesting class. The change that has come over China just in the years we have been home is prodigious. The Renaissance Movement becomes a reality when you find that in a small group like that every one of those men is thinking about what the future of China will be, and really believing that Bolshevism will be the way out. [I guess we should say Communism]. They are scrutinizing every kind of social institution and cutting away with the past in a way that is simply revolutionary. We read about it at home, but you can't be in China a week without feeling it in the air. The students of China are awake and thinking." [Lloyd reminded me here that one of the members of that class was condemned as being a Communist and was executed, by the government. They were very hard on Communists at that time.]

April 16, 1922. "Another accomplishment this week was the purchase of a birds bath tub! We were quite sure our garden vista needed a little bit of stone work to be the crowning touch, and perhaps I told you about my seeing just about what I wanted one day, out in front of a shop. It was a big square of stone with a deep hole hollowed out of it, in which they pound down a wooden hammer with their feet, to polish the rice. You can imagine how the shopkeeper nearly burst with excitement one day when I told him I wanted to buy it, and to cap it he sent over an apprentice with it who was exceedingly near the line of being a half wit. He was Launcelot Gobbo in the flesh. Shakespeare must have seen him in a former incarnation. He never ceased his silly giggle from the time he came into the yard till the time he left, except occasionally to turn it into a downright guffaw. To think that we wanted a polishing machine in the first place, and then to think we wanted it planted under a tree, and to think we had spent all that money for something

60

to plant flowers in. It was all too funny. We hadn't dared tell him it was for birds to take baths in. A bath tub is regarded with wonder akin to awe when it's for a human being, and to provide one for birds! The servants are all speechless with the marvel of it. I may have to use it for Ding Hsiang (the gateman's stepdaughter) after all. Anyway Lloyd has filled it with cement till it is a nice depth and I can hardly wait for it to be dry enough to test out whether or not Chinese birds will avail themselves of bathing privileges."

April 21, 1922. "In the spring of 1922 we went up to Kuling to see about some property we had there. "We had perfectly gorgeous weather for the trip up the mountain. Went right up Monday evening, making everything by schedule time. It was so blessed to leave that old stuffy smoky train for the ride through the cool spring air, up into the foothills, which were so gorgeous with azalea and wisteria that they fairly made me ache. I kept wishing we could have had such weather for you all—of course we were going up about two weeks earlier than you did, so the lower part of the mountain was in the height of glory, while the top part was still in the earliest and tiniest of leaves. Both Lloyd and I think that the view we had of the waterfall deep down in the ravine, and across to that great steep of mountain wall hung with wisteria and scattered over with the most brilliant of azalea was as fine and wonderful a sight as ever we saw. It was about six o'clock and the long level rays of the sun were still touching the waters of the mountain spring, turning it into silver, while one whole side of the mountain was in black shadow. Far, far below, seemingly a part of the mountain itself, were the roofs of the old monastery adding a picturesque touch to the scene. It would be hopeless to try to make anyone see it for the first time by mere description, but you have seen it and you can imagine."

April 30, 1922. "So much has happened since I wrote my letter a week ago, I'll plunge in at once to the visit of the World

61

Student Christian Federation delegation. It was quite an episode in our existence. I think I told in a letter to Mother that when I got down from Kuling, I was met by Netta at the doorway and shortly told that I was to entertain four of the delegates instead of two. That was because most of the men had to leave town for one reason or another just at this time, but I, being well chaperoned by Mr. and Mrs. Van Doon, the Dutch delegates, could take in single men. I went across Saturday to meet them with Netta in the B.A.T. [British American Tobacco Co.] launch. It was a most interesting group which descended from the train. There was the Hindu, Swami Dass, who was so astounding to all around that I wouldn't have given up a sight of those faces for anything. He was black as a coal, and wore a light blue turban with a streamer. You can imagine what that was to the man in the street, who'd never seen such a specimen in all his life before. Then there was delightful Ella McNeil, an Australian girl, who was an old friend of mine [I'd met her up in Kuling the summer before], the representative from Holland and his wife, young and typically Dutch of countenance. A tall, stalwart Australian gentleman named Mr. Robinson, with a deep cleft in his chin and the most cockney of accents. A Japanese, who was such a mild specimen that I decided he must have been chosen to prove the Japanese are truly peaceful in their inclinations. And a fine-looking middle-aged person named Sharman, who proved to be the man who wrote 'The Harmony of the Gospels.' It was decided that I should take the Australian and the Japanese in addition to the Dutch, and I tell you I felt like a real old timer when I led them up the bank and began to arrange for their baggage. I never had had four speechless guests before. [Lloyd was away.] They were glad enough to get to our house and rest a bit before dashing over to the YMCA and giving the first addresses. The big YMCA auditorium was crowded, and we could see there was going to be more than the ordinary amount of interest in these students, representing as they did the thought of so many countries. A schedule was planned that night with Mr. Liu, the Chinese secretary, taking charge. Netta and I gathered with the rest of them in Arthur's study and felt tremendously important to be thus representing our husbands. Sunday the delegation went around to various churches throughout the city. Mr. Robinson came to us and gave a good talk on the Christian attitude toward war, which is his main interest, as it is of everyone who thinks, of course. Only he has been through the war with Allenby in Palestine, and I seem to hear in him the voice of those who knew whereof they spoke. He was a Philip Gibbs himself, only more radical. It was a most interesting experience.

"Then that afternoon there was a huge meeting of students in the Methodist Tabernacle on the lake, built while we were home. There Miss McNeil spoke very well about Responsibility of Youth, and the necessity of taking a scientific attitude and weighing the accuracy of statements, and getting at facts instead of hearsay. She knew of the recent student anti-Christian attitude, and they listened attentively to her wholesome advice. Then Mr. Dass spoke about Gandhi and India, and it was most stirring. He is a real orator, and the Chinese students, who are all asking and reading and thinking about Gandhi, as about no one else, sat there enthralled. Our guests had to dash off to see a civil governor after that, so Netta asked if they could all have supper here in our Summer House instead of going way back to her house. Of course I was game, but I must confess I was a bit excited when I got back home at five to find that I'd forgotten to tell the cook that there was to be six o'clock supper, and twelve people to feed. Lao Den was on hand, but he simply didn't know how to work a Summer House supper, since he never had done it, and whenever I had a moment to think in Chinese, between mad spreadings of sandwiches, I had to tell him what to do next. I had almost achieved the calmness of despair, when I found two secretaries here, plus Netta's two infants, making sixteen in all. I tell you it was some hustling. The end of the story is that we did it, and got the crew over in time for the seven o'clock meeting. It was a mighty nice way to inaugurate the summer house, which proved perfectly capable of managing that crowd, with space for as many more. We have tea out there frequently now and love it.

"But that seven o'clock meeting was the most memorable one, for it gave the students a chance to ask Dr. Sharman questions. I had had a vision of the hesitating way in which question boxes occur at missionary meetings, and wondered if it would go. I needn't have worried. No sooner did Dr. Sharman pause than all over the huge audience of about a thousand or more, up jumped eager-looking students just bursting with questions. Some came in English, others in Chinese, to be translated. The first one I remember was something about an explanation of the books of Daniel and the Revelation. There was another about Christ's brothers and sisters. There was another about miracles; another about prayer. It was the most intensely interesting group, and Dr. Sharman was absolutely the man for the place—a thorough and devoted Bible student with a liberal background of thought, who had conducted Bible classes for years in the University of Chicago. Tuesday evening we had an outdoor community supper at Dr. Kahn's with speeches again from those poor delegates who certainly had to work their way; only this time it was under the lanterns on that lovely cool compound, quite different from the hot crowded stifling hall. The whole thing made us realize more than ever that the only hope of the world today lies in the spirit of Christianity. At that assembly in Peking they said one of the most hopeful aspects was in the friendliness of the groups which could get together and discuss in spite of the greatest of political differences."

Just at this time Arthur and Netta Allen of the YMCA and their two little boys moved from their quarters outside the south gate of the city to live with us for an indefinite period until housing could be built for them. This meant that Arthur would be much nearer his work in the city and that we would have the companionship of delightful friends, as well as their

64

rent allowance to make repairs on our home. I tell of the new members of our family in the following letter: "My household has swelled enormously in the last three days. First came Towser, a big yellow and white combination setter and collie from Baldwin. He's a gift, and we love him devotedly already. He is supposed to be very foolish, but I really think it is mainly due to his having had no particular master or mistress to attend to his education. Now he has fastened himself upon me, and I positively don't move without his moving too. He's a lot of company.

"Also on Wednesday Netta and the infants and two servants arrived [Arthur was at some meeting in Shanghai] so we have more to think of than merely the dog. They are all comfortably settled upstairs, in the two back rooms, and we're all getting on beautifully. The kiddies are darling, and as good as gold. Netta has splendid discipline. Then Wang Nai Nai is the most cheerful amah in the world, and everyone is happy to have so much going on."

May 15, 1922. "Of recent days the main excitement has been connected with three large boxes of silkworms, which one of the schoolboys gave to Lloyd. I never had watched them go through all the processes to the finish, and find it almost impossible to go more than an hour without hanging over the little objects. We have a hundred or so. When they first came they were small creatures living in one small box. Then they expanded into a large box, then into two boxes, then three, and now they are crawling everywhere making their little nests up on the curtains or any old where they want to go. It was exciting enough to see them grow from little wrigglers into great fat white worms, just in the process of eating leaves. And how they did savor those leaves! It took the attention of all of us combined to get enough right from the trees in our own front yard. It was a dramatic moment for us all when Wang Nai Nai came into the dining room, her face full of importance, and

65

announced that the worms were beginning to spit silk and where should they do their spitting. Since then we have been kept busy fishing them out of the box and putting them on the paper stretched across a bowl, where they are supposed to run back and forth and make a round piece of silk which you may all behold one of these days. We left the large majority, of course, to use their silk to spin cocoons and lie dormant till next spring, when the life process would be repeated.

"Wednesday afternoon I spent in making calls on the school girls' mothers. One of the homes was that of the Chinese manager of Asiatic Petroleum. It was a huge Chinese house, and the odd thing was that from the time we first stepped past the man at the door we didn't see a living soul till we thought we must have entered the palace of the Sleeping Beauty herself. That in a Chinese house is a most unusual experience. We wandered through room after room, high, clean, empty, in the best Chinese style, and at last, without having heard a sound, found ourselves in front of a guest room where the women of the house were sitting. You know how stiffly Chinese guest rooms are arranged, and there they were sitting around the wall, doing absolutely nothing. It gave me a sudden insight into the barren boredom of the life of many Chinese women of the highest classes which I won't soon forget. Their faces hardly moved a muscle as we came in, though I knew they must be glad of something to break the monotony. I didn't know who they all were at first, but found later that there was a grandmother, wife and concubine. The latter's room was shown to me, and they used an unfamiliar term to describe her, whereupon I made the pupil most embarrassed by inquiring who she was! For the pupil was at home, and the one bit of brightness in all that gloomy abode. She is a sweet unaffected child, apparently utterly unspoiled by all her high estate. She stood in the middle of the guest room feeding her silk worms, which was, of course, a bond of union. She took us all through the house and then led us back to the guest room, where we

66

were fed the usual tea and cakes with the addition of a nice new kind made of flour, sugar, sesame seeds and lard, all mixed together and then, uncooked, moulded in the bottom of a teacup. The flour is heated, they said, and the result is a perfectly delicious little powdery cake."

May 23, 1922. "It seems to me that I closed my last letter by telling you that I was about to have a meal at the Governor's. And have it I did. Netta teaches English there twice a week to the Governor's niece, and when Mrs. Brockman was here gave a party at which I met her pupil and her Chinese teacher as well. Hence my invitation to a meal at their home, with Netta. I was naturally delighted to go, for that kind of an invitation doesn't come every day, and I had never even been in the Civil Governor's yamen but once. It is located out near the gate where we take the ferry across the river, and is fronted by an imposing gateway at which are lined up a row of guards. Our rickshas went right on in through the gate, along a straight driveway edged with trees, and soldiers' barracks on each side. That ended apparently in a big foreign-looking brick building, but we skirted that and kept on and on, past all sorts of buildings till we came to an entrance past which the rickshas couldn't go. There we climbed out and then had quite a walk through interesting-looking courtyards with imposing guest rooms on all sides. I began to think we never would get anywhere, but Netta had learned the way, and at last we found ourselves being greeted by the teacher and the sweet-faced sixteen year old Miss Yang, and then out came flying the Governor's three little girls, all dressed up like butterflies. They had on exquisite silk coats which came down to the floor, with gay ribbons and flowers in their hair, and such giddy shoes. They were a regular little bunch of flowers, and simply beaming with the excitement of a party which was to end with a movie, staged by Arthur who was to arrive after supper with the machine from the Y.

"We had been invited for four, and arrived at five, just an hour and a half ahead of anyone else! It was perfectly polite and all right for the rest, too. Anyhow I had plenty of time to see their semi-foreign guest room, with its chairs and tables and cabinets filled with all sorts of exquisite pottery and bronze. I was particularly taken by two lions carved out of bamboo roots in such a way that the little rootlets made a shaggy covering of hair all over them. Then there was a marvelous framed picture carved from wood. It represented some sacred mountain, covered with little summer houses, and paths and trees, all standing out from the wooden background in bold relief, and marvelously carved.

"After talking and eating all kinds of cake and fruit they took us out to the garden back of the house. That had all been filled in so it wasn't far from the level of the top of the city wall, and was full of flower beds in good condition. There were two summer houses there, on little artificial hills, overhung by trees. They took us up into one of them, and I was simply entranced with the view. They showed me where they had planted the flower seeds I had sent them and which had all come up better than mine, I grieve to say. And at last the rest of the guests arrived—Mrs. Johnson, Mrs. Draper, and Dr. Kahn and another doctor from the Hospital. Then we sat down to another lot of cakes and fruit, and shortly after that was over in came a lot of turnovers filled with essence of rose leaves and mei hwa, an early spring shrub. I was practically filled up before the real meal was announced, which was served in a big separate room, surrounded by glass windows opening on the garden. We were all lighted up with electricity and there was a grand piano over in the corner. Very grand. So was the food though I can't give much to sharks fins. It was all served in foreign style with knives and forks, but was licking good Chinese food—a very acceptable combination. From there we went back to the guest room for more cakes, and to wait for the movies. We were all feeling well filled and lazy, and at that point Dr. Kahn suddenly decided that she wanted me to dance! There is no gainsaying the doctor when she wants something, so at last Netta and I got up, hummed a waltz, and proceeded to dance for the company, much to their joy. The little kids sang Chinese songs, and at last when we had seen the movies and went to pay off our sleepy ricksha men, we found we had been at the Governor's exactly five hours!"

September 24, 1922. "One afternoon Lloyd and I went out of one gate near the school, to get a boat on the river. There was a grand wind, and we wanted to sail, but the boatman for some reason decreed not.

"On our way, just outside the gate, we passed the big building in which is Nanchang's most famous bit of literature. We'd never either of us been in, and ever since I'd heard the story I'd made up my mind to visit the place. It seems that long years ago a Magistrate of the city had a daughter who wrote such wonderful poetry that all who heard were amazed. One day the proud father staged a feast to which he invited many eminent scholars, and asked each one to bring a poem. A great many people went and it was a very big time indeed. The poems were read, fond parent expecting to have his daughter's at the end to cap the climax. But a young boy stepped forward with such a marvelous poem that all were dumbfounded, and daughter's contribution wasn't even given a hearing. That poem became immediately famous, and was printed in all the National Readers, so thousands of school boys know of Nanchang as the place where it was written. Naturally I wanted to see it—it having a huge building as its shrine. The soldiers at the gate welcomed us cordially, and we were led past a big entrance court. The wall at the end was carved with characters telling this story in detail I suppose. Then we were led on around to the back of the building, past some bedrooms occupied by recumbent policemen, to a pair of almost impossible stairs in a black, absolutely unlighted part of the building. The stairs were

69

each one a different width and a different space apart. Poor old Towser simply couldn't get down them in any ordinary manner, so he just plunged, when it came to the return trip. It may be the idea to make the navigation so difficult that the place won't be bothered much. Anyway, the great room upstairs, when we got to it, was quite impressive from its huge size with nothing in it but a few benches, and a side of the wall, perhaps 18 or 20 feet high, painted gray to look like stone, and carved with old-fashioned characters not one of which we could possibly recognize, but we knew this was the poem. But good for China, I say, to show its respect for learning in such an evident fashion."

October 4, 1922. "Monday morning Lloyd and I had a very instructive time sight-seeing in the city with our teacher as guide. It adds a lot to have him along, naturally. Our objective was the Orphans Home, run on an endowment, and an institution which has been going for years. I'd heard something about it from Dr. Gale, who is called in sometimes to look after the wet nurses—I don't know whether they ever worry about the health of the babies or not. It certainly didn't seem so! She told me that the babies are brought in when they are tiny new-born infants, and usually are taken away to be servants or wives for the sons of country people who are too poor to buy one and so raise one, instead. We knew we were approaching the place, for in the open space in front of the doorway were sitting a group of women, who seemed to have come in from the country in wheelbarrows. I think they may have brought in their charges to be looked over, and get their money for being nurses, for I understand some of the babies are farmed out. I was prepared to have my heart wrung—I'd heard enough about the place to know that. But really it beggared description. We walked along narrow dark passageways, past a wall in which was set something which looked like a revolving wooden pail, with an opening cut in one side in which the baby could be put and then the tub revolved to an equal-sized opening in the wall.

There the baby would be received, and no one the wiser as to the mother. Such a tragic little bucket!

"Then on past that into a long narrow courtyard, with a series of rooms opening from it. The rooms had plenty of fresh air, at least, since the partition from the court was wide open. In each room were ten or twelve wooden cradles, full of unspeakably horrible rags, once stuffed with cotton as comforts, but now the cotton was all exposed. In each cradle were two tiny babies, one at each end. And oh—such pitiful emaciated little heads as some of them had, I never even imagined. I suppose there is a tremendous loss of life among the little things. As Lloyd said, it could never be anything but a survival of the fittest. Any child living through those first three months was to be congratulated. The wet nurses sat around in heaps—about ninety of them, to two hundred babies, if I remember my statistics accurately. They administer nourishment by leaning over the cradles, and sometimes you'd see two infants clapped on at once. All around were spread out the diapers—supposed to be drying after being washed, but they still looked like floor mops. It really was terribly depressing. I never wanted to do anything so much as to clean up the place, and Netta said it worked on her just like that. The most that can be said is that it saved the babies from death. It's interesting to think they are all girl babies!"

October 12, 1922. "We had a beautiful time on Friday when, at Mr. Den's invitation, we went out beyond the South Gate, into the country for the whole of a most lovely day. The sky was clear and blue and the air bracing enough so walking was a joy. I hadn't been in that direction since we went together, mother dear, and you were in my thoughts many times. Our destination was a Taoist temple beyond the cemetery where we went that time. It's about five miles there, they say, but it didn't seem as far as that. We straggled along in a procession that I wish you could have seen. Mrs. Den and the two women

71

teachers went as well as myself, so we had two wheelbarrows to grace the occasion, and one of them with a tremendous squeak. Then dear Mr. Den had brought his accordion, and wherever we went we had those peculiar strains to add buoyancy to our feet. He carefully explained that he could walk better to music. So *Go tell Aunt Nancy* and *Yankee Doodle* mingled with most of the hymns in the hymnal, added to the gaiety. There were some school boys and several teachers and Towser, bounding about through everything and thinking himself in the seventh heaven, though he brought utter consternation to the rustics. I think they must have thought him a tiger! Our wheelbarrow man was entranced by him. A dog who could understand our commands was beyond his comprehension. He took to issuing commands himself, and whenever Towser started a little farther afield than usual he would shout 'Taudze, dsou goli' [Come this way]. You have to realize the wolfish nature of most Chinese dogs, which are never called anything but "dog," to appreciate the situation.

"We stopped and ate queer things in a tea house along the way so it was almost one before we saw the white walls of 'Clear Cloud Temple' in the distance, overhung by magnificent camphors and bamboo. The temple itself isn't much, but it is quite modern and very clean, comparatively, and in one of the courts is an old, old cassia tree [cinnamon in case you don't know] that supposedly dates from the Tang Dynasty 1200 years ago. It is quite the thing for the gentry and scholars of the city to stroll out there and have their pictures taken at the foot of the tree.

"There were a lot of interesting things in the temple itself, many of them given by Nanchang officials. The place of honor was given to portraits of the Military and Civil Governors of last year, and how Lao Den did swell with pride as he announced in loud tones, 'There is the picture of the governor who had a meal at our house last spring!' In fact Lao Den was in high feather all day, for this was near his home and he knew every stick and

72

stone. We wouldn't pass a Widows Arch or a brick house that he didn't push his way to my side and announce the name of the family connection. There is a real democracy in China that comes to the surface on such leveling experiences.

"We wandered around and looked at a fish, about a foot long, carved out of solid jade, and the scrolls of lacquer with characters of blue porcelain inlaid, and I discovered an interesting contrast of two pictures of the temple itself. One was a modern and quite accurate water color, after the style of those innumerable Japanese ones. The other was a most delicate one in the real Chinese style, utterly lacking in Western perspective, but such a thing of daintiness and beauty that I somehow came nearer than ever before to appreciating the true inward beauty of Chinese art. There was no comparison in the decorative value of the two.

"Another entertaining feature of the temple were the quantities of little plaster figures of monks and gentlemen of all types, who had their lineaments copied with amazing accuracy. It seems that there are such sculptors connected with the idol factory. I'm perfectly crazy for Lloyd to have his image made, but it costs $5.00 per, and seems a little like making a graven image, as it is. But it seems they make the faces without looking at the clay at all, simply looking at the person's face. The Chinese who were telling about it said they poked the clay up their sleeves while they were moulding it. Seems quite remarkable—possibly apocryphal!

"Lloyd and I ate a foreign lunch under the beautiful camphor trees outside the temple, while the rest ate their noodles inside. Then we started back home, stopping at our own Church Cemetery, which has been all nicely terraced off from the endless miles of other dreary graves, with a stone cross in the center to mark it. We sat there and Mr. Den played *For all Thy Saints* and it was good to feel something expressive of Christian

73

hope in the midst of all that vast expanse."

December 26, 1922. "The 'pageant' of the birth of Christ given by the Lower Primary boys for the 'ragged Sunday School kids' [the poor children of the neighborhood who had no money for an education] came Sunday night and was a scream. Nobody else knew it was funny but just Lloyd and I, so it really didn't matter. But when the wise men held a lighted flashlight up to their eyes like a telescope and peered through the unlighted end to see the star it was almost one too many! They passed it solemnly from one to the other so everyone had a chance to see the phenomenon. We had forgotten to bring over gifts for the Wise Men, but I found they were all provided—one with the top of a toy wooden apple, another with a three layer tin basket of which he let the third boy have one layer. But even that didn't matter! If you could have seen me do strong arm work on getting those children to sit down you would have recommended me to the police force. Of course we were dealing with raw material which had never had to sit down in all its life before, so there was no wonder that they didn't quite understand. They each got a package of cakes and an orange at the end, having to climb up on a high platform to do so, while Mr. Den dressed as Santa Claus pranced up and down with a cane to knock the fingers of the ones who were struggling to crawl up instead of using the steps. I found Lloyd utterly steeped in perspiration at the end of the performance and took him home to listen to the Victrola Christmas records, to calm his spirit."

January 2, 1923. "Friday afternoon Lloyd and I were invited to the wedding feast given for the daughter of a church member. It is one of our very best church members but his family have never had anything to do with us. His brothers have really persecuted him, so he finally took his name out of the ancestral book, or whatever arrangement they have, thereby losing fifty dollars, but saving himself from the non-Christian performances he would have been forced to join in. So we know he is absolutely true blue, but with his family non-Christian and the bridegroom also never having been near the church, it was impossible for them to have any kind of a Christian ceremony. I went with some fear and trembling, fearing they wouldn't care much for my presence, and believing it might be a chance for me to get a little opening at least in a friendly way, which always is the first step to getting anywhere.

"It was a delightful surprise to be met with the greatest cordiality and be led at once to the bedroom where the little bride was sitting on the bed all clad in her wedding garment of bright red satin, with all the awful embroidery of modern China. I saw the wonderful hat she was to don the next day, covered with round glittering beads and waving ornaments. She had a most responsive face—I liked her so much, and the old 'popo' or grandmother, who had brought her up in the country. There was a lot of conversation before the feast was ready. The mother of the bride told me about her bad times with a strange malady which has been seizing her for some years. It sounds like epilepsy, for when it comes upon her she falls down senseless, and is evidently sick in bed for some time. The last time she struck a marvelous cure—though I had some difficulty in being sure what it was, for it turned out to be swallowing a piece of very old copper cash, one a day for three days in succession. Then she got well! Now what would you do with that! After the feast they went out into the street to buy something which they informed me was a very fragrant kind of medicine to be dissolved in her bath water, for the bride was to take a bath. Did I take a bath before I was married, they wanted to know. When Mr. Den promptly informed them that foreigners took baths every day they were too stunned to speak for at least five minutes.

"We were getting along famously, and they seemed to like me as well as I liked them. So I was much pleased to be invited to come back the next day and see the bride get into her chair. In all my years in China I've never seen anything but a Christian marriage, so you don't know anything about it either. I took my camera and set forth about one the next day. The first thing that I saw in the guest room outside the bride's door was the red embroidered chair which was to take her to her new home, and in front of it a wooden bucket containing five red wicks, in oil, lighted. Over the bucket was a bamboo sieve, full of little open places which I knew were meant to represent so many little eyes to keep off devils.

"The first thing on the program was to take pictures, and how I hope they turn out well. It was the chance of a lifetime. I took the chair, and the bride with her two attendants, who are women of good fortune, with husbands and sons. Then I took two family groups of the old lady with her sons and grandsons. I never have any luck with pictures in courtyards, but breathed a prayer over all these and hope there will be some success.

"There was another wait of an hour or so before the time arrived for the poor tired little bride to be carried off. I invited all the females to come and see me—and the house—on Monday afternoon, which they eagerly consented to, and had a long talk with the old popo, who was so friendly and even peered at my stockings to see how far my underwear came down into them. Finally came the time for the bride to mount the chair, and the fifes began to blow and the drums to be banged. The first ceremony was performed by the attendants who came out with lighted wicks and went all around and in the chair as if hunting for something. They were on a still hunt for devils, forsooth, and finding none the edict went forth that the bride was to be produced. I saw the uncle making a bee-line for the bedroom, and was informed that the bride couldn't set foot to the floor, but must be carried out, and in a minute out came the uncle with the lady, who was good and hefty, in his arms, and dumped her in the chair. Then the front of the chair was all pasted up with big red papers, on which were written the family name and so on, and insured the arrival of the delivery without having been tampered with en route. At the same time somebody produced a little dish containing rice and tea, which was to be thrown after the chair to insure the new family always having something to eat. Throws a little light on our own quaint superstitions, doesn't it?

"They had asked me frequently if I was going to weep, and I had answered that I was willing to try, but refused to do it out of my nose as they made the motions. I showed them how we pat our eyes when we wish to inform the world of our sorrow, but they continued to clutch at their noses whenever tears were mentioned. Mrs. Den told them that foreigners didn't weep, on such occasions, but marched down the aisle, beaming on the world and holding their newly acquired possession on the arm. It really did sound a little flapperish, I must admit. Nothing like that here. The bride wept loudly as she sat in the chair, and all her brothers and sisters and mother did likewise. Then the chair was picked up with the oddest twisting motion, and wriggled through the door like a snake. I'm not quite sure why they did that, but think it was to avoid devils, probably, who move in a straight line. I should think the poor bride would have had a dizzy spell to contend with as well as everything else. No sooner did the chair get out of the room than a carpet was spread down, a chair put on it, and a little bundle of wood wrapped up in a red cloth put on the floor in front. Then the old popo who had suddenly been transformed from a beaming hostess to a wailing one was helped to the chair where she sat with her feet planted on the wood, and wept copiously and loudly. I couldn't make out what that was for till Mrs. Den explained. The word for 'wood' has the same sound as the word for riches, though the character is quite different. This little performance was to typify the fact that the riches were not to leave the home along with the daughter!

77

"Then I ran out to the front door, where the chair was still standing in the street, and suddenly my heart sank down into the pit of my stomach as I thought how that child was going to be picked up and carried quite by herself to an absolutely strange place, and worse still, to an absolutely strange man. Am I glad we do things differently."

VII

There was one city in our diocese which we were extremely eager to visit, and in the spring of this year, 1923, we were able to do it. I will introduce my letter telling of our trip to Chin Teh Chen with a short description to show why we were so interested in this particular city.

Centuries ago a deposit of kaolin was found in the northeastern part of our province, which was so superior to any other in China that soon Chin Teh Chen, the city located near it, became the one important center for the manufacture of porcelain. Other cities might decorate the product, but the porcelain itself was sent by circuitous routes up the Kan River and overland to Canton or other southern cities, and also distributed along the whole length of the Yangtze and from there all over China. The porcelain was all made and decorated by hand.

Since it was in our diocese it seemed to me that there might be an opportunity to go there and that arose when the clergyman, the Rev. Bernard Tsen, arranged for a series of evangelistic meetings in which he wished Lloyd to take part. Moreover he sent a telegram which had me all agog. "Come with consort. Help evangelizing." When had I ever before had such a title! This was the time to go, most certainly.

At this point Bishop Huntington came by on a visitation and reported that all the launches as they arrived in Nanchang were being commandeered for soldiers who, for some reason, were being sent to the south of the province. Our chances to leave looked slim, and I was, I found, truly disappointed. So much so that I suddenly decided we must go by a Chinese junk even though it would take six days to make the trip and we would be late for the meetings. Still, if we went at once, we could get there for three days of them at least.

May 19, 1923. "Of all the varieties of boat travel that I have
had, lead me to this, in spite of the fact that we killed three bed
bugs, fattened on my blood. That really is the only fly in my
pot of ointment, if fly it can be called. [We finally found that
by standing the legs of our cots in tin cans with a little kerosene
in them, and tucking a mosquito net carefully around our
mattresses each night, we could at least diminish the attentions
of these visitors.]

"We had all our provisions ready and the basket of food all
packed and lists made out so when we made this decision to go
it didn't take us too long to get underway. How we did fly
around, getting Mei Ss Fu to order the boat and get his things
ready, packing our two big waterproof bamboo boxes which
have our names woven in Chinese characters on the side, have a
tray in them, and hold as much as two week end cases; Lao Den
dashing in at the last to ask if I'd remembered my typewriter
and camera and to press two fans upon us; Wang Nai Nai asking
if we'd taken soap—and off we started about 3 p.m. We took
Mei Ss Fu, the Allen's boy, because he can cook.

"Netta went down with us to the shore to see our boat, so
she could picture us all the way. I'd imagined a little black hole
in which we were to settle ourselves for six days. What I found
was one of the better type of junks, with an arched hold divided
into three compartments, two of which were to be our own
private possession, and divided from the rear by a white curtain.
The front compartment is large enough to hold our two camp
cots, crosswise of the boat. The back one is the living and dining
room. On each side are shelves, at least three feet wide. It's
wonderful how useful those shelves can be. We have our
bamboo boxes on one end, and leave the rest free on one side
for a dining table. On the other side we have departments—there
is a library containing everything from Walter Hines Page and
Fosdick to Chinese tracts. Next comes the bathroom—wash
basin and soap dish, and the indispensable below. Then comes

the optical department with the camera, tripod and field glasses. And there is still room enough to spread down pillows and recline, while the other one of us sits on the wicker chair we brought along, placed on the floor between the shelves. Dangling from the rafters are rain hats, umbrellas, knitting bag, lantern. You never have seen such a complete and shipshape arrangement. Whenever we don't have anything else to do we sit around and admire ourselves!

"Most important of all, there are windows, a row of boards all around above the shelves can be taken out, making perfectly grand cross ventilation. The front end of the boat is open when we fight hard enough, so we have an airy bedroom. I mention this particularly for the 'lao ban's' hobby is to batten down the hatches. It almost breaks him up not to put up those front doors at night, and nothing but the most peremptory treatment suffices. Three times did he attempt it the first night, and only the fact that I was awake a good deal and heard him creeping up kept us from waking up smothered.

"At our rear floats the American flag—to keep the soldiers from seizing our boat. We let the 'lao ban' have it as soon as we got aboard, and about three hours later we discovered that he had run our beloved Old Glory up the mast upside down! Not only have the stars fallen but the heavens as well. We saw some females at the Methodist compound gazing fixedly in our direction before we waved, and think they must have been considering it a signal of distress.

"We're supposed to be the only passengers aboard, but needless to say, we aren't. There are four regular members of the crew, which includes two able-bodied men, one old man who steers in the rear, and a fourteen year old boy who giggles his head off at us in general and the field glasses in particular. Then there is a slightly demented women who never utters a word, who is said to be the boy's mother. She disappeared a few

81

minutes after she got aboard, and when I went on deck I found a plank had been shoved to one side and there she was, down in the black hold underneath—'down among the dead men'! When night comes the board is placed back over her prostrate form. Occasionally I stamp on the deck and demand of the lao ban 'Is that woman under here?' and am relieved if he can hastily reply that she is in the rear. It seems too much like a too early interment. Then there are two regular passengers as well as Mei Ss Fu. We occupy completely two thirds of the boat. The remaining eight take what's left over. Crowded but cozy!

"The next topic—our food. The stove is a charcoal burning one, shaped like a flower pot and of the same material as one. That reposes under the back deck, and there our meals are cooked. Fortunately the hours of our meals and the crew's don't coincide. Mai Ss Fu's kitchen table becomes his bed at night, and is a most convenient arrangement for he merely lifts up the curtain and pokes everything in to us without ever setting foot into our dwelling. I forgot to say that a four inch ledge around the outside of the boat is the passageway so that no one comes into our rooms without an invitation. They do poke their heads in the window or through the back curtain in a way a trifle disconcerting, but they usually pick a rather harmless hour of the day. To return to food—Mei Ss Fu cooked the most delicious fresh fish yesterday, and we had rice and a green vegetable and bread and butter and raisins for dessert. And last night you never ate better 'flannel cakes,' as Lloyd calls them—pancakes, real thin and oh so good. We ate them with scrambled eggs and had prunes for dessert. We just long for meal hours to roll around.

"Our mode of locomotion is so varied that just watching it would remove any monotony from the trip. When we left Nanchang we were being rowed along by those long curved sculls at the front of the boat—splendid exercise in leaning over and back and pulling as both Lloyd and I can testify. We take our daily dozen assisting. Then when the shallow places come—moderately shallow—two long poles are produced with hooks on the end. You stick them into the mud and then run along from the front end of the deck to the rear, pushing as you go—leg exercise of the best variety. When the water is still shallower they tie ropes to the top of the mast and pull, walking along a tow path. That's quite a bit faster than either of the above methods! When the extreme of shallowness is reached, as at present in the middle of Poyang, the whole crew roll their trousers to the vanishing point and get out and push the boat walking along through the water and we go flying—comparatively speaking. Of course the fifth method would be a south wind, were there one, but so far it has eluded us. Little Lao Ban stops giggling long enough, occasionally, to whistle for one—or rather squawk—and yesterday morning when we helped him he was rewarded with a few fitful gusts. Mostly not.

"Scenery: I should think this would be the last topic. You know our general direction is northeast, and to accomplish it we sail down the Kan River, through the delta country into Poyang Lake, where we are now after nearly two days of traveling. It's now about noon of the third day. We've enjoyed every minute of our time and could contemplate an indefinite amount of it. When we left Nanchang we went along long level stretches of shore with an occasional charming looking temple and wondered why we never had explored that region on our two feet. Then the next morning we found ourselves in the delta country with nothing on all sides but great fields of grass. They use the grass for fertilizer. Carry off great loads of hay to rot. Lloyd and I got off and walked for an hour along the tow path to get an appetite for lunch. Another advantage over steamboat travel.

"By late afternoon we were in the lake, but still so surrounded by long stretches of grass-covered land I kept thinking it was the river. About five o'clock we put up at a town which had a perfectly delightful temple with a tindze [cupola] on top giving a view in four directions. If we take these pretty temples away from the country people we must give them tindzes for their churches. We had seen another interesting village lying along the high land back of this one, and since we were to spend the night at that town we decided to take a walk and make an exploration. It had been a gray day, but the sun was peeping through the clouds, the air was sweet and fresh, and the view of all these shining sheets of water was really lovely. You remember how it looks from Nankang Pass on Kuling and at last we were in it! How we did enjoy that walk along the bank, past cottages surrounded by bamboo and overhung by the most beautiful old trees. The courtyards were very untidy, but I couldn't find it in my heart to pity the inhabitants in the least. They certainly are the most sensible people in China, excepting perhaps the boatmen.

"Then suddenly it came into view—a long white shining temple and back of it a fairy grove of trees so old and gnarled and with trunks so gray that I think now I know what a grove of old English beeches must look like. But this was here all by itself and we had found it. We kept on to the village and the people were turned almost speechless. When we asked them questions they simply gaped up at us for the first five minutes. Then they asked what on earth the tripod was that Lloyd was carrying. The sight of the way its legs pull out made more of a hit than the camera, even. They took us along and showed us the village well—a great fine well which is evidently the center of the life—and where, incidentally, all the water carriers were Rebeccas.

"Then we turned back again. Thinking about the multitudinous number of such villages there are in this country, and how interesting they would be to work in and how much they need our schools and our teaching—we're beginning to wish we could be transferred to country work. I can't imagine anything more worthwhile than giving what we have to such villages as

84

that. And we could picnic in that grove behind the temple."

My next letter, telling of our visit, has been lost, but I remember something of those experiences even after forty-eight years. On the sixth day of travel we noticed that the clear waters of our mountain stream were no longer running over pebbles but over broken bits of crockery and porcelain. The whole stream was lined with the discards of the centuries of making china. It made us realize that we were at last approaching Chin Teh Chen, and suddenly at a bend in the stream, there we saw it, far more imposing than I could have pictured. Seventy-two kilns, and each one with a great tall brick smoke stack reaching high into the sky. It seemed most incongruous to see the sign of what looked like an industrialized area in the United States after these days of travel through remote country, and to realize that this important city had only small launches and junks to connect it with the outside world.

We were met by Mr. Tsen and his wife and given a hearty welcome to their home. It was good to leave the junk which was now surrounded by all the confusion of a port, and get to our church center. I know that we had arrived in time for some of the meetings and that we were impressed by the number of interesting and intelligent people who attended, but my outstanding recollection is my trips on foot through the city streets, much cleaner than I had seen in any other Chinese city. I was told that everyone had a job and I saw that there were no beggers. I was fascinated to find that I could see the china being decorated in the small shops, open to the light and to the gaze of the passersby also. I was told that the art of decorating certain types of china—the willow ware, or the "mille fleur," or the imperial yellow—was handed down from one generation to another in one family.

We went into several large warehouses and saw the way the china was wrapped in wood shavings for shipment to America, where rice straw was not permitted because of possible contamination. For shipment in China, rice straw was used. In any case the bundles were so skillfully packed that they could actually be dropped to the floor without danger of breakage. It was in that shop that I saw a huge crate just packed with a Baltimore address.

I watched the potters wheels being turned and cups and vases emerging almost miraculously under those skillful fingers. I saw long trays—really long narrow boards—covered with articles ready to be placed in the sun to dry. The kilns were heated by pine wood since only that wood could produce fire sufficiently hot. Occasionally the heat was too uneven and a whole firing would be spoiled. This was a kind of product which called for the utmost skill, and that skill had been achieved through generations. Incidentally we heard that it was a criminal offense to burn pine in any home in the area, for it all must be conserved for the use of the kilns. And also, incidentally, when I started to follow Lloyd into one of the huge kilns which wasn't being fired that day, I caused consternation. One of the workmen barred my way, and Mr. Tsen explained apologetically that it was a superstition that no woman could be allowed in one of these structures or the next firing would be a total loss. I learned my lesson. On our return we had favorable winds and made the trip in four days instead of six.

Later two of our women in the diocese visited the city and returned saying they thought the group of church members and inquirers the most hopeful and interesting of any center in our diocese they had seen. Miss Gregg had addressed a group of about six hundred men and women on the subject of "Progress." I have this letter to jog my failing memory.

The Chin Teh Chen trip was a high point not only for that year but ever since that time, and no doubt the present porcelain which we saw recently in Hong Kong, made in

86

Communist China and alas, decorated most crudely, was also a product of that city.

May 12, 1924. "It was bright and sunny here on Sunday, for the greatest of wonders, and a lot of people at church. There they were told to come back at two in the afternoon to go out on a Poster pasting expedition, distributing anti-opium literature. All the churches except one were united in the effort to get this across, which was a very good thing aside from any effects the literature might have. The school band headed the procession and made a special hit, for people flocked from near and far as they paraded through their appointed district in the city. Mr. Den had one paste brush and the Senior Warden the other and they must have been quite a sight, sticking these posters up on every prominent position. By the way, we got more information about this opium deal from the consul in Hankow when Lloyd was there. I told you, didn't I, that the military governor had started a great opium combine, licensing the sale of it throughout all the province subject to taxation which he got. Of course the official statement was that these taxes were 'fines' but the more lamps a place had the smaller the 'fine,' one lamp being five dollars and two being six, and so on. Also the editor of one of the Nanchang papers whose friend came to Lloyd and Arthur to plead for protection for him, for he was in danger of his life, had found and attempted to send to Shanghai the documents [not for publication] which appointed district supervisors in the province to collect the tax, and informed the dealers just how to get the opium. Lloyd and Arthur got this editor out to the Nanchang Hospital with his head in bandages disguised as a patient, and from there he escaped in a little boat, so there is one brave man saved to the world. Mr. Johnson got these documents and sent them to the Consul at Hankow, who told Lloyd he had sent them to Peking to the ambassador, and it was through the publicity given them there that the Kiangsi gentry went time after time to the President to protest, and finally raised such a rumpus that the bureaus throughout the city have been closed and there was a rumor of impeaching the Governor! We really are quite proud of Kiangsi that it didn't merely supinely acquiesce in all this. The traffic is much worse in a good many other provinces and they might just have said nothing could be done. As it is there is a great deal of feeling in the city and Lloyd said that there were many signs of approbation as they distributed the posters. One group of students broke into spontaneous applause."

Jan. 16, 1923. "This has been a week of important arrivals, even though I haven't had home letters. In the first place, Wednesday morning in came the model of the buildings for our new church and school. The Bishop left Tuesday, so it was a little tantalizing to think he couldn't have seen it, but we certainly have had a time with it. Lloyd is so choice of the precious thing that he keeps it under lock and key, and I realize my privileges keenly in the fact that I know where the key is. The whole group is about four feet long, and each separate story lifts off, so we begin at the bottom in our demonstrations and work up. And demonstrate we do, I assure you. All the workers and most of the Church members have had one. The wonderful part is that we never get weary of showing it off. Of course I know that after my early training nothing that looks so much like a doll's house could possibly weary me, and my only grief is that I can't get inside the thing and see what it looks like from within. It is made of wood throughout, of course, but the roof with its turned up corners and all looks surprisingly realistic. Mrs. Den came over with the first batch of people to look it over, and gave it the name which is destined to stick by it in this family—'little temple.' She also had some good suggestions to offer about a bathroom opening off the school room so all the little girls could have a chance to take baths in winter and summer alike. Just pay a few cents for hot water.

"Yesterday afternoon was quite a corker for me. First from two on I had a group of six women getting ready to take their examinations on Friday to become Inquirers. [That was the first stage in becoming a church member.] They have been coming here regularly to my class Wednesdays, and it has been a great joy to me to teach them the first principles of Christian living. They are very receptive, and I believe are going to make genuine Christians. They were followed by a class of little girls who also want to become Inquirers, at four o'clock. In the meantime George Lin came to learn typewriting [I said in the beginning I was going to teach the touch system, though I didn't know it, but I just lent him my typewriter and some book about the touch system and let him work it out.] and Miss Heng to have Netta teach her her English lesson. Also a school boy to see if his mother could come and call on me, and a committee of foreigners and Chinese to meet in Lloyd's study. Just as I finish my third hour of teaching in Chinese in comes Mr. and Mrs. Djing to make a call and ask for a note to Dr. Blydenburg at the hospital. At 6:30 I fall into a rocking chair by the stove and say I never want to speak another word of Chinese!"

VIII

Lloyd was blessed with a deep-seated appreciation of beauty in whatever form he found it. In his early days he experienced it especially in the Virginia country-side. He never had any self-consciousness about expressing his joy in the loveliness of his surroundings, though he did remember that some of his college classmates laughed at him for it.

He had found great beauty in the arts and crafts of China, and it was a continuing joy to him that we could embody much of this in the church building he had supervised in Nanchang. He felt that for every reason a house of worship dedicated to God should make use of the best in Chinese art. The school buildings and parish hall were well designed and functional, but St. Matthew's Church was truly beautiful. The Rev. Fletcher Howe, an architect and clergyman of our mission, had made the plans. Lloyd writes of the building in the following letter:

"The parson contractor of the firm is glad to tell you that the new church in which most of you have had some share is at last an accomplished reality.

"We have had in mind from the beginning to make this a house of worship in which our Chinese brethren would feel at home—Christian but Chinese in atmosphere. To accomplish this we have made the roof of Chinese tile with the characteristic upturned corners, and for the interior decorations have used Chinese designs throughout. The exposed roof beams, instead of following the Western style of triangular trusswork, are built up of the typical Chinese horizontal and vertical members, and are supported on two rows of lacquered columns along the aisles. The camphor wood paneling of the chancel, the reredos, the windows, and the pew ends, are all developments of one pattern of Chinese lattice work. The altar, bishop's seat, clergy stalls, etc., are all adaptations of Chinese furniture.

The Chancel of St. Matthew's Church, Nanchang.

"In symbolism the Chinese have a real advantage over Western lands in the use of the Chinese character. It is true in the West we have used scriptural quotations, Latin or Greek mottoes, and monograms in our ecclesiastical decorations, but the Chinese character is a word picture in itself, with a perspective and richness of association that far surpass the Roman letter. Moreover, their ideograph is a highly developed work of art, though to the average Westerner, whose only familiarity with those 'hen tracks' comes from the Chinese laundryman's cryptic slip, this may be hard to realize. At any rate we have depended on Chinese characters mainly for our suggestive symbols in the new church, and it is enough to say that the Chinese Christians find it good.

"You may remember that in order to economize our limited land area we put the church on the second floor, and so made room for the parish hall below. This hall is a well lighted, airy room which will seat about four hundred people. It is already

91

proving its usefulness as an assembly room for Sunday School, lecture hall, place for social gatherings, game room, etc. Moreover the church can now be kept entirely as a place of worship.

"We held our first service in the church on Easter morning, and a right happy time it was, with all its hopes and promises of new life which we trust will center in, and radiate from that place.

"The following week there arrived delegates from all over the diocese, about sixty in number, to attend the first meeting of the Diocesan Synod ever held in the Province of Kiangsi. With our one foreign residence and no boarding school it was probably a foolish thing to attempt to entertain so many, but by giving our Easter holiday then and by turning our class rooms into dormitories, borrowing beds and furniture from the schools and hospital of our fellow missionaries in Nanchang, and by calling on the Y.M.C.A. restaurant to feed most of the Chinese and some of the foreign delegates, we were able to manage it. The meetings of Synod were comfortably taken care of in the new parish hall. Outside of the sessions there were numerous entertainments, sight-seeing tours, and boating parties on the East Lakes, managed by our church members or provided by Methodist and Y.M.C.A. friends.

"But the focal point of this busy assemblage was Sunday morning, the first Sunday after Easter, for it was then the church was consecrated. In the congregation were old Christians who had gone through the early years of discouragement and even persecution, younger members, school boys and girls, pastors and church members from other Christian groups of the city, and delegates from nearly every parish and out-station of the Diocese of Anking. In the procession which had formed in the parish hall and marched in through the center aisle of the church were the Bishop and clergy of the diocese, including for the first time two deaconesses. As those prayers, so full of meaning and association, were said, asking God's blessing upon all acts done in His name in that church, and upon everyone who should come seeking Him in that house, we could not but think of the faithful company, thousands of them in all, whose prayers and gifts had gone into its building.

"Of course the significance of these buildings depends on the use to which they are put, and that lies in the future. The present demonstration in China is symptomatic of a growing national consciousness. Out of it should emerge eventually a more definitely Chinese Church, and fortunately we have a new building with a Chinese atmosphere to suit the need. But the period just ahead will probably be one of the most difficult the church in China has had to face. The need of China for Christ is as great as ever, and thousands of Chinese are deeply convinced of this need. In a spirit of sympathy and humility we can help them."

The year 1924 held for us the height of joy in the birth of our first baby, after previous sorrows and disappointments in the hopes of having a family, and the depth of sorrow in losing this baby in November of the same year. The following letter of 1925, written from Siasconset, Massachusetts in the summer gives some detail of our life at this time.

"Our baby Edward fell suddenly ill from a very acute intestinal infection, and after a week of struggle slipped back into Heaven, leaving behind him aching loneliness and heart-break, but at the same time a new sense of our nearness to the other world, and of comfort in the promises of life everlasting. Along with the memory of the anguish of those days is mingled that of the help we found in our friends, Chinese and foreign, who came to grieve with us as they had rejoiced with us such a short time ago. Our constant prayer is that the people we have come to live among may learn through this experience something of the peace and hope which is possible for us as Christians even in the presence of death.

"But the shock of such a loss after the illness of the summer proved harder for me physically than I realized, and when a cable came from the Department of Missions urging us to take an early furlough our doctors advised us to plan for it. So we started out on what proved to be a beautiful calm voyage, leaving Shanghai May 25th, with Bishop Roots and the Edmund Lees for traveling companions. It was just five days before the riot broke out which precipitated so much agitation, and which has been causing us to think almost as much of China as of our joy at being home in peaceful America again, with our dear families. I'm thankful indeed that we could leave before this trouble started, so that we have only the most heart warming expressions of good will to remember."

SECTION II

THE REVOLUTION CHANGES OUR LIVES

1925–1930

I

When we arrived in China in 1915 the Chinese Republic had been established for only four years. Sun Yat Sen had been the leader most instrumental in bringing about the fall of the dissolute and almost impotent Manchu Dynasty, and it was expected that he would be China's first president, but when he found that the Northern Element was most unwilling to entrust the country to a Southerner, he withdrew in favor of Yuan Shih Kai, who held the office at the time of our arrival.

As a matter of fact, there was no strong central government for all our years in China. It has been true of the history of the country that after the fall of a long-entrenched dynasty, there is a period during which the government is divided and the real control is in the hands of local leaders. This was true for our era. "The War Lords"—or military governors, were the real rulers, and the country was divided into areas over which each one had almost complete control, with only nominal allegiance to the central government.

When we arrived the traces of Manchu rule had been quite thoroughly obliterated. The men had cut off their queues, a style of haircut demanded by the Manchus of their subjects, foot-binding was discouraged and in many places abolished, and the large areas where the Manchus had lived, both in Nanking and Nanchang had been turned into vegetable gardens. The curio stores were full of the outmoded embroidered garments formerly worn by Manchu officials. It was amazing that such a complete change could have happened in so short a time, but

97

this, we knew, was the effect of a long-overdue revolution.

It is sad for the history of China and the world that there was no group strong enough to lead the country into the ways of democracy. There was so much hope among the young people at this time, and we saw it change during our years into bitter disillusionment.

We became aware of the encroachment the various powers had made on China's suzerainty as soon as we arrived. Shanghai, the largest city in the country and the most important commercially, had been divided into "concessions" by England and France, and those areas were governed by the Nationals of the countries involved. The boats which we traveled on up the Yangzte were run by British companies. The foreshores where they tied up in the cities along their route were all controlled by the British. There was one Chinese shipping company, but as they weren't allowed to touch at the British docks and had to unload at places which were inconvenient for us, we rarely traveled on them.

The import duties were administered by Westerners, to insure the payment of the indemnity required of China after the Boxer uprising, when much foreign property had been destroyed. The post office was also administered by Europeans.

It was terribly humiliating to the pride of China that this should be the case, and much of the anti-foreign attitude which dominates China today had its roots in the events of the 19th century. It was only occasionally in our first years that we were aware of this feeling, since for the most part our church members and students were eager to learn about the West, to adopt some of our customs and learn the English language. The future belonged to the West, they felt; China had too long been shut away from the currents which were sweeping the world during the 19th century. The young people wanted to learn all they could, particularly about science, and to be able to speak English.

With this very slight background it may be easier for those who read our story to understand the political situation—"the P.S."—as we began to call it, which involved us for all our years in China and which began to affect us particularly in the fall of 1926.

We had returned from furlough with our son, Lloyd Rutherford, Jr. in January of 1926, to find the usual welcome from the members of our station, and nothing greatly changed. I found one letter to my mother written from Kuling in that summer, in which I wrote that it was our happiest one since we had been married. Little did I know what lay ahead of us in that year and in those to follow.

We heard during the summer that the Southern forces under an able young general named Chiang Kai Shek were gathering strength around Canton to begin a march north, presumably to drive out the war lords and attempt to unify China under the Nationalist Party, or Kuo Min Tang. In early September we heard that their large army had reached the Yangzte River, had seized Hankow and Hanyang, but that Wuchang, across the river from Hankow, a city surrounded by a high wall, was holding out against them. The wall was turning the city into a fortress. We became anxious for our missionaries who were under siege.

It became obvious that Nanchang, as the capital of Kiangsi Province, would be the next point of attack. In spite of this news, I decided to accompany Lloyd to Nanchang when he returned after his vacation. We both feared separation more than a siege, especially when the whole situation was so uncertain. We arrived without any incident and had started to begin our fall work, when we discovered that the city was getting panicky. At times a wave of rumors would sweep the city, people would begin to run through the streets, and the merchants would close and padlock their stores in broad daylight. No one seemed to know what was happening. Communications with places up river had been cut, and we were very ignorant as to the true state of affairs.

Then, one evening in September, 1926, we found that our staff next door to us had decided to accept our invitation of offering them a place to stay in an emergency, and the women and children were arriving to spend the night, bringing their own bedding and sleeping on the floor of the living rooms. Our house, protected by the simple fact that we were American citizens and as such shouldn't be molested, offered a haven of security they craved. From that day on the numbers kept increasing until one night we awoke to the sound of machine guns operating not only across the river, but actually in our streets. Our house filled up with refugees, and the next day we heard that the Southern troops had arrived, the Northern army had withdrawn, and that the take-over we had dreaded had already happened, and with almost no fighting.

We liked the looks of the Southern troops as we saw them in the streets, young, energetic and active, going about their business of occupying the government buildings, putting up posters denouncing the war lords and pronouncing a regime of government "of the people, by the people and for the people"—as I wrote in a letter to my mother.

But as that week wore on, we realized that things were not as stable as we thought. The fighting across the river grew in intensity and then came a night when the air was shattered by the sound of gunfire as we had never heard it before. I pulled the baby out of his crib and we all lay prostrate on the floor, well aware that bullets could pierce the windows much more easily than they could our heavy brick walls. There we lay without sleep until next morning told the story that the

Northern troops were back in force, having learned from their intelligence that the city had been taken by a very small vanguard of the Kuo Min Tang and that the main body of troops had not yet arrived to reinforce them.

Then followed terrible days for our city. The Northern army was back, looting the houses, raping the women, taking vengeance on those citizens who had welcomed their enemies from the South. Our huge basement was filled with refugees— 300 or more—who came for protection. They quickly banded together to buy rice, and set up a stove under our back porch where the long lines would march past with their rice bowls twice a day. The gate opening on the lake behind us was a godsend for disposal of sewage. To realize fully the dangers to the inhabitants in the siege of a Chinese city you have to understand that there were no sewers in an interior city like Nanchang. Each morning the human excrement was carried out in buckets, one on each end of a carrying pole, and was used eventually to fertilize the fields of vegetables or rice. When the city was under siege, as Nanchang was now, the gates were closed and sandbagged, no buckets could go out or food come in, so in a short time everyone was threatened by starvation and pestilence.

It was in the midst of these surroundings that I wrote a letter to my family which tells in vivid detail the happenings of these days.

"Family dear   Begun Tuesday October 12, 1926
"Will it be too harrowing if I share with you what I'm living through just now? Lloyd wrote Mother a few days ago, so you know the South has come back in numbers and has completely surrounded the city for the last four days, with nothing going out or coming in and all business paralyzed—as has been the case for the last weeks, as far as the latter is concerned. Our refugees are here in greater numbers than ever, and everyone is

101

fearing a siege like Wuchang's—so yesterday when the Chamber of Commerce asked Lloyd and Arthur Allen [the Y.M.C.A. secretary] to go out of the city to try to take a letter to Chiang Kai Shek to ask the Southern Army to move away from the city so the gates could be opened and the danger of famine and disease lessened, they felt it was a real opportunity. They tried to get out yesterday afternoon, but the soldiers, who have no discipline, disobeyed commands and opened fire just as they were about to climb down the ladders which had been tied together for them to get from the top of the wall to the ground, so there was no hope then. But they've just started out again now, the two of them, carrying a huge American flag, to try their mission again. They will go out Tan Tai Men, on the northeast, and walk along the foot of the wall, while the military commander will walk along the top, to see that there is no firing while they are out—that is, from the Northern troops. The danger is that the Southerners won't respect the flag. They didn't when Bishop Gilman and Dr. Wakefield went out on a similar mission for Wuchang, and they walked along the foot of the wall in a shower of bullets, but fortunately weren't hurt. There was the Yangzte River between them and the Southerners then, however. Now I feel the danger of their situation so much, and am so powerless to help, that as usual I take refuge in pen and ink. I feel so alone even in the midst of three hundred! But in spite of the danger I'm really genuinely thankful that such an opportunity has come to them to do something for this sorely beset city. I don't know how they could even attempt negotiations if it weren't for these men of ours.

"But I am not the stuff heroes are made of, and I have inward shudders everytime I hear a bullet whistle. They probably aren't over the wall yet, so there is continuous firing, but nothing like the terrible battle from the wall last night and early this morning. I woke up at 5:30 perfectly convinced the South had slipped into the city somehow. Machine guns, cannon, revolvers, rifles, hand grenades—I've learned to distinguish them all and they were all going at once around Tan Tai Men, not more than half a mile away. The refugees are so terrified. They won't come out of the basement, and I saw some men running back and forth yesterday with their heads wrapped up in blankets. There are two tiny windows in one of the basement rooms, and twenty people in the room, but they closed the windows and filled them with bricks till it's a wonder more of them didn't die of asphyxiation than bullets.

"Just in the middle of the above sentence the firing grew so hot and so many struck our house that the cook came flying in from the kitchen to hide, and old Chow came in with a bullet from the room just back of this. My hands turned perfectly cold—I've been looking at my watch every five minutes to see where the men were, probably, and I thought that having them go out might have precipitated more firing instead of stopping it, as they promised. I've been in torment for fifteen minutes, but at last a calm has settled over this city—only occasional sniping now. Evidently the command is being obeyed.

"My imagination is working every minute, seeing those two tiny gray figures, and that blessedly big American flag, walking steadily along the foot of the wall right into the face of those bullets. Things started up again for a minute over at Tan Tai Men—I wonder how long the truce was supposed to hold. These Northerners are such off-scouring—

"At this I went out and played on the porch in the sunshine with my blessing of a baby—and as it's now a quarter of seven and no one has come to tell me of wounded forms, I'm quite sure they are safe somewhere. Lloyd, bless him, told me before he left to realize that if he were hurt I'd know about it—also that he might not come back for the night. They also both of them gave me their keys. No wife sending her husband to the trenches felt more uncertain of the outcome than did I. There were so many targets there, and here only one. But oh! I do so hope that something will come of this. The men told me as they left that the Southerners are firing from Baldwin and Nanchang Academy [on higher ground] which is why the bullets have been coming into the city all day. Now that I know the direction to expect them from I feel so much safer. We have great rice bags and dirt bags in the north windows downstairs, and a mattress in front of the kitchen door. I've just had our springs and mattress brought down to Lloyd's study, and there the baby and I will sleep, as much for companionship as anything else. I know now that our bedroom isn't in the line of fire. But my herd-instinct is very active just now. Somebody's wet nurse downstairs was shot in the arm as she was getting wood in the back yard this afternoon. You never saw such a lonely place as that same backyard since then. And now the milkman wants to bring his nine cows here to hide! I've agreed to two, but we cannot have such a herd plus our 300 refugees. He got down on his knees to me, too. Then he wanted to know if I wouldn't give him a little sign saying 'Milk bearer to the Holy Catholic Church' for his house. The grown men are afraid to bring the milk to us each day, but they send it by a little rascal no taller than the joint of bamboo in which he brings it. He was held up by a soldier, too [he's been coming every day even since the firing began Thursday] but he sassed him back and came on unhindered. Isn't it lucky the Chinese think milk only fit for babes and sucklings!

"I sat out there on the floor of the porch in the sunshine this afternoon, with my adorable son on a steamer rug, and listened to the whine of bullets over my head, and thought about how this really was one of the 'events' of my life—I trust not to be frequently repeated! Also I reflected that Hillside Avenue in Englewood was lying there in sunshine and golden leaves, just as last year and Bergendahls having the same sodas, and the Hudson Drive doubtless just as lovely—and Mother probably sitting at her desk that minute writing me a letter. [No—I know it was the middle of the night, Mother.] And here I was

104

collecting bullets and trying to protect the lives of three hundred and enforce health regulations and send out the First Aid kit to the wounded wet nurse, and mix up Dryco for her six months charge, who was an only child with a 40 year old mother! Could it have been only a year ago that my main worry was about a certain stretch of road on the way to the hospital which wasn't as smooth as one would wish it to be? Lloyd and I got almost hysterical at the memory.

"Miss Chang, my dear Miss Chang, came over to help pass the afternoon with me, realizing the strain I was under. Charity Tzen had done the same this morning. Their sympathy means everything, really. Yesterday when I first got Lloyd's note, I asked some of the church members to come in and we had a little Prayer Meeting. It was a help and comfort and I know they have been with me this afternoon. But all this page I've been meaning to tell you about the baby. I laid my handkerchief on the floor by chance, and suddenly Miss Chang exclaimed, 'He is blowing his nose'—and sure enough he unmistakeably was. He had found the hankerchief by himself, and put it up to his nose, which he was rubbing violently while he sniffed. He kept it up for 15 minutes, too, only laying it down to roar with laughter with us. I never imagined he could be so clever. He really hasn't had his nose wiped a great deal, either. He takes a brush now and tries to brush his hair with it—but refuses to put on his hat. He doesn't care for hats.

"I've just finished eating my lonely supper, and it's a comfort to come back and talk to you again. Mother, I'm glad of my Economy Cook Book with its war recipes. I made a real success of an applesauce cake without milk, butter or eggs. We have heaps of margarine, so fat will be no problem; two bags of flour, enough tinned peas and tomatoes to open a new can each day for a month, and two cows on the place. Our worst difficulty will be for eggs. We have two chickens, but they aren't the laying kind. By saving our small supply carefully it's been

105

lasting along for desserts. Isn't it luck that my supposed year's supply of canned food was in the store-room. The real tragedy of a siege would be the Chinese poor, of course. Of that I won't think. We very possibly won't have a prolonged one. Though we have soldiers in quantities they aren't supposed to have much dander. They really want above all things to get away with their loot.

"I wish you could hear the chatter in the front room where our thirteen still assemble nightly. It is a very mixing up process, this being besieged. I've just been in talking with Mrs. Den about the relative merits of Dryco and Klim, and in pops the amah now to ask where I'm going to sleep. She is vastly relieved to hear it's to be in the study. They couldn't, any of them, bear the thought of our being 'way up in the top of the house, and say they can 'place their hearts' now they know I'm to be on the first floor with my baby. I haven't heard any firing for five minutes. Perhaps we can really get some sleep tonight—though I'm going to miss my Buddy a great deal. Oh how I wish I knew how things were with him!

"The baby will be a year old in a week. I'll trust we'll be so situated I can think of it. He is to have a big cloth cat I bought in Kuling, and some beads on a string. May's last letter said you'd been out to buy him some presents—and how long it's been since we've had mail or will get any. Lloyd begins to think of the newspapers he'll have to absorb. It's my chance to make him do headlines only.

"It's half-past eight now and I must go to bed. We've been going at eight the last few nights, for our sleep has been so broken. I'm glad I didn't go earlier, however, for a delegation of four of the men have just come in to tell me they represented the rest of the group in thinking of me and my anxiety and remembering Lloyd and Arthur in their prayers. Wasn't that dear of them. Then we had prayers together and they left. Now you know it's good to remember there are such thoughtful people among the Chinese as well as all these wild militarists.

October 13th. "The end of another long day, and still no men! What has happened to them. I still think nothing serious or I would have heard—but I'm wondering now if the South isn't detaining them as hostages or something, and they won't be able to get in till the siege is raised. Pleasant prospect! I'd imagined Lloyd going through a siege without me, but never my going through one without him. However, there has been constant firing—sniping—all day long, and it would certainly have been a risk for them to come in through it, so I'll just remember how I exhorted them not to take any *unnecessary* risks, and try to hold my horses and ͵ny heart.

"Such a night as I had! Of course it was lonesome not having Lloyd or knowing how he was faring, and I kept seeing his face looking at me so plainly I was afraid it was a bad omen! But things continued fairly quiet without, and I got to sleep and slept until two-thirty, when I was awakened by the most terrible fusillade of bullets, pouring right over the house. Evidently the South had set up machine guns in Baldwin and was simply raining them on the city. I felt convinced we were the enemy they were after, too, so certain did it seem that every bullet was headed our way. Whereupon I proceeded to have a nervous chill. Really there are none of the manifestations of fear which I have failed to produce. I feel sure I am descended from a little white rabbit! Anyway I hauled myself into the front room and there held hands with my Chinese lady friends and felt better for the company. Through all this horror I have to keep reminding myself that it was Western civilization which taught the Chinese how to do all this—machine guns and all. I wish they hadn't learned their lesson so well. I went back to bed again, but not to sleep—too much going on. Cannon and machine guns fifteen minutes walk away aren't conducive to slumber. But that son of ours slept sweetly behind his Morris

107

chair cushion barricade, and woke sweet as a peach.

"Queer how this kind of situation affects one's attitude toward familiar things. I find myself now thinking of my home purely in terms of brick walls thankful that we have them and wishing we had more. Windows are at a great discount—I understand now why the Hopkins north wall contains not a window, though formerly I scorned the plan. It must be a little haven of refuge these days.

"Then to think that our old friends, Baldwin and Nanchang Academy, have become places to be feared and shunned. At least I suppose these bullets come from there, though Ben Schmidt [a Y.M.C.A. secretary then in the city] seemed to think this morning that the Northerners were quite capable of firing them on the city themselves just to keep things lively.

"It was so nice this morning, when I was sitting on the hall floor with the baby feeling so discouraged to find a bullet had broken a pane of glass in what I considered our safest direction, to have the front door fly open, and in pop John Littell. [He was the son of a missionary from Hankow who had come from Harvard with his brother to spend the summer with their parents. They'd gotten caught in Kuling and couldn't go up river because of the fighting, so they came down to Nanchang.] Did I write you he is spending nights and some days guarding the church property? He had come through the city and was glad to sit down to a breakfast of shredded wheat and pancakes after three days on rice. He had been up on the bell tower and looked over the city. He could report that Baldwin and Nanchang Academy were still intact. I was certain they had been demolished by cannon last night—and also tell me the origin of all the fires burning around outside the city. Those devilish Northerners are burning out all the little shops close to the wall, so they couldn't be hiding places for the Southerners. At least that seems to be the most likely reason. And when you consider that the poorest shop keepers in the city are the ones who crowd around the walls in the suburbs, you see why my adjective is mild. Our sufferings are of little account in comparison.

"John says he'll take Mr. Liu and go to the General Headquarters tomorrow morning to see what can be found out about the whereabouts of the men. Blessings on John. I'm glad his mother can't see him now.

October 15th. "Yesterday I didn't write—my heart and mind were so fully occupied. They've come home!—and nothing else really matters now we're safe and together again. I never realized that so certainly as now. I got up yesterday morning feeling that I *must* find out something about those men of ours, and determining to send Mr. Liu and John to General Headquarters to see what they could learn. But suddenly the news came winging down from the housetops—where one of the doctors was viewing the landscape—that two foreign men were nearly here—*our* men—with the American flag above them. I rushed out on the porch to find most of the three hundred in the yard ahead of me. They all drew back, with that instinctive sense of a dramatic setting which the Chinese seem to possess, and made a path for me, down which I rushed to the hands of my beloved. [Not the arms, under the circumstances!] Pretty worn and weary they looked, too, and such a tale as they had to tell. We realized then that the firing had ceased, and knew that an armistice is in progress. The relief to our tired nerves is almost unbelievable. But now for the men's tale.

"They got outside the gate going down on those ladders with the officer above them, and the firing stopped for awhile on the part of the North, but suddenly the soldiers up there on the wall saw some Southerners retreating to cover in the lull, and immediately opened up fire, which was returned with interest by the South, and there our two men were right in the middle of it. My mental picture at that time, as I heard this perfect fusillade, was all too true. They fell flat on their stomachs on the sand, with the flag in the same ignominious position, and there they stayed until the firing let up a little. Then they beat it as rapidly as possible back to the gate. When they got there, however, they decided not to go in, but to hunt for the Southerners and see if they could find them out in that direction, east from the gate, where there was no firing. The North had sworn there were no Southerners there, but you know that bull-dog Buddy of mine. And sure enough, after they had walked about a mile through the village they found some Southern soldiers peering over a sand bank. The soldiers took them in charge and brought them to their officer, who in turn led them to the Headquarters, in the south, a school about three or four miles outside the city. There they handed in their letter, and there they had to stay for two nights and a day before they could come back with the reply.

"They were much impressed with the earnestness and alertness and general intelligence of these Southern officers. They are aflame with enthusiasm for the gospel of the Kuo Min Tang, and are keen to free the country from the burden of these wretched Northern officials. He said they seemed really concerned for the people. Certainly they are the only army which has ever come near us which has given a thought to the populace. They evidently had lost very heavily in men in their two attempts to storm the wall. Once anyway their men actually climbed up on it—and very probably have retired to reconsider.

"We hope and pray that they may decide to bend all their efforts on the railroad station, and places along the line, so isolating Nanchang and forcing a surrender. But in the meantime the Northern ruffians are getting in great quantities of rice and ammunition, prepared to withstand a great siege, while the people can't buy rice for love or money. No rice shops will open

110

for fear of being immediately looted by the soldiers, who are going on their brutal way murdering individuals ruthlessly in their demands for money. Yesterday we got a new influx of refugees, every one of whom had just been looted for the third or fourth time. Truly the cup of bitterness of this people is full to the brim! It was impossible to turn down people yesterday, they were so pitifully in need. One of them was a graduate of Peking University, a former student in America and Germany, and a Professor in that fine Southeastern University who came bringing his sisters, all students, after horrible experiences. Every one of them would rather face the terrors of bullets which are far worse a menace here than in Chinese homes, than be subjected to the brutal treatment of these insufferable soldiers.

"During these days of respite we're bending every effort on making this place a refuge. We want to put sand bags on all the north windows, and a mud wall to protect the north exit of our cellar. Lloyd is in now discussing plans for water, fuel and food with a big committee. They are taking most of the responsibility for this refugee station. You don't know what a joy it is to feel that we can do something to help out in a situation of such pure horror. This place is a heaven and haven to these so sorely beset.

"Saturday the 16th—and still peaceful—as far as the return of the South is concerned. The soldiers keep on looting, and as our friends begin to emerge we hear horrid tales of murders and pillage. If these 'braves' stay in here much longer this city will be an empty shell. It's Sunday now, and I can't write more because yesterday Timmy [our postal commissioner, a delightful Welshman named Thomas Gwynn] came in with the good news that the railroad is running again, and we'll have some mail today after two weeks. This will give me a chance to get away to Kuling with the baby, and after much cogitating we've decided it's the wise thing to do. Lloyd is out now getting what information he can, and tomorrow I'll try to make the get away along with most of the inhabitants of this city. It will be a rabble if ever there was one. Hope little Lloyd will survive the process. But the chances are that the South will be back—perhaps with big guns to try to blow the wall to pieces—and in any event it's wise to go while I have a chance and the way is open—only *how* I hate to leave Lloyd here. I've been a help as far as contriving food is concerned, and could share responsibility when he has to leave. John Littell is going to stay by, like the brick he is, and Timmy Gwynne may come in here to try to keep the post office running. They won't be lonely, and in some ways it will be easier for Lloyd to have me out of it. If only it weren't such an indefinite sentence! I realized last night that you'll none of you get any Christmas presents till Easter, in all probability.

"Goodbye to you and always remember this news is a whole month old. Probably all will be quiet before this reaches you and I'll be all settled down with Netta.

> Dearest love,
> Marian
> Lloyd"

Nanchang, October 20, 1926. "Still here, my dears, and thankful to be so. You'll probably be quite upset when you see the heading, so let me tell you about it and why I'm not freezing off my nose in Kuling. As soon as there was a rumor of my departure all the ladies in sight, nearly, wanted to go too. I felt somewhat afflicted when Mrs. Den, due to have a baby in a week, joined the number. But about that time we began to hear things about the trip. You were packed in so tight that no one could sit down the whole way, and the train moved so cautiously that you didn't arrive in Kiukiang till ten p.m. [instead of the usual three or four p.m.] Then, there being martial law in Kiukiang you continued to stand on the train a la sardine, till morning. Pretty picture.

"So then I thought about a launch—but the only one not commandeered was stuck on a sandbank and unseaworthy. So gradually I decided that home was the best place after all!"

Methodist Compound, October 30, 1926. "A new heading for you. At last I was seized with the same epidemic as the rest of the world and have taken flight! Not as far as I intended at first, but I'm really glad my intentions were cut off. I believe it was Monday [it's Saturday now] that Lloyd and Arthur got a letter from the Southern general [Chiang Kai Shek] saying they were coming back! Said they'd waited for the North to retire and they hadn't done so, so please to tell them to beware, or words to that effect. It was more in the nature of a threat, and not so awfully significant, but enough so that Arthur and Lloyd took the letter to the Chamber of Commerce and Dan Liu [our clergyman] decided to ship his wife and children to Anking. We sent the school teachers, too, and Lloyd took them all over to the train, there to discover a foreign gentleman of the Brethren Mission, all ensconced quite comfortably on the mail bags with room enough for me if I wished his escort. So back Lloyd flew, across the river and city, and arrived breathless to tell me to pack up my clothes in fifteen minutes and make a dash for it.

"Imagine packing for Kuling in fifteen minutes! But I did it, a kori for me and one for Little Lloyd, and the amah got shaken together somehow and off we started, Lloyd carrying the baby for ricksha men are a scarce sight, these days. We found the Methodist launch waiting for us, and chugged across the river, only to discover that for once the train had left on time, three quarters of an hour before. But Lloyd still wanted to be rid of us, so we returned here to Mrs. Johnson's [on the Methodist compound] and settled down in her parlour. She is a dear to take me in, for I make the 7th outside her regular family! She has a lot of people who are helping the hospital. But she makes

113

me feel very much at home, my friends all gather around out here, I go 'out for tea' nearly every afternoon, and lead a very carefree existence. My only trouble is to gather together all the odds and ends left out of my 15 minute packing. You can picture us now at the Johnsons with Buddy coming out every day to bring letters and things I hadn't packed and tell the news. We take the letters down to the river bank and sit under a tree while a cow regards us from a distance and the little goats nibble near out feet, and it's all so sweet and rural that it's doing me a lot of good. Little Lloyd is just bursting with health and good spirits again after the setback of his cold.

"*SUNDAY NOVEMBER 7th, 1926.* Capitals all the way across for since I wrote the above a great event has happened. So much that I can hardly realize it, much less express all the joy and relief and hope that fills our hearts. Yesterday the whole day was quiet, with no fighting. Lloyd didn't come out but wrote me a note saying that it looked less like a siege of the city, and the Northerners might be leaving. That really seemed too good to be true, however, so I didn't think of it too much but sat and sewed on the big American flag I've been making [at Mr. Johnson's request, with Betsy Ross stars, thanks to you, Mother] and prayed and wondered. The least inkling of hope that there wouldn't be a siege made me so overjoyed that I knew what the fear of it had been—long days shut away from Lloyd, starvation for all the city, looting by the soldiers, and pestilence, in all probability. Wuchang's story was enough.

"Last night Mrs. Johnson came in after dinner to say that she heard the most curious fighting outside. The shots seemed to be going in the air, accompanied by the sound of shouting and calls and marching and excitement such as I've not heard before. Immediately I thought 'The Northerners are evacuating and this shooting is to cover their retreat.' But Mr. Blasner came in to assert that the Northerners were retreating back to the city [they had moved about twenty miles outside before this where

114

they were facing the Southern troops] and a big battle was on. So my heart went lead again, thinking this must mean a siege. But oh! my dears, as it turned out I was right, only the shooting—the queer shooting—came from the firing of ammunition dumps across the river. Before the retreat all these things were burned.

"Mr. Johnson came in not long after to say that some Northerners had jumped over the compound wall—that there undoubtedly would be a lot of shooting around and we ought to go to the basement. I compromised on the hall, where the baby and I were both surrounded by brick walls. As though this excitement were not enough sweet Mrs. Wang, the Japanese wife of a fine doctor, president of the Y.M.C.A. who is staying here, began to have her baby. Imagine the Southerners arriving at the city wall and this baby we'd been expecting, all getting here the same night. In spite of all the scampering of feet upstairs I lay me down in peace and slept the first part of the night when suddenly I was conscious that the hall was full of Chinese men, gazing on my recumbent and fortunately, beflannel-night-gowned, form! Dr. Wang was with them and I heard his excited voice call up to Mr. Johnson, 'Mr. Johnson, the Civil Governor is here!' Mr. Johnson came down to receive his distinguished guests and found that the tuchun [Military Governor] was among them. Fortunately they hadn't come as boarders, but wished to leave by the boats in front of the compound. They were so scared that the whole crowd got into one sampan, and that couldn't be floated for a long time. Then they got aboard a launch without a pilot, which promptly stuck on an island a short distance away. Retreating Chinese generals are a bit humorous. We know one boat upset and some were drowned, but think it was the body-guard. All this is far from clear as yet, and all this I got this morning.

"I was awake a lot in the night, heard cannon rumbling past which I *hoped* was retreating Northerners, but feared might be

115

advancing Southerners. At last daylight and certainty. The North had evacuated, having lost Kiukiang and all the railroad, Sun Chuan Fang [the war lord in charge] has fled to Nanking and all this province is in the hands of the South. The people are so relieved and so happy. We ate precious apples for breakfast, may have a goose for dinner, and begin to realize what it will mean to have established peace and order again. After the personal safety of our family and friends my mind instinctively flies to the fact that the streets can now be cleaned.

"The South will have a challenging job to build up again this poor looted city with the schools all turned into barracks, the precious and all-too-rare equipment smashed, and the horses stabled in the court-yards. Business is terribly upset, all the paper money foisted on us by the military practically worthless, and a general paralysis of everything stable has taken place for two months, nearly. But our prayers have evidently been answered for this was exactly the way we would have chosen our rescue to come, first the fall of the railway and Kiukiang, and then a rapid evacuation. Those Northerners even had to cast away their suits and bedding, some of them. This morning when I went out to look the landscape o'er I found two poor wretches down by one of the gates near the river, kotowing to me and shivering in the wind. Three of the Northern officers are in the cowhouse and four in the basement. At last they are tasting some of the bitterness of which they have inflicted so much.

"And what a victory for these little men in khaki, to accomplish so much against such odds. They never could have done it if the people hadn't been with them, showing them bypaths and lending them aid.

"Just now another episode. Mr. Johnson has just come in to say that the Southerners are searching the premises for

Northerners, and will soon have the house inspected. I've moved in to sit here by the baby. Oh when will all this be at an end! The fact that these Northern officials are hiding, four of them in the basement, doesn't make it much easier. Here comes a group of about a hundred armed men, over the wall! They are a wild-looking bunch, too, and are demanding to search the house. They've just been all through the house up to the attic, and then demanded the basement. We knew that four Northerners were there, so its been a bit ticklish. They also knew the civil governor came here formerly to hide, and thought he was still here. So they've certainly been making a hot time for us. I wasn't a bit afraid, for some reason, told them all to be quiet and not wake the baby, and to be careful of Mrs. Wang, who had given birth to one last night. Imagine meeting a hundred such wild-looking specimens at the door and automatically saying, 'Hush!' to every one of them. They didn't wake up the baby either. They're very dirty and very excited, and Mr. Johnson, who is tired to death, is having a time with them. Mrs. Johnson has just saved the lives of the four by her quick wit. When the soldiers had finished searching these upper floors they asked where they could get into the basement. I told them there is an outside door. There is an inside door, too, and while Mr. Johnson was holding them outside, Mrs. Johnson got the Northerners up the stairs and into the study closet. Then finally the basement was searched and revealed no Northerners. After that the prisoners were run down the stairs again! I assure you this business of standing in the hall casually looking out the window while all this was going on was far from pleasurable. I keep wondering what may be going on over at our house. Nothing like this, I'm sure.

"Mr. Johnson kept saying he would surrender the men as soon as they sent a responsible person, but he was long in coming and in the meantime the soldiers kept getting madder and madder. They pulled their guns on Mr. J. any number of times, and talked so loudly and so angrily that we really

117

thought his end had come. Finally I believe someone came of officer rank. Then the soldiers rushed into the basement and found these poor devils, dripping with sweat and positively ashen. Such a commotion. Mr. Johnson tried to keep them there, but finally they were dragged out, but not until rifles had been shot off right in our back yard, and one right in the basement under me. By this time I had sent the baby out into the compound, but when the fighting started up I decided the place for me was with my child. I knew my amah would be in the forefront of any executions. Sure enough, there she was surveying all the rabble, horrified but fascinated. So I grabbed my boy and have just been over to Mrs. Brown's with him. There they listened to my horror tale—none of their houses had been searched—and wished I had stayed in the city. Mrs. Libby was left to guard the hospital gate in an emergency and had a wound on her arm from a bayonet which one of the soldiers scratched her with as she attempted to keep them out till a major or someone in authority arrived. It's the truth that this Southern army does not have the respect for authority and certainly not the respect for foreigners that the North has. They evidently have become convinced that the tuchun and civil governor are not here, and are just leaving.

* * * * * * * * * * *

"Monday morning, and last night we got a full account from Mr. Johnson of what had happened and how yesterday morning, when he came down to breakfast he found on the front porch three shivering wretches, one of whom proved to be Gen. Yoh, who in attempting to escape the night before had been upset and dumped in the water. Mr. J., for humanity's sake, let him hide in the basement even though he knew he was the head devil who had given permission to his troops to loot the city. So it was *that* criminal we were protecting. The soldiers knew from Yoh's bodyguard he had left at the gate that Yoh was in the compound, so no wonder they refused to leave! Also they saw his wet uniform hanging on the line drying. Mr. Johnson was determined to surrender him to no less an officer

118

than a general, who would be responsible. He finally had to let some lesser officers get him but not until he had the name of one of them on whom he could fix responsibility. [Mr. Johnson had studied law at one stage in his career!] These officers seized the two lower officials, let one unimportant man go, and then skipped off to let their men do as they pleased with the general. We thought they would cut his head off at the least, but not so. They fell to at once and stripped all the thousands of dollars off his person, and then fought like cats and dogs for possession of it! A fleeing general is covered with it, as they knew, and they were after that more than anything else. Well, the long and short is that they carried the general off and I hope they'll hang him high as Haman, and not just because he was the cause for our having one of the worst days so far. The soldiers ransacked the hospital, too. It was all brought on by harboring this political prisoner, and I believe that it shows this is not the thing to do.

"Yesterday was horrible but today apologies have come from the head men for what this irresponsible group did, and the world seems oh! so peaceful and worthwhile again. The little boats are all out on the river, the fishermen are mending their nets on the shore, the chrysanthemums are at their height of beauty, and a ton of fear and gloom and hopelessness has rolled off from every heart.

"They say the city gates will be open tomorrow and the next day a train will leave. But I'm not going to wait for that to mail this letter. What tomes I've been perpetrating since the war!" [We found that the soldiers whom I had requested not to waken the baby were part of the army which attacked the foreigners and looted their houses a few months later, March, 1927, in Nanking.]

II

From that time on we began to get a clearer picture of the composition of this army which was rapidly taking over the country. We had found that there were Russians in key positions, and there was no doubt that there was a large element of Communism in among its members. Before long we found that the various crafts were being organized into unions which were then better able to demand their rights as workers. Each day processions marched past our gates, and the slogans they displayed had much to say about ridding the country of the "running dogs of imperialists." The Allen's amah next door, from Peking, who had lived through the Boxer uprising, begged us to leave. She felt sure this group was out to destroy foreigners as that had been. We suddenly found that to be a Westerner had changed almost overnight from being a person able to give protection to being one who needed it. Even our servants were organized into a union and told to demand higher wages, but as the head of that union was a cook for some good mission friends of ours, the demands were not overwhelming as they were in some cities.

All through these months the missionaries were uncertain as to what they should do and had frequent meetings to discuss how to meet this threatening situation. We heard at one time that General Chiang had addressed a large and important gathering and read the Communists out of the Kuo Min Tang. We wondered if this could be true when there were so many evidences of Communism in the city. We found later that this had indeed happened, and at that time the first rupture had been brought into the open between the Kuo Min Tang under General Chiang, and the Communists. The personal secretary of General Chiang Kai Shek had been given the text of this speech of the general's and had been asked to translate it into English to be sent to the English newspapers in Shanghai. The secretary had asked Arthur Allen to go over his English and put it into good form. I believe that Arthur spent twelve hours getting this accomplished, probably having an idea even then that this was a most historic document.

It was this split which caused the communist branch of the Army to march on Nanking late in March while General Chiang and the forces loyal to him had marched on Shanghai and taken possession of that great city. It was the attack on Nanking in April, 1927, known in history as the "Nanking Incident" which caused us finally to flee from Nanchang and begin our career as refugees.

On January 22, 1927, Lloyd wrote, "It is interesting to be living in the midst of a real revolution, though it's not always exactly comfortable. The parade of about ten thousand students, laborers, soldiers, and citizens which has been streaming past our door for an hour and a half is in a way a pageant of what is astir in China today. 'Down with foreign control in China': 'Revise the unequal treaties': 'Take back the Concessions': were the slogans yelled from hoarse voices in a rhythmic antiphonal chant. Next came a unit of soldiers with their band playing the song of the Nationalist Party to the tune 'Are you sleeping, Are you sleeping, Brother John?' The group of enthusiastic students which followed, you could hardly believe were really shouting the same tune to the syllables, 'Do re mi do, Do re mi do,' etc. What a weird bit of unconscious Western penetration in the midst of this intensely Nationalistic parade. Almost as surprising as those modish beehive bonnets the 'new women' are now wearing above their bobbed hair, on the streets of staid old Nanchang.

"What does it all mean? Well, on a thumb nail, it means:

"(a) Militarily, that Chiang Kai Shek, 38 years old, disciple of Sun Yat Sen, has put a group of his school-trained officers at the head of a compact little army and started north from

121

Canton biting off huge chunks of territory formerly held by the Northern war lords or Tuchuns.

"(b) Politically, it means that this army is infused with Dr. Sun Yat Sen's 'Three Principles of the People,' embodying his idea of how the people of China may reclaim for themselves.

"(1) National Power (break the power of the foreigners over China).

"(2) Political Power (overthrow the war lords).

"(3) Social Power (outlining a scheme of socialistic control over land and factory production).

"Along with this comparatively moderate right group, there is a more extreme left party whose program cannot be distinguished from that of the Third International, involving world revolution, the overthrow of capitalism, free love, and all the rest. Widespread agitation among laborers and farmers is one expression of the new nationalism. Every day sees a new strike and overnight a score of new labor unions is born.

"(c) Internationally the movement has far-reaching consequences. The Peoples' Party, or Kuo Min Tang, is determined to regain for China control over all of her territory now administered by foreigners, and in general to abolish all treaties which give to foreigners rights which Chinese do not enjoy in foreign countries. They have already taken over the British Concessions in Hankow and Kiukiang as part of this program. The Nationalist Government clearly declares its intention to protect foreign life and property.

"(d) As to Christianity and the Mission Schools there is again a wide diveristy between the left and right wings of the Peoples' Party. The extreme radicals would close every Christian

122

institution, and in fact abolish all religion. The right wing, represented by such men as General Chiang Kai Shek, and the majority of the military leaders, stand for religious freedom and desire the Christian schools to continue, though under government regulation. So far we have had nothing that could be called persecution here in Nanchang. In some parts of the country, however, the missionaries have been driven out or held as virtual captives, while the Chinese Christian leaders have been led bound through the streets and reviled as 'foreign slaves' or 'running dogs of imperialism.'

"In Nanchang we have had our troubles. During Christmas week the Anti-Christian Association held parades and made speeches on the streets. In spite of this we were able to have our Christmas services undisturbed. In fact I have seldom felt so really the presence of Christ in our Christmas worship as this year. It was a time of real peace and joy in the midst of much hostility and turmoil on every side, and the beautiful presents, which came this year from the Diocese of New Jersey, added greatly to the pleasure of our pupils.

"A few days after Christmas the Christians of the city held an open forum meeting at which Bishop Birney of the Methodist Mission led the discussion on the topic 'Christianity and the Three Principles of Sun Yat Sen.' To this meeting the Anti-Christian group were invited and they came. There was a fair spirit of give and take in the discussion, and no disorder. Some of the anti- made vitriolic speeches denouncing Christianity, capitalism, and imperialism. In their minds the three were inseparable. On the Christian side two speeches by officers of the Nationalist army were notable for their courage and for their constructive Christian spirit.

"Our St. Matthew's School building was commandeered for officers quarters, and has been occupied for about two months. This has greatly hampered our school work, but we have been able to carry on after a fashion in cramped quarters. We hope to have all the soldiers out before the beginning of the new term. It remains to be seen how the anti-foreign feeling will react on our school then.

"We have been more fortunate than some in the city in that our church has been left untouched by the soldiers. This has made it possible to have our services as usual. Some members have stood the test of the present rough weather and some have not, but I feel the church is really stronger for the testing.

"That there has been some wholesome thinking done by our Christian group was revealed in the questions presented for discussion at the retreat which we held last Saturday: 'What is the relation of Christianity to the Revolution?' 'Why did the Church come to China?': 'What is the attitude of Christianity to Labor?' 'How can the Church in China become self-supporting?,' were some of the questions brought forward.

"It's an interesting time, as I said to start with, but it's a new day for the foreigner, a new day indeed. Instead of being a person of special privileges, able to protect hundreds of Chinese citizens from looting, violence, and, some seemed to think, even from bullets and air bombs by his mere presence, he now has to retire very much into the background of any movement he wishes to help. We feel we have a real and important place here for all that. Just to be able to help our loyal Chinese friends and fellow Christians see their way through the throng of baffling new situations which press in on every side is privilege enough in itself. Then there is also the chance of keeping in touch with some of the fine young officers, some of them returned students, some of them Christians, some of them scorning religion, and by every friendly contact which offers keeping open the avenues of friendship and fellowship in the midst of so much narrow national prejudice and misunderstanding. Surely this is in itself a job amply worthwhile."

III

Later I wrote from Unzen, Japan, where we had been invited to share their cottage by our dear friends, Claude and Margaret Thomson.

September 10, 1927, "I wonder if I can condense into a few paragraphs the incidents which occurred after that most eventful morning of March 25th, 1927 when a violent ring at the door bell disturbed our slumbers, and our dazed minds had to suddenly adjust themselves to the significance of the tale which Mr. Johnson of the Methodist Mission, just arrived on the night freight from Kiukiang, was pouring into our ears. We had begun to feel so settled in our home and work again and as though we had weathered the gales of revolution. Miss Monteiro had even arrived two days previously from Anking to start special classes for the women, and now—this! Nanking foreigners attacked by the Southern Soldiers, possibly many of our friends killed; property looted and burned; all the foreigners in the Yangtze Valley to be withdrawn to Shanghai as rapidly as possible, since this might be the forerunner of a great anti-foreign uprising.

"It was all so hideous and so unexpected, but fortunately we had too much to do to take in its full significance. Two hours in which to dress, pack up what we could snatch, eat breakfast, turn over the work to the Chinese staff, and say our farewells, was not conducive to much meditation. Our packing was of the sketchiest variety, but our servants turned to with the best of spirit to help us through, and somehow by the time the wheelbarrows squeaked up the walk we had seven boxes and trunks ready for them, and enough toast and Klim [powdered milk] for the baby's journey to Shanghai. When a group of our nearest and dearest Chinese friends gathered around us the meaning of this leave taking came over us as we saw their tearful faces, and realized all that was devolving upon their shoulders.

125

It was a comfort to pause for a few moments in the doorway and lift up our hearts in prayer for those who were taking up the burden, as well as for us who were fleeing into unknown dangers.

"The day was fortunately rainy, so there were few coolies at the Kiukiang station to be a possible source of trouble, and by evening we and our belongings were safely stowed aboard a river boat headed for Shanghai. 'Packed' would perhaps be a better expression, for there were over three hundred foreigners crammed into accommodations meant for eighteen. My memories of those four days and nights are mercifully blurred by the fact that I have never learned how to sleep on the floor, expecially packed as we were like sardines, and lulled by the snores from the fringe of gentlemen on our outskirts.

"On arriving at Shanghai we found the mission ladies at St. John's University working with all their might to prepare Seaman Hall, one of the dormitories, for the reception of the up-river refugees. By the time the Hankow and Anking groups arrived a few days later a great deal had been accomplished, and we could go into rooms equipped with beds and stools and use any means in our power to make them look cheerful and homelike. Those weeks at Seaman Hall were a most interesting experiment in cooperative housekeeping—we might almost say communism—and the result was quite a triumph for the American ability to work on committees. Eighty of us, for a time, were fed and sheltered there, with even such details cared for as were offered by the 'Self-Service Shoe Shining Parlor.' Everyone, from Bishops on down the line, waited on tables, washed dishes, or made beds. We proved to the world that we had not lost the ability for manual labor in our palmy days of many servants, and undoubtedly it was good for us to keep occupied when leisure gave us the opportunity for so many despondent thoughts.

"We were among those who decided to stay in China, hoping that we might be able to help in some way our Chinese friends up country, and at all events to be able to keep in touch with what was going on. It was a great satisfaction to have Mr. Liu, the Chinese clergyman at Nanchang, come down for a week in June with news of events to date, and to know that the church services were keeping up and that attendance was remarkable good under the circumstances."

The middle of June found us setting out for the beautiful resort of Unzen, in the mountains of Japan, where we were invited to share a bungalo by our dear friends the Claude Thomsons. We have had a most peaceful, healthy, summer, after the horrors of that last year in China. We lived quite primitively in a cryptomeria grove, beside a beautiful brook tumbling over great mossy rocks. The baby thrived in the sweet good air, and we felt quite made over and ready to face whatever the coming winter might have in store for us. We decided to stop in Shanghai. We hoped to have a few rooms of our own somewhere, and try to set up some semblance of a home after months of refugeeing.

Lloyd's letter of this date followed mine, and told of the advance of the Southern Army after the Nanking Incident. It had separated into two parts and advanced north like "two tines of a fork," one from Nanking, the other from Hankow, with Peking "the juicy morsel at the end of the fork," their objective.

However, as they moved farther north, it became evident that there were serious difficulties within the two divisions of the Kuo Min Tang, and Hankow, representing the radical group began assembling force to attack the army under Chiang Kai Shek, operating from Nanking.

The split occurred right after the Nanking Incident, when five foreigners were killed, practically all foreign homes were looted, and ten houses belonging to foreigners burned. Dr. C. C. Wu, Minister of Foreign Affairs of the Nanking Government, intimated that the attack was planned by the Communists probably to provoke reprisals by foreign powers and consolidate the country under Communist leadership. The result in reality was that the most moderate element rallied around General Chiang.

A temporary coalition was formed when Borodin, the Russian Communist and leader of the group in Hankow was expelled and sent back to Russia. At the demand of the Hankow group and in order to form this coalition, General Chiang was also dropped for a short time, though later he got back his power and the Communist element had to retreat to Southern Kiangsi, a few hundred miles south of Nanchang. Their occupation in this locality and its results fill many of the later pages of this story.

One result of all this fighting and uncertainty was the depreciation of the paper currency, which had four issues within one year, each becoming worthless in a short time. Fortunately the crops were good so there was a sufficient supply of food if you had the money to buy it.

Through all these dangerous times our clergyman, the Rev. Daniel Liu who had taken charge when the Rev. Kimber Den went to the U.S. for study, kept the church free from soldiers and even protected our household belongings when the soldiers arrived to loot them. He insisted that they must bring the officer in charge, who, at Mr. Liu's request, sealed up the gate, and "by tact and real courage" Mr. Liu kept the soldiers out of the house until he could move all of our belongings upstairs, and rent the lower floor to the Commissioner of Education.

Lloyd ended his letter "This is the Church's trial by fire but the real church is not consumed thereby. Rather there are evidences of the strengthening of Chinese leadership, and a new realization on the part of many Christians of the meaning of the Cross of Christ and the love that shares with them their sorrows. Many, too, are holding to the belief that in this hour of national hopes deferred, there lies the hope that Christ may be found with His way of life which is the only solid foundation for any full national existence."

In September we returned to Shanghai and settled into a house on the beautiful St. John's University campus, where we prepared for the arrival of our new baby.

Lloyd realized that Bishop Huntington, also a refugee, needed his services in various ways. Later on in the fall he was able to go up river to visit Nanchang, returning in time for the arrival of Mary Katherine Craighill on November 18, 1927.

The following excerp throws light on the way the uncertainty of the political situation was bringing about the emergence of Chinese leadership, more noticable in our up-river diocese than in Shanghai.

May 29, 1928. "(Lloyd) came right down (to Shanghai) from the Wuhu synod, and was much cheered and encouraged by the good spirit and sense of responsibility shown there by the Chinese. Sixty delegates and only seven of them foreigners (Western missionaries) shows where the brunt of the work is resting these days. Lloyd was the only foreign clergyman there. He and Dan had worked out a set of Canons changing the whole organization of the diocese, so a Chinese general secretary shares responsibility with the bishop, and under them there are a good many committees, each composed largely of Chinese. Oh, — I forgot the Standing Committee which is the real working group at the head, and of which Lloyd is a member. Lloyd was very much pleased with the way these measures were voted on, for they were all preceded by intelligent discussion and passed after deliberation. He says the result is that if all the foreigners in China had to leave, the work in the Anking Diocese is still organized to go forward."

General Chiang, once more in charge of operations, was able to drive the Northern element far enough west so that he could form what seemed like a fairly stable government, with Nanking as its capital. Lloyd went back to Nanchang again after Christmas, returning to get me and the children in the late spring and take us with him to Kuling, where we settled into the little home we had bought some years before. He spent much of that summer in Nanchang. One of his tasks in the early fall was to clean our house after it had been lived in by various officials. Our cook told us that one of them was Chu Teh, the famous Communist General. We wished he had left his name in our guest book.

The changes which were taking place in the outer aspect of Nanchang at this time were an indication that we were in a truly revolutionary period. The old wall which had surrounded the city for many centuries was pulled down, and the bricks used to pave a wide boulevard encircling the city. The main streets were in the process of being widened so that motor vehicles could be used and even pass each other. It meant the ruthless tearing down of countless facades of the largest stores in the city, and we heard there was no recompense for the owners. Some of the smaller shops were left with such a tiny space that we marveled at the dogged persistence of the occupants, who put up additional shelves reached by ladders, and carried on. Men and women walked together on the street. There were even some girls in the police force.

It was indeed a new city to which we had returned, but the situation was by no means settled. We were quite aware of the Communist forces gathering strength only a comparatively short distance south of us. We knew they were anti-foreign and very cruel and that they regarded foreigners as people either to be exterminated or to be held as hostages in exchange for their demands. It wasn't the most peaceful setting for the arrival of our third child, Peyton Gardner, in the fall of 1929, but no matter how upset the conditions, we were delighted to have one child born in our home city of Nanchang. Through all the turmoil of those days the new hospital at the Methodist Mission was being built, and its grand opening, when hundreds of the citizens poured into its halls, came at exactly one day after Peyton's arrival.

We felt very conscious that we were living dangerously, with that large army of hostile Communists so close, and our children so vulnerable. We were quite happy when Bishop Huntington urged us to take our furlough in the summer of 1930, hoping that by the time we returned things would have settled down. We packed up once again to leave our city, but this time with the joyous prospect of having the children to show to our welcoming families.

Any parents of young children can appreciate what we faced in traveling with "three under five," but in China travel was far less simple than in America. There were rickshas and sampans to be negotiated, each parent carrying a child. There was the long ocean voyage when the mother of the family lay prostrate with seasickness and Lloyd began to realize the truth of the old saying about woman's work being never done. Finally came the arrival at San Francisco, with our homeland looking dear and familiar and peaceful to us, and utterly unfamiliar and exciting to our four-year-old Lloyd, Jr.

Two months at camp in Goshen Pass seemed like a bit of Heaven to this weary family. Here our children were claiming their heritage of beautiful Virginia country, of pine trees and blackberry picking, of playing on the rocks in the pool with numberless cousins, of seeing Doc Hall milk a cow by the back porch and squirt the milk, still unboiled, right into their

132

The Craighill family on furlough — 1930.

mouths. After the numerous children were tucked in for the night the parents sat on the porch telling stories, laughing, forgetting the cares of the world as darkness fell and Hog Back Mountain stood out in bold relief against the sky, with the fire flies dancing their magical dance through the cedars.

We ate batter cakes and sausages, Virginia ham and biscuits topped off by watermelon. What a furlough! I still feel the peace and relaxation of it after those years of turmoil, as I write this forty-one years later.

SECTION III

REBUILDING AND RURAL RECONSTRUCTION

1931-1937

I

We came back from our 1931 furlough leaving behind us a country in a state of despair and disillusionment from the Depression. We were to return to a country which was full of hope and expectancy. The large group of Communists were still in Kiangsi, not very far south of Nanchang, where they remained until they moved their forces far to the Northwest on that incredible expedition, known as the Long March, in 1934-35. However at this time General Chiang Kai Shek was again back in an increasingly certain control of the country, and was surrounded by a group of young Western-educated men, who were eager to implement the Revolution. Along with them, I found later, were men of very different ideals, Germans and Italians, looking to lead China into the ways of Nazism or Fascism. General Chiang was to try to maintain an uneasy balance between these two widely diverse groups until the war with Japan changed the entire situation.

On our return to Nanchang in the spring of 1932 until the outbreak of war with Japan in 1937, we were living in the midst of it, and our lives were controlled in large part by our locality. From having lived in a huge medieval city, far remote from political developments, we found ourselves in the very center of them.

After that memorable summer in Virginia we went to Englewood, New Jersey to spend the next months of furlough at the home of my mother and sisters. This was the era of the Depression and we began to realize why we found such numbers of men along the New York streets, trying to sell apples or pencils, anything to gather in enough money to keep them from going on relief.

Our return trip across the continent in 1931 reinforced this awareness of the Depression because we had the long transcontinental train almost entirely to ourselves. Very few people were traveling at this time as we saw during our daily trips back and forth from our Pullman to the diner through nine almost empty cars. Our berths were close to the observation car and that became an ideal playroom for the children, tossing their balloons around with no one to be annoyed by them.

Bishop Huntington was due to go on furlough and wished Lloyd to take over the diocesan office in Wuhu during his absence. His title would be "Bishop's Commissary."

At last those long six weeks of travel ended and we arrived at Wuhu, a city about two hundred miles up the Yangzte from Shanghai, important commercially for the great amount of rice which was shipped from its ports to all parts of China. The Bishop's residence, which was to be our home for nearly a year, was on top of a hill outside the city, with a magnificent view of the river. We wished the house hadn't been surrounded by narrow porches with heavy brick arches, which cut off some of the view as well as the light.

The mission owned many acres of land which stretched away below our house, dotted with trees and shrubs. On a rise of land at some distance in front of us was a large boarding school for boys. Across a lane from our compound was one where the Sisters of the Transfiguration [an Anglican Order] had their convent. Sister Constance, one of their number, was a trained nurse and had opened a clinic for the poor people in the neighborhood soon after her arrival. Later she added a work room where the mothers could come and do the beautiful

138

designs of cross stitch on grass linen, which made that industrial work known far and wide. There was added a day nursery to care for the babies and a grade school for the older children. It was a flourishing concern in which we were much interested.

The next months were marked, politically, by the increasing threat of Japanese aggression. Manchuria had been seized by the Japanese, and during our year in Wuhu they attacked Shanghai, resulting in terrible destruction and bloodshed. We became fearful that we might once again have to flee. China was forced to accept humiliating terms of surrender. We banded together with our Chinese friends to boycott Japanese goods in retaliation for the Twenty-One Demands and this continuing hostility. My letters of this time are full of speculation as to what lay back of all this. Japan had seized Manchuria. Could they actually have as their aim the subjugation of all China, reducing her to a colony and requiring that she purchase the goods which Japan manufactured? It was a most disquieting possibility and we spent many hours wondering about what the future would bring forth.

Lloyd became immediately involved with the duties of his new position, glad that occasionally he could say, "This can wait for the Bishop to decide." I now began on my career of teaching the children, starting Lloyd on the Calvert School First Grade course, and giving Mary Kate some kindergarten.

In June, 1931, Lloyd made his first visit to Nanchang to see how work was progressing there. A printed letter to friends in the United States tells his story.

September, 1931. "A recent trip to Nanchang, after the family was safely stowed in Kuling, gave me a chance to get back to mother earth as it were, to come in touch once more with those interests which have brought us back half way around the world. That crowded third class coach on a hot summer afternoon was slightly different from the Santa Fe transcontinental limited on which I had last traveled, but for all that there was a strange sense of elation at being once more on the way back to Nanchang.

"The hospitality shown me by the Rev. and Mrs. Quentin Huang during my stay with them was of a quality more often found in the Orient than elsewhere. Not only this spirit of hospitality, but the good taste, the cleanliness, and the Christian atmosphere of that home are bearing witness among an ever enlarging circle of friends.

"I was glad to be back in time for the commencement of St. Matthew's School. I had come at this time especially to make an address at the closing exercises of the school. It was good to see the teachers and the older boys whom I had taught. The school has been registered during the past term, but the religious worship and instruction has been in no way interfered with by the educational authorities.

"At the morning services the following Sunday I had an opportunity to preach to our congregation with about 85 present. Six were baptised at that service, among them four from the graduating class, which means that seven of the nine boys in that class are church members.

"One afternoon Mr. Den and I went out to see the new Leprosarium which was built during the turbulent year that I was gone. The barbed wire entanglements through which our motor bus passed a few miles out from the city was grim evidence of the danger of communist attack which had threatened our friends so often during that year. From quite a distance we could see the new leper hospital which is situated on an isolated hilltop. The $8000.00 for these buildings was contributed: $5000.00 by the China Mission to Lepers, and $3000.00 from local Chinese. I found forty lepers there being cared for in clean, wholesome surroundings, ten men in each of four cottages. They look after their own quarters, do their own cooking, plant gardens, etc. Though the Christian instruction is at present somewhat irregular, they are hoping for a chapel with regular religious services as the next step. The Rev. Kimber Den is the chairman of the local committee and the prime mover in the enterprise.

"The work among government school students under the Rev. Quentin Huang I felt was in especially encouraging shape. Though figures are not always significant yet I felt that statistics plus spirit in this case did indicate some worthwhile progress. There are over 180 members of the Students Club, of whom 37 boys are also members of the Pure in Heart Society, which means that they are definitely striving to follow our Lord in His way of life. Worship and a course of instruction are parts of this new life for them. Though the latter society is less than two years old there are four or five of its members who are preparing for Baptism. From Mr. Huang I learned that a number of the club members were formerly quite anti-Christian, but now that they have come to know what Christianity is they have definitely changed their attitude.

"While these various aspects of the church's work naturally occupied the center of interest for me, the world was hearing of Nanchang for other reasons. For the time being it was the little capital of China. President Chiang Kai Shek had taken up his residence there, and had brought an army of 300,000 to deal with the red bandit armies, who had entrenched themselves in the mountain strongholds of southern Kiangsi. Either these communists armies had to be defeated or else the Nanking Government would eventually fall. Fortunately, by his vigorous measures, President Chiang has captured every one of his enemy strongholds, though much remains yet to be done in rounding up and disarming various scattered bandit groups."

II

Toward the end of July China was involved in another, and not man-made, catastrophe. I write of this in a letter to my mother from Kuling. "As I sit writing I hear the running of many waters, the rushing of the big brook along the lower part of the valley, and all the many drains and brooks flowing into it, the dripping from all the eaves and gutters and each individual leaf. The whole world sounds like a completely saturated sponge being gently squeezed over a tub. Never have you seen anything so wet as poor old China in this past week! The first pour-down came a week ago, it flooded on Monday, poured on Tuesday, rained off and on on Wednesday, and so on and on. It even had the nerve to thunder storm on Thursday. We simply couldn't believe there could be a week of such steady rain, ending in a grand finale of cloud burst yesterday and today. We're almost afraid to read the papers for fear the news of floods will be too terrible. You hear of 4000 people being drowned in Canton when their homes were swept away."

The mighty Yangzte continued to rise all summer, pouring over its bank and the dikes built to keep it in check, producing a flood even worse than the one in 1870, which was the worst in recorded history. The country people in the vicinity of Wuhu took refuge on any high ground available, and our hill, surrounded by a long brick wall, was excellent for their needs. The wall provided the solid prop for them to use to fasten mats woven of split bamboo, which gave them shelter of a kind for all the months until they could return to their farms the following spring.

The doors of their farm houses were hung on leather hinges and could be easily removed. It was these which had been turned into rafts to take them to safety as the waters rose. Whole families could crowd on them, as well as bags of rice and piles of straw, to be poled across the rising waters to any higher land available. About 3000 farm families surrounded our compound, which rose up like an island in a lake 120 miles wide and 180 miles long. Here and there were dotted other hills, topped by mission compounds or houses of Western business men—that area outside the city had been too exposed and lonely for the Chinese to wish to live on it, so it had been available to these comparatively recent comers. Fortunately the walled city was also on fairly high ground, so the shop keepers continued their business as usual by simply moving their wares to higher shelves and covering the waters below by using their shop doors as false floors. Their customers arrived in sampans. When we returned to Wuhu the middle of September, I found that we stepped directly from the steamer into a row boat and were rowed through our front gate until we could walk a plank to dry land on our hill.

Toward the end of September, 1931, an exciting piece of news was reported. The Lindberghs were flying out from New York to make a report to our government about the extent of the flood, and one of their stops in China would be Wuhu! A dinner for all the Westerners was planned as a welcome for them at one of the largest homes on the Hospital Hill. We listened for the plane all the morning of the day they were due to arrive, but when nothing happened, the welcoming party of Chinese officials returned home. Shortly after their departure we heard the drone of a plane and the Bishop's secretary, Mildred Capron, without a moment's hesitation, climbed into a sampan and started in the direction of the sound. By the time she had arrived the plane had already alighted, and Mildred, a reception committee of one, received the Lindberghs.

The dinner that night gave us a chance to meet our distinguished guests. Mrs. Lindbergh's home had originally been in Englewood, and my family knew the Morrows well. After dinner Lindy wanted if possible to get a weather report from the gunboats lying at anchor in the river, well upstream from the hospital. Dr. Hyla Watters, a remarkable surgeon and head of the hospital, offered to contact them by means of Morse code and a large flashlight which she had used for this purpose at other times. We followed her up the stairs and onto the balcony of the house built on the highest land of that hilltop and here watched fascinated as she flashed her signals and got a response from the gunboat. She turned with satisfaction to make her report. The weather would be good and no rain or undue wind expected. The Lindberghs were delighted and Anne, who knew the Morse Code, began to think of adopting her method. This whole trip, with the recommendations they gave our government for relief procedures, has been told in Mrs. Lindbergh's book, *North to the Orient.*

Lloyd's work as chairman of the famine relief committee in that vicinity was very important and he spent hours of time helping to organize the farmers into teams to rebuild the dikes, receiving their pay in bags of wheat sent by the United States. The Chinese people are independent and self-respecting, and much preferred to work for their supplies, rather than have a handout.

It was a wonderful act of Providence that an immense quantity of shrimp was found in the flood waters all during that fall and winter. We knew this had prevented starvation and we began to think of shrimp as the manna of our flood era.

It wasn't until April 1932 that the return of the Huntingtons made it possible for us to go back to Nanchang and take up our work there again. We were housed for a time at the Methodist mission while our own home was repaired after two years without occupants. Then we settled in and began to open up the contents of 83 pieces of luggage which had in some way accumulated. That included a basket of kittens but didn't count the children.

III

The year 1933 was a most important one for Kiangsi Province and for the development of the Mission Work there. General Chiang Kai Shek arrived, rented a house on the Methodist Compound, and settled in to conduct a thorough-going campaign to "exterminate" the Communists. As the Communists withdrew farther and farther south and east large areas of territory were left with few inhabitants, and those needed a great deal of help. Most of the able bodied men in the area had either gone with the Communists, won over to their cause, or had been killed. There was great need of rural reconstruction, and during this year plans began to take shape in which the Christian forces would undertake this work, using money supplied for the most part by the government. It was a very unusual situation which faced the Christian Church. A book published in 1970 by James Thomson of the Harvard faculty, entitled, *When China Faced West*, goes in detail into those years in Kiangsi from 1927 to 1937, and constantly refers to George Shepherd as the main source for his material. Our contact with the development of a rural service union has been written about in my letters of that period and will be quoted here to show not only the relationship which all this had with the Nanchang Mission, but also to show the development of the Shen Kung Hui [or Chinese Episcopal Church] in the city at this time.

In January 1933 I wrote, "Monday an unknown gentleman from the government headquarters called here and said that Chiang Kai Shek was coming and they would be glad to borrow our kitchen stove. I murmured that it was something which we used a good deal and couldn't really spare, at which he said most urgently that they would use it for only a week—the implication being that we could certainly get along without it that long. Now there really are a good many things I would lend that gentleman for I like him, but the kitchen stove is not one.

145

However, I remembered our old one was over next door and I said they could have that though goodness knows it is not of presidential timber. But the man appeared relieved. It occurred to me that they might just as well use a Chinese stove, but when I said something to that effect he answered that a foreign house must have a foreign stove, and to that there was no reply to be made.

"This week has been just as cold as any we have had, which is saying something. The lake has continued frozen, and we are wondering if any of our vegetables will be resuscitated. How the Chinese stand it, I can't imagine for they really aren't keyed up to such weather. Anyway they know how to protect themselves from it better than we do, though I adopted some of their methods before I went out calling with Miss Chang on Friday and Saturday. Just for example, I had on two woolen undergarments, a heavy wool dress, three sweaters and my heavy coat over all. But in spite of that my legs would have frozen if I hadn't remembered those wonderful spats you gave me, May, and which were absolutely the thing. I shall never be parted from them again. With socks over my wool stockings, spats and zippers my legs were as dainty as was the rest of me. Lloyd threatens to take my photograph in that guise, but I'm afraid you would never send me any more of your hand-me-downs if he did.

"When one is so fortified, and with such a good companion as Miss Chang, New Year calls are a lot of fun. Everyone has more or less cleaned up for the great day, and the little boxes for cakes are all filled, and in addition all sorts of dainties are on tap. We literally ate our way from house to house. I came home so stuffed with eggs boiled in salty tea and lotus seeds boiled in sugar and lichee nuts and mandarin oranges and sticky rice balls cooked in sugar syrup that I really looked with lack lustre eyes at our perfectly good supper. I also came home with the feeling that China New Year is an institution which must be preserved.

146

The government says it just doesn't exist, but believe me it does. I don't care what they do to the calendar, but they must preserve the gaiety and relaxation which such weeks bring in the middle of the cold weather. It gives a chance for laborers away from their jobs who never have even Sunday off, to get back home and foregather with their relatives once more. And it does give such a holiday feeling to everyone. The sun came out yesterday and it was much warmer, and really it was fun to walk the big streets. Only a few stores were open, and those only a crack, but the vendors were out in all their glory with all kinds of firecrackers and the grand paper lanterns for the children and little candy men which they formed most charmingly and unsanitarily while you stood and watched. We called on one church member who has one of the stores which was reduced to a mere hole in the wall when the street was widened, but which they have extended vertically since the spacious courtyard is a thing of the past. She insisted on showing me the whole house, which consisted of three little rooms set one on top of the other, and reached by the most precipitous flights of stairs, with the treads not more than four inches wide. She pushed and the apprentice pulled and I managed to ascend them and still more wonderful, descend. It was worth the effort for I finally reached the roof and looked out upon the streets in their holiday array, and it was quite a sight."

February 19. "One night Kimber and Quentin came in for the reading of the Laymen's Report, and we heard later most interesting things about the way they are organizing the drive against the Communists. Chiang has been emphasizing the fact that it must mean co-operation from the whole city. He says he has just three months to give to the campaign, and that this is their last chance to get rid of the menace. He also says that the reconstruction is as important as the military campaign, and that it must be considered in the light of real enlistment. When a man undertakes to reorganize a city vacated by the Communists he must not suddenly feel called to leave on account of ill health. Such a man will have two assistants, a doctor and a coffin, sent him. He can use either he is required to, but he must stick on the job! One way they are using to get the people aroused is to have the whole city canvassed for money, as well as having numbers of speeches made daily on all the principal streets. Kimber and Quentin are in on the speech making, and Quentin, I know, goes out every day at two for his turn. It does seem as though they were going at the thing with more efficient planning than they have used before, and also as though there were more chance of their accomplishing something drastic.

"One event we are thankful for, Kimber reported to me that night. An anonymous giver in Nanchang has offered to support twenty additional lepers in the hospital (60 in all) if the Mission to Lepers would furnish the additional housing. That they have now agreed to do, and Lloyd is even now making the plans for the one additional building needed. It is such a splendid piece of practical Christianity going on there, that I am most happy to have its scope increased."

February 26. "While we were eating dinner Monday noon Chow Gia Sau came stamping in as fast as her stumps can carry her to tell us to come quick and see the procession. We flew to the gate, and what a sight it was. It was part of the effort they are making to arouse the citizens to help in the Anti-Bandit [or Anti-Communist] Campaign, and every walk of life was represented in the procession, half of whom were dressed as bandits themselves. They had their faces painted up most grotesquely, and wore red bands and leggings and sometimes carried spears on which were impaled the effigies of the poor villagers. The bandits were tied by strings to their captors, and all sorts of beasts and bands and people on stilts and people in cages and bandits with wooden boards around their necks were led along. They had burning paper houses and burning thatch and dear knows what else. It was half gruesome, half ludicrous, but wholly gruesome when you knew how very real all these things were only a hundred miles or so away. Let us hope and pray that the extermination they are aiming for will happen, though I prefer absorption to extermination as an ideal. A lot of wounded have come in already, poor souls, and on a cold rainy day like this I just agonize to think of the suffering and misery all around us."

March 25. "One of the real events of the week was getting word from the Department of Missions authorizing the use of $20,000 Chinese currency from the Shanghai lease rentals, which are always kept for buildings, for the building of a plant to house Quentin's work for the government school boys. It will mean one main club building which will have room for girls' and women's clubs as well, and back of that a church which can be converted into a recreational center. There will be space on the roof for a tennis court for the girls, and in time there may even be a swimming pool, making use of the lake water. We are simply too excited and happy over the prospect, and you can imagine how Quentin and Lloyd get together and make plans most of their waking hours. The gift is contingent on five thousand being raised locally, but they seem to think that will be quite possible, and have a bit over two thousand already in hand."

April 2. "This makes me think of a booklet Lloyd got the other day. It is descriptive of the 'addition' which the government is making on the old graveyard land next to the Baldwin School. It is all written up with plans for bungalows and sketches of formal gardens and maps of streets and plans for civic centers until you would think you were in California itself. After seeing these plans I am simply speechless with amazement, but so many amazing things have happened in this old city in the last six years that I put nothing down as impossible—even to formal gardens. One real achievement has been the planting out of any number of trees along all the new

149

roads in the city—really good trees, not just willows as of old. These are all marked with a little board warning people to leave the trees alone, and the shop-keepers are each responsible for the trees along their land. For years they have planted trees and for years the wicked little vandals have broken them off. Now we do trust this scheme will work. [Which it did, when the shop-keepers were made responsible for the trees.]

"Last night we had a very nice meeting here. The Discussion Club died while we were in America. We felt it either should be revived or something of a similar nature substituted. There are many very fine and rather lonely returned students here in town who need to have something done for them, and we foreigners need a little more gaiety. So we finally started in, Lloyd and I, and the rest have rallied around in good style. By limiting the Chinese to returned students we could handle the group in our living room, and our house is central enough so the Chinese who don't know us very well are more ready to come to it than to go outside the city. We are going to call it a China Study Group, and will have short articles read about aspects of Chinese life. The Chinese can contribute to that and feel they are more of an authority than we are, so it makes a nice give and take atmosphere we couldn't get in other lines of study nearly so easily. Last night there were 22 here and we read an article on the Chinese family system which started up a lot of discussion. We are wondering how much a permanent change in family life has been made in this province, which has been under Red rule for so long [five years, we reckoned]. Mr. Hsiao, a graduate of Harvard, who is head of the public works, was here and told us many interesting things."

May 16. "Last night the China Study Club met here, and Dr. Wu gave in English a tremendously interesting lecture on tuberculosis. He has charts and showed lots of X-rays and the whole thing was most concrete and pertinent. He has been able to accomplish remarkable cures by operating on a nerve which

150

controls the diaphragm and makes the lung rest, as well as by a method of pumping air into the lung. It was most interesting to see the pictures of before and after taking this treatment. He is a thoroughly fine person, so simple and humble. It happened that one of the men here that night was a Dr. Chu with a degree from Oxford, who was in charge of the provincial Department of the Interior. He was so interested that he wants to get Dr. Wu lined up in a program of a province-wide anti-TB campaign. Who knows what an evening's entertainment may bring forth?"

Dec. 11, 1933. "A nice Mr. Liu, interested in the road development in China, led Discussion Club Friday evening. He's a Civil Engineer, returned student as all the Chinese in this group are, and quite high up in the National Economic Council which is projecting this road-building program. It embraces seven provinces, and will in time link together the whole country with a splendid system of roads. He told us just how the finances were managed, and then showed maps on which were shown these 'trunk lines' — all of them have parts under construction but a great deal has been done. They have tried to use as much as possible the shorter provincial roads already finished and link them up in a real system. It certainly is a most tremendously needed development, and it was most encouraging to think it was actually being done. And that Mr. Liu is one of the nicest young men you could find anywhere—so polite, so interesting and really a gentleman."

Dec. 16. "After Mrs. Johnson's papers at the Mothers Club on the teaching of unselfishness to children, one of the women rose up and gave voice to her difficulties. 'I believe in everything Mrs. Johnson said, and I try to practice it, but how can I when not one of my relatives or neighbors has my point of view or has any idea what I'm getting at?' It's the enormous difficulty of the Chinese family system, with neighbors constantly around looking on. 'The Mothers' Club must reach out and inform more people of new ways to treat children,' says she. Others of them echoed the same idea. At that point Quentin appeared to say that Governor Hsung, our very up-and-coming governor, had asked if a group of official wives he was organizing might attend the meetings of the Mothers' Club and learn of us. So of course we said they might, and felt that here was a way to let our influence be felt a bit further." [They were of course none of them Christians, and the members of the Mothers' Club were Christians.]

Dec. 3, 1933. "This past week has been more than usually busy for we have been having the Home Week with a meeting every afternoon on some topic of Christianizing the Home, ending up with a grand old Child Welfare Exhibit yesterday afternoon in the big gym, at Baldwin. Two of the meetings were outdoors—at Dr. Hwang's on Tuesday and here on Wednesday. [Dr. Grace Hwang was a physician at the Methodist hospital.] There must have been several hundred people at all the meetings and I'm sure a lot of interest has been aroused. The most amusing meeting to me was Friday, when one of the Methodist pastors pronounced that he was going to tell them the new way to bring up children. He is a first rate actor, not to say mimic, and he proceeded not only to tell them what not to do, but to show them most vividly why they weren't to do it. 'Don't rock your babies,' he began. The audience audibly gasped. They had never heard of such a thing. Then he proceeded to rock himself violently to and fro and show just how it addled the brain! The next admonition was not to 'mind the baby.' Another gasp from the audience. Of course the man was mad, but very amusingly so. He then told them not to carry their babies! As half the women there were doing that very thing they looked a bit nonplussed. He ended up by telling them not to mind if their babies cried, and showed in the most concrete and vivid way just what splendid exercise a baby received in the process. The audience rocked with merriment. Then he quizzed the children on the front row. 'Is crying good or bad?' 'Good,' they roared back. 'Do we want our babies to cry or not?' 'Want them

152

to cry,' they whooped ecstatically. I was in stitches. What do you suppose the great undistributed middle class there present thought of it all?

"Yesterday's exhibit was really good and I bank rather heavily on that for making the real impression. There was a very good exhibit of foods, assembled under their vitamin content, and loan exhibits of toys from the few shops in the city where they are sold, as well as things we have had made here, and stuffed animals. We had rocking boats and bean bag boards in the middle of the gym floor, and the best exhibit was seeing how the children enjoyed using them. Grace and I had charge of the furniture exhibit, with pens, individual beds for the babies, little tables, chairs, etc. The greatest interest was in Grace's baby bed with a very practical scheme for keeping a baby covered with bed clothes when sleeping by itself. That seems to be one of the reasons nearly every Chinese baby is tucked in somewhere with the parents. As I was in the process of demonstrating for the five hundredth time, a woman looked at me very proudly and said, 'I know all about that. This [pointing to the doll in the bed] is the baby Jesus and this little bed is the manger.' "

Sept. 11, 1933. "Yesterday I had two interesting lots of information. After church I had dinner with Mr. Chang Fu Liang, Secretary for Rural Work on the National Christian Council, at Ruth Green's in Kuling. We found out from him what the committee is planning in regard to work for rural reconstruction in the various 'hsiens' [counties], when they are cleared of the Reds—[or 'if'!] Mme. Chiang has asked the church to make out a program, and Mr. Chang and others are highly interested. As he said, if the Christian forces can meet and conquer Communism on this basis, it will be the first time it has been done anywhere in the world. Other places have merely conquered—or delayed—the advance, by force. Now, can the Church meet this challenge? Can Christianity meet the laborers of China with a program which will appeal to them even more than Communism has done? It's such a huge and engrossing and important question—is anything in the world more so, now?—that I'm thrilled to think we will be in the center of it. Mme. Chiang's idea was for the missions to co-operate, but this committee thinks it more desirable to have a separate committee of legal status through which Christian and the best of the non-Christian forces can work. It is highly probable that many Americans would give to it—such a valuable experiment—as well as the Rockefeller Foundation, and others. I'm glad it is being undertaken by someone other than our few Nanchang missions. They'll probably start in just one demonstration center and work out from that. In the meantime the hsiens are still very much in the hands of the Reds."

From Lloyd to my Mother—Sept. 12, 1933. "I found things going ahead very well at Nanchang when I got back. Kimber had been holding Wednesday night prayer meetings on our lawn during the hot weather and the attendance there and at the Sunday services had kept up remarkably well. St. Matthew's School has opened up with an enrollment of 156 pupils—all we can take care of. I am to have general charge of the religious education both in school and in our children's church this year, and I am planning some improvements as a result of our summer conference on religious education.

"The Vestry has just decided to abolish separate seating for men and women in church, and last Sunday they all appeared with their wives and husbands [we have two women on the vestry] and sat together to inaugurate the new system. We are laying special emphasis on Christianizing the home this year too."

Sept. 24, 1933. [We had come down from Kuling.] "Coming into Nanchang from the station gives us an idea of what this old city is preparing for. Such crowds of soldiers everywhere, and

154

hardly a ricksha to be had for love or money. All the coolies have been sent out to work on the huge aviation field they are rushing to complete, and we hear that in a few weeks the forty aeroplanes purchased from America will all be stationed here. Won't we be in the thick of things then. Lloydie is *so* excited about the bit of news. As we came along past Baldwin we saw ten armoured trucks drawn up along the roadside. They say it's a perfect sight to see those ten thousand men at work on the field. I wish I could go out to see it, but it's been far too hot to do anything but settle and take baths. I've taken at least three a day—of a sort. And how we have tubbed the children—I never saw anything dirtier than they have been. They drip with perspiration even sitting still, and wipe it off their faces with their grubby hands until they look just like mulattoes."

Oct. 2, 1933. "It was last week that we had a note from Mr. Johnson saying the Assistant Military Attache of the British legation from Peking was arriving, and could we put him up. We have plenty of room so have been housing him ever since. He's a nice Scotchman—Capt. Dewar-Durie, with a good sense of humour and quite easy to have around. He has a nobby little Highlander's uniform with the amazing cap, but unfortunately left his kilts behind him. He seems to be limited in his interests to only one field—and that the military—but possibly it's good for us to rub up against such. He is busy most of the time making official visits and trying to get as much information as he can possibly cram in. He wants to start for Foochow [this was a city in our province, not the well-known city on the coast] tomorrow and then on to the places south, to see as much as he can of the military preparations. No one quite knows when the drive will begin, but the field is evidently nearly done, and they are doubtless waiting for that before the advance comes. That field I saw better on Saturday, and it is an amazing sight. There must be 20,000 laborers all in this area a little over a mile square and giving an impression of human labor in the mass which must be comparable to that in the building of the pyramids. You've seen that many people sitting still at a ball game, but can you imagine seeing them all at *work*! I wish I had a movie to show it. No camera could begin to do it justice.

"Capt. Dewar-Durie ran into another Englishman and brought him over Saturday for lunch, and then we took him out with us to the dedication of the new chapel, at the Leper Hospital. He is the Reuters Correspondent—a Mr. Yorke, who has come to Shanghai to do some research for the Institute of Pacific Relations and whenever he has a holiday he goes off to report a Chinese war. He is an eccentric duck, but quite likable. I believe he was imprisoned twice in Jehol, and when he was here five weeks ago he went everywhere that anyone not Red fears to tread. He went to Changsha by bus, and as far south from here as buses run.

"He is long and lanky and loosely clad and looked so funny on a little bicycle which he hired to go with us, and which he pedaled with his heels rather than his toes. The occasion for our visit to the Leper Hospital was a delightful one after all the military preparations on all sides. They have enlarged the hospital to take in 20 more patients, and the new chapel which was dedicated at this time will be a gathering place for the lepers on all occasions, their one public room. It seemed odd and sad to have them unable to join with us in this service. The chapel is high with a lovely view in all directions and a bell tower atop.

"I was surprised to see how much work had been done around the city since last I went out. A new road all around, and a big moat which will be a boat canal as well as a means of protection—and something to reduce the danger of floods. In making this aviation field they had dug up any number of graves, and we took some pictures of the huge piles of bones lying beside the road. Skulls and crossbones enough to make

156

you have nightmares except that I'm used to it, though I did dream that night that the Communists were after me."

Oct. 10. "The landing field is all finished and the Big Drive about to begin, though the aeroplanes are not yet here. Our Capt. Dewar-Durie will leave tomorrow for Nanking and perhaps return here later. We expect George Shepherd and the Chinese representative of the National Christian Council next week, and the Hollands the week after. I'll keep both my guest rooms in order for Nanchang is simply crowded with guests of the government, largely. Ina Johnson has two German military advisers, and the usual pilots of the planes, and last night in came a delegation of three new ones—the adviser of developments from the League of Nations, the Health Adviser, also from the League, and a couple of lesser lights. We no sooner read in the paper of an important personage arriving in Shanghai than he pops up in Nanchang. I much prefer to let my mind dwell on the reclamation projects than on all that must precede it. Ina says the talk by the German advisers of extermination of the populace in the Red Areas is enough to make your blood run cold."

Oct. 25. "I got word that our guests I had been ready for, for several days, had arrived while I was at a meeting so I rushed over here to find nice George Shepherd and Mr. Chang here. Since then life has been just one thing after the other, and most interesting truly. George you never met, but you remember Dr. Shepherd, his wife. After being in Nanchang two years they lived for years in the interior of Fukien—until the Reds finally ran them out in 1930. George is a most delightful raconteur and has told us many things about the joys of living close to country people, where he is known and loved, I'm sure, by the whole countryside.

"But mainly George has told us about life as it is lived in that great area of China, in Kiangsi and Fukien, which is a Soviet

157

government and has been for three or four years. He knows more about the working of the Soviet than any other foreigner in China, I feel sure, and has been asked here by the national Christian Council for that reason—to help in these rehabilitation schemes. He says he can tell them what they *can't* do, anyway.

"His tale is a revelation to most of us of the thorough-going Leninization and the complete dedication of the Reds in that territory. As he says, it is an almost uncanny mixture of good and evil, and hard for anyone to analyze. He told of their complete absorption in their cause, by which they endure every hardship. Graduates of colleges, returned students, Ph.D.'s—all mixed in with the Red Army, all wearing only two garments, straw sandals, no bedding at all [sleep in straw or huddled together] and no one, not even Chu Teh, getting more than $3.00 a month. Graft is unknown and practically no immorality in its grosser senses. They allow no waste or splurge of any sort, limit the amount spent on weddings to $13.00, allow absolutely no silks or satins, tear up any silk bedding, burn up every book and destroy everything which isn't flatly utilitarian. It's a great leveling down process. Every deed has been burned, every landmark destroyed, every indication of life as formerly lived obliterated as much as possible. All the landlords and wealthy have fled or been killed, and every man of brains is frowned upon if he gets ahead of his fellowmen in any respect, whether by getting a little more rice or a bit more pork than his brother. Only two bowls of vegetables are allowed at a meal. All individual initiative and rewards for it are done away with. As a result a territory formerly exporting quantities of rice hasn't now enough for its own existence. I could go on indefinitely about all this and of how absolutely the country is at grips with this system now—the end of the struggle to decide whether China will or will not be Communist. One interesting thing is that in plans for reconstruction of these areas the government is hoping to keep many of the Communist ideas—reforms, perhaps, would be better. But the crux of the whole thing, and the knottiest problem, is what to do about redistribution of land. With the whole land redistributed and landmarks gone, who's to say how it's to be put back, and do they want the old landlord system with many of its old evils?

"George got most of his information last fall at this time when he went back to visit in the neighborhood of his old city, which had been taken by Reds and then freed from them. He spent a lot of time talking with the people—and then one fine moonlit night the Reds suddenly surged back again and he came within an inch of being captured. He and his pastor with him had to walk 65 miles in 24 hours, over mountains all the way, and the only way they escaped was by keeping on these mountain paths instead of on main roads full of Reds. And a captured foreigner is practically a dead foreigner, these days. He lost 15 pounds in that walk!"

Oct. 25, 1933. "On Monday along come Bishop Huntington, Virginia [his wife] and Dr. Harry Taylor—to be here for the big meeting to make plans for rehabilitation on the 31st. Fortunately Harry will bring a camp cot and bedding, for the Hollands are planning to stay for it and it looks as though Monday and Tuesday we'd be 'fairly full'—I'll have nine guests in addition to the family! You see now the why and how of large houses in China. I'll have to put Harry, Mr. Chang and George all in the room back of this [the living room] with the privilege of washing their faces in the little room at the end of the hall. Not exactly luxurious but we'll manage somehow and they won't be censorious. There is nothing in their 'bedroom' now but some book shelves! I borrowed two beds today from one hospital and will get comfortables tomorrow from another. It keeps me hopping both literally and figuratively to keep up with it all.

"Lloyd and I have been making the most of the beautiful weather having perfectly delightful bicycle rides. He had told

159

me of the new military road built around the city this summer and how pretty and quiet it was, but I had no idea until he took me out Friday just how much of an opening into the world of beauty it would give us. We've always felt rather shut in in this old city with its wall and now with the wall down, there was nothing particularly pretty to see. But about two miles out of the city, completely encircling it from river to river, they have built this very good road. We can get on it in fifteen minutes from the house and in an hour go through lovely real country scenes. Farmers threshing and cutting grass, even plowing for winter crops. Green fields, big camphor trees, little shrines to the god of the harvest. Mounds covered with ancient graves. Just the kind of peaceful country life that is so restful and satisfying to the soul. I kept exclaiming with rapture at the perfect picture of harvest scenes with the distant blue hills as background and overhead the typical quiet autumn sky with silvery rippled clouds. Then we suddenly swung around a corner and found ourselves with the real climax of it all. On top of the dyke along the river on the north of the city, since it was just at sunset, we could sail along with the radiant sky ahead and the loveliest view that one could imagine of sailboats on the river with the nearby hills in the background. Such a joyous and almost magical experience. For fifteen years we've longed to get some views of the river other than just from the Methodist compound, and here at last we have a chance to see the most beautiful part of it which we've always longed for in vain. We flew past an old temple which we remembered we had once reached after spending half a day in a boat. We can do that whole circle from the house and back in an hour. The next afternoon we went out just to the river and back. This time we had Peyton and Mary Kate on the book rack of our rears, and Lloydie proudly riding on his own vehicle. Such a wheeling family you never saw. I didn't wonder the whole world stopped to stare with amazement and then to grin with appreciation. I thought we really were worth it. I could foresee many nice expeditions in the future.

160

"The plans have come for the new Student Building next door to us, so one of the contractors who would like our job wanted Lloyd to see the $129,000 barracks he is building outside the city. Yesterday we rode over to see it. It's a huge place, for he's been renovating old ones as well as building new. It gave me rather a turn to have him reply when I asked who the sloppy-looking soldiers were who were living within it, that they were Communists imprisoned there. I was in a hot-bed of Communism for fair. They all looked just like our usual soldiers—I thought somehow they would look different! We decided to come back so we could see the canal they're digging around the city, also for purposes of defense. That goes along this military road part of the way and is a perfectly mammoth thing, and the earth thrown up from it makes a regular city wall, and all along its edge are gray forbidding towers of reinforced concrete full of little openings for guns. This city is the most fortified place I've ever seen in my life. These pillboxes dot the whole country side. It's a regular Verdun. It shows most evidently that the government realizes it must not lose Nanchang or it loses all. We hear many more planes have arrived and imagine the campaign is about to begin in earnest. There has already been hard fighting in various places. It's the most difficult kind of fighting, for the enemy has all the advantage of knowing the mountain fastnesses and of having the help of the people and of being able to make ambushes and surprise attacks. But the government is certainly pouring in troops—thousands are coming in every day. I hear the train frequently is not open to passengers, which may account for the fact that neither the piano tuner nor the other guests I spoke of have turned up.

"Our British captain has gone on to Nanking, and the amusing Reuthers agent has gone too. He is sending in all the reports to the papers, though he has only about 20 words of Chinese, and his only interpreter and investigator a pseudo 'boy' who has not more than 100 words of English. But what news he

161

does collect, and how his imagination does work! He obligingly told us what accounts of his in the paper we should and should not believe."

Virginia Huntington, the Bishop's wife had arrived with him for her first visit to Nanchang. I wrote of her Nov. 3, 1933, "She writes beautiful poetry which Vida Scudder and Florence Converse want her to publish [Miss Scudder, in the English Department at Wellesley, was an author of note, as was Miss Converse.] She has just written a paper for the Living Church on Barth and his theology, and with it all she is the sweetest and most unassuming person."

Nov. 3, 1933. "She got a taste of our manner of life these last weeks on that first afternoon, I remember, when I suddenly found Lloyd requesting me to have tea served for the eleven guests who were having a Committee meeting in the living room. Mr. Lobenstine and some others had arrived from Shanghai [he was the Executive Secretary of the National Christian Council and I think P.C. Chu came down from Peking University, but I can't really remember]. It was a most interesting group we had gathered together that afternoon, and we had Mr. Lobenstine and Mr. Chu for dinner that night with the Huntingtons.

"Tuesday was the day for the all-important meetings. They left the house at nine and didn't arrive back till five, when they were late for a 'Welcome Tea' at the church, followed by a delicious feast at the Kimber Dens. The first hours they spent with the provincial chairman, Governor Shong, where he asked the Christian group to help with organizing and administering refugee relief, as they so often do famine relief, using government funds but being an independent group and incidentally giving a witness to Christianity by honest administration of the funds and adequately meeting the needs. It's a big job—and makes me think of what the Smith Unit was called on to do in

162

France during the war. Mr. Johnson will probably give full time to that, and he wants Lloyd to do the same.

"The other plan took shape during the noon meal with Mme. Chiang, when the dozen men completely fell victim to her charms as well as her exceeding ability. She is a very remarkable person. The upshot of that plan is that a certain section of a county is to be turned over to the National Christian Council, probably under George Shepherd and Mr. Chang Fu Liang, to administer. They will get the Madame to have the right kind of magistrate appointed and will make a plan of development, covering a five year period, spending money raised among Christians by Mme. Chiang and the other Christian groups. It will include education—adult and children; farm experimentation and administration; simple training in hygiene and care of sickness. With those men getting after it I think it will be a most interesting and worthwhile scheme and will, I trust, be the spark to kindle other projects of a like nature. As Mme. Chiang said, the issue before the world, anyway before China, is whether Christianity or Communism will prevail. This is giving the Christian Church an opportunity to prove that it has a message for the underdog as well as does Communism, and is a very real challenge.

"The next day was presumably the Huntingtons' last in Nanchang. We had made many plans for it, but at ten Tuesday night came a phone message from the Madame who had gone to Foochow that afternoon, about eighty miles away, to be with her husband at his headquarters there. She wanted the whole group to go by motor to Foochow the next day to spend the day there and have a movie taken! The Fox people were here to get a film. So at her summons the whole group departed. The Huntingtons changed plans to stay a day longer, and everything else stood aside. They got home about five that afternoon after having had a most interesting trip. Foochow is in a lovely location, and of course it really doesn't happen every day that one dines with the Chiang Kai Sheks! They found the general very much of a person, too, giving a sense of power, and authority as of a truly big man. No small talk, they said, but when he did have something to say doing so very directly and definitely. After lunch they all had their pictures taken—and those films are now being rushed to America for development and will probably be shown about as you get this letter! Wouldn't it be fun if you could see it and hear the General making a speech and the Madame translating *very* freely, much to the relief of the foreigners, for they distinctly did *not* want the General to say they were there to help him fight Communism!"

Nov. 19, 1933. "Dr. Chu has come up to continue his talks and plans about the Kiangsi reconstruction program [later called the Kiangsi Christian Rural Service Union]. There are experts here from the League of Nations likewise making plans. It would be so fine to have some such Christian demonstration given as the National Christian Council is planning. The Chiang Kai Sheks themselves will give fifty thousand for it, and the National Christian Council will raise another fifty thousand among wealthy Chinese Christians."

Nov. 26. "This week has been famous for entertaining a guest with a hobby, and that same hobby is the collecting of ancient porcelain. It seems that Nanchang is one of the best centers for getting the rare old china made in the Sung dynasty, over a thousand years ago, when porcelain was in its earliest beginnings. Lloyd and I had wondered mildly about these queer old things we had seen in the curio shops, and which looked like ancient funeral urns, but we had to wait for the arrival of Dr. Tsu [at that time a secretary of the National Christian Council] before the whole realm of the collectors began to open up before us. Curio men gathered in our hall day after day, silent and respectful, and would open up tin boxes from which would be taken a little brown or a lovely gray-green bowl which Dr.

Tsu would fall upon with exclamations of joy. And the amazing thing to us was that these little creatures were worth in some cases hundreds of dollars. We went out to the shops with him on Wednesday, and were ushered into back rooms where we had never penetrated before, and shown some of the most precious things, ready to go to Shanghai. One little pitcher about four inches high, the color of an egg shell and very shiny, was priced at a thousand dollars! There were two tiny bits of porcelain for rubbing up ink, each about an inch high, worth several hundreds. Of course Dr. Tsu didn't buy those, but the man was perfectly wild from our penniless point of view, and must have spent at least five hundred dollars for these little fragile things. He said he had spent two months salary and I can easily believe it. He got some beautiful pale blue bowls, as thin as paper, and with a wonderful glaze. Little conventionalized decorations were cut in the biscuit so that the light shines through them when you hold them up. The shape is like what I will draw in the margin. Of course the wonderful thing about it all is that these things have been preserved for all these centuries in some ancient graves. They were buried with the people when they died, otherwise they would have certainly been broken a thousand years ago. Dr. Tsu got them to throw in three inferior bowls when he made some of his purchases, and gave them to us, so we have at least three pieces of genuine Sung porcelain.

"When Dr. Tsu was here before Mme. Chiang had been interested in his purchases, so he wrote over and told her of his collection this time and asked if she would like to see them. She replied that she would, and invited us all three to tea on Friday afternoon. The Madame has her reception room on the second floor, very comfortably furnished and with a cheerful open fire. We had some delicious tea and cakes and then Dr. Tsu spread his wares before her. She realized that the things she had bought were not of the best, and before we left she had asked Dr. Tsu and me to go shopping with her the next day. But before that we had had a talk about so many interesting things. She got Dr.

Tsu to go over some of the books she had been getting to read in her hour of devotional study which she has every morning with the general. She is anxious to get things which are available in Chinese and which will be of the greatest help to him in these hard days he is facing. She talked about how much her devotional life meant to her—how in her busy days she had just had in Shanghai it had been crowded out, and how she had missed it. She is very charming, with an excellent keen mind and with it all so much of earnestness and such a real religion that I found her a most unusual personality. How we do pray for them, and how much they need our prayers. She is reading Fosdick's latest book on *Religion As I See It* and liking it very much. She had just finished reading the life of Huie Kin, one of whose daughters was Mrs. Tsu, and had liked it too. She lent it to me before I left, and I am finding it most interesting. Doesn't it make one realize the latent possibilities in every little ragged Chinese farmer boy riding a water buffalo, as he was doing once on a time.

"It was quite exciting next morning to be called for by the 'First Lady of the Land' and roll along in her auto to the alley leading to the curio store, the best in the city. I thought surely her leather coat, blue and red scarf, matching cap, not to mention her distinguished air, would give her away, but it didn't seem to. They brought out all the lovely things in the shop and I decided she had very good taste for she liked the same things I did! Also if she liked something she didn't really care whether it was of the most intrinsic value or not. We left without buying anything, but in the afternoon Dr. Tsu went back and got the things she wanted, and when she sent here for them that night, a big basket of Nanfeng oranges came too, as well as candy for the children. She is a very thoughtful person, always doing little things like that for people.

"The General was in the room next to us while we were having tea, and as we left both Lloyd and I glanced in at the

166

open door where he was sitting alone at his desk. The room was full of maps, otherwise very little furniture. He sat there with his head thrown back, looking off into space, deeply and it seemed to us sadly meditating. We thought of the burden which rests on his shoulders, of the difficulties he is facing and of all he is trying to do, with little help, and we did feel for him. Those are two great people whose task I do not envy."

Dec. 3, 1933. "Thanksgiving dinner was at Ina Johnson's this year. There were 35 of us at the tables, for we had invited the Russian Archangelsky's of the Salt Gabelle [the tax on salt, which was administered by Westerners at this time], as well as the three American aviators of the Chiang Kai Sheks' and the five League of Nations experts who are here making investigations for the government. One, Dr. Stamper whom I sat next to, had charge of the National Health program in Jugo-Slavia. Another, a Dane, is an expert along lines of rural work. There is a German who was a fine burgomeister somewhere and lost his job under Hitler, and a Czechoslovakian as well. Talk about your International House—for of course we had the Wus to add the Chinese touch. [Dr. Wu, a Chinese, married Miss Penny-packer, an American nurse.] Our place cards were little silhouettes of a Pilgrim father and the rooms were lovely with chrysanthemums. There was a service first in the Baldwin parlors where the children sang sweetly, and Daddy sang *O Lord of Heaven and Earth and Sea* very beautifully. The young were seated next to their various 'aunties' and had a grand gay time eating as much as they wanted to.

"It was very interesting to me to get the reactions of Dr. Stamper to the various types of Mission work he had seen. He is mainly interested in institutional work so hasn't investigated us much, but he certainly is scathing in his criticism of the Methodists for having two hospitals in both Kiukiang and Nanchang. In each case I think the Women's and Children's Hospitals started first, and now in these days of decreased

167

mission funds they still cling to both plants, out of sentiment. 'Vat de Chinese need is lessons on co-operation, and I ask you, vat do zey get from the missions?' asks he with a fine white scorn which I could not but echo. 'I know you have two American Schools in Kuling, I saw them myself. And the teachers they do not speak. Vat is dat, I ask you?' [This second American School is run by the Lutherans who think most of the rest of the missions are so liberal as to be on the verge of damnation, but again I agree with him that it is a scandal.] It doesn't help any to say, what is quite the truth, that many schemes of cooperation with other missions which our own bishops out here are ready for are foiled by the church at home. He is most scathing of his condemnation of Hitler and of the way the churches are doing anything the government asks of them, apparently.

"Dr. Stamper thinks that what we call Communism is really an agrarian uprising and that the question of land tenure must be dealt with by the government if there is to be any real peace and prosperity in China. It seems that in his own country all large landlords have been abolished, and he feels that that must happen in China. He says that in Kiangsi only half a million dollars in taxes are paid by the rich business men, while five millions are paid by the desperately poor farmers. And in Szechuan they are collecting taxes due twenty years from now! He feels that most of our uplift work in China is far too much for the classes and not at all for the masses. He quotes the Peking Union Medical College which has a class of thirty medical students [a Rockefeller college], and he has discovered that it takes one hundred and fifty thousand dollars [American] to pay for one of those diplomas! Isn't that simply appalling. And at that the doctors rarely go back to work for the people, or if they do are so discontented with the difficult conditions that they go back to the port cities again."

Dec. 11, 1933. Lloyd wrote to my mother: "We have

168

naturally been alarmed over this recent flare up in Fukien, and I don't now know how it will turn out. A large element in the Southwest want to get Chiang out but I can't see that they have anyone better to offer or as good. He is the best hope of stability between north and south, and most of those who want to put him out are those who want to control the political jobs themselves.

"What is really needed is agrarian reform or even revolution but I don't believe this is to be expected from any of the military contestants and even if the Communists got the upper hand, the country would be thrown into such a turmoil that Japan would probably step in and take over control—or try to do so. The danger of this latter event may yet bring the contending factions to some kind of compromise."

IV

The year 1934 was another year of great political activity in Nanchang, with all its attendant impact on our home and work. The highest officials in the nation were gathered into our city, a series of roads were being built to connect us with Shanghai and points west and south, and the Christian Church, represented by the National Christian Council, was being asked to take a part in the rural development program, which was recognized as a very important aspect of winning the farmers, who represented 80% of the population, away from Communism into acceptance of the Kuo Min Tang. While the Christian Church was being asked to have active participation in this fashion, the government itself was undertaking a much more ambitious operation of a similar nature, which would cover a much wider area of our province than could possibly be attempted by the Christian forces, weakened as they now were by the Depression in America which hampered any programs for extension.

Nanchang, we heard, was to become one of the two 'model cities' in China, with Loyang, in the far west, the other. The fact that it wasn't a river port, had never had foreign concessions, and yet was a center from which roads could radiate in all directions to the large cities of the coast and on the Yangtze, and connect with railroads to the north, made our city, once so isolated and comparatively untouched by Western ways, an area of great activity.

One unusual aspect of all this was the formation of the New Life Movement, which tried to change the age-old customs of the Chinese populace into ways more in accord with Western habits. It produced great and sometimes rather ludicrous activity and proved to be a very superficial movement, but it received much attention during this year. Another effort, concentrated in Nanchang, was the program to clean up the lakes which occupied the center of the city. Our house was

170

located on one lake and faced another, so this whole program was very literally at our door. Some of my letters tell of this.

Feb. 4, 1934. "They are cleaning out the lake back of us, and later will do all of the lakes. It certainly is a new day in China. First they had about fifty men, each with his bamboo foot pump, pumping the water out into the adjoining lake. As it got lower the people went in with baskets and caught fish, and such a 'hot time' [a Chinese expression for excitement] you never saw. The whole lake was lined thickly with people watching the sport of bottomless baskets being clapped down over the miserable fish, thus rudely deprived of their native element. Our 'boy' got eight of the 'mud fish' and the pussies got fifteen. Of course it was a great day for the young—and to think that we had a back gate opening right out onto all this!

"Now the whole mud bottom is exposed, and they are preparing a track with cars to carry off the mud—the richest fertilizer for miles around. We're having it spread on our garden and expect to blossom as the rose.

"The reason for all this is that the League of Nations Engineer adviser felt it was a great danger spot in the city. They are making a series of pipes by which they can control the outlet and at times of high water, flush out the whole series with clean river water. Since all the drainage for the city runs into them, it certainly is a good idea, but as a matter of fact they never have really seemed like a menace to us, breeding neither smells nor mosquitoes."

March 5. "We are not only 'knee-deep in Spring' but in mud as well, in Nanchang. It's wonderful to be a model city, but has a few drawbacks in the process of getting that way. I've told you how they had decided to dig out the mud from the three lakes here in our neighborhood, and I'm beginning to think that cleaning out the Augean Stables was a cinch in comparison.

171

After pumping out all the water by foot pumps, literally thousands of coolies have been burrowing into the black filth of centuries which covers the bottoms and trotting away with two little basketsful of mud on the ends of their carrying poles, to be dumped out either on the great sandy waste which is to be the New Nanchang, outside the old city wall and near Baldwin, or into a smaller pond which, I am glad to say, they are filling up. They haven't finished one lake yet, and there are two more bigger ones to be done, but I hear they are going to bring in a dredge for the biggest one. All I could think of when I heard it was how jolly that would be for the children. But it certainly is a new day in China when the city calmly decides to spend $300,000 Chinese currency [perhaps $100,000 U.S. though exchange fluctuated] for a scheme like this where the only incentive is to have better sanitation. Quentin says he has been promised four boats for his Club—which we will borrow occasionally—and we will by that time have forgotten how we have 'slapped down in the mud,' as Peyton says. I believe conjugation should uphold him in making that verb 'slip, slap, slopped.' Of course in the process of transportation enough mud has overflowed the baskets to make our path unbelievably bad as we pick our way to Baldwin. But what strawberries and roses and asparagus we should have with all this Chow Dynasty fertilizer spread abroad!"

Feb. 4. "The Chiang Kai Sheks will soon return, we hear. First signs were the preparations at the house next to the Johnsons on the Methodist Compound, including the gobble of a turkey, and today we hear the leopard and tiger skin rugs have been airing. Evidently the anti-Communist campaign is to start again speedily. We had wondered when they left if they would return [they had gone to Fukien to put down an uprising] and it seems they are to. Certainly the Communists have by no means been 'wiped out.' "

George Shepherd had been in Fukien during the uprising

172

there, and had visited Shanghai on his way back to Nanchang. I reported the result of his visit in the following letter.

"In Shanghai George discovered how many people are interested in this project of Rural Reconstruction, and how significant they feel it to be. A group of bankers, including the most influential one in the whole city, came to see him and Chang Fu Liang, and wanted to find out all about it. They say the thing they want most of all is a peaceful country, where they can have a chance to invest their funds in developments of all kinds. To have this they believe that the farmer must be given a chance and that the troubles will never be settled by military force alone. They wanted to know what program the Christian Council had, and how much it would be able to open the eyes of the government. As a matter of fact they have an excellent chance to do something very significant, we feel, and the eyes of all China will be on this experiment. Of course the government is going to attempt a much larger program of its own. How this of the National Christian Council will gear into it we don't know. But it's a new day in China when so much thought and effort goes into the peasant group.

"George and Fu Liang started out Friday on their first trip to the country—like Caleb and Joshua, to spy out the land. They expect to be back in a week and we can hardly wait to get their reports. They were happy to be able to get their passports without any delay, and will go down to a place within a few hours by bus from George's old station. By these new roads put through this last year a place anywhere from six to ten days trip away from Nanchang, frequently inaccessible, can be made in *six hours*! Not yet, of course, for the country is still far from peaceful and only military buses go to many places. But the Communist cause is definitely on the run, and as far as anyone can see the back of their military strength will soon be broken. The great question is what stand the government will take on the causes which have given rise to all this. Chiang is here now, and I have great faith that he is beginning to sense the real source of the conflict.

* * * * *

"Well now, to go way back on my tracks, the day before New Year's Day, in came George and Mr. Chang, back unexpectedly early from the front. We could hardly wait to get their report, which was so important for our plans. They came back thus early because there was fighting not far from the place which they were investigating. The Communists were making quite a desperate attack but the government troops were holding and the farmers didn't seem much concerned about it. Since then we've heard that the Reds have been pushed back and a good deal more territory freed, including the place where the Shepherds lived their several years in the interior. George made some interesting reports about their findings—one in regard to the exceeding care with which the fortifications have been made all through that part of the world. He says there isn't a remote hilltop or mountain peak which hasn't its pillbox, and one out of four of these is constantly guarded, so that in case of trouble the alarm may be given. The surprise attacks have been the government's undoing in the past, and this is their way of preventing them. Then he found the people much more friendly to the government than before—in fact they were quite anti-Red. He thinks it due largely to Chiang's School for Officers which he held at the foot of Kuling last summer, and in which they were told to regard the welfare of the people, as well as taught how to climb mountains. Anyway a change has come which is all to the good.

He says it will be rough hard pioneer existence, and feels that it will take strong devoted men to do the job, but there is so much interest in rural work now in China, and so much response on the part of young people, as Communism shows most clearly, that he believes he'll be able to get his group by going around to the schools and colleges, making his appeal and enlisting their support much as Dr. Grenfell gets his groups for

174

Labrador. That means he'll get a youthful lot of workers, without family ties, who can endure the hardship and isolation much more easily. He wants to make a kind of fellowship of his workers."

Mar. 5, 1934. "Speaking of progressive measures, we certainly are taking them in gulps of late. Under General Chiang's supervision and with his backing the 'New Life' Movement has been launched in the city in a kind of whirlwind campaign which is fairly taking our breath away. All the clergy and religious workers here have been enlisted in it, as well as every other kind of leader, and the program has in it much of moral reform. It has lots of health propaganda, too. They are using all the public halls in the city for two weeks solid of lectures, and are getting all kinds of charts and tracts and having exhibits as well. I am supposed to be a secretary, on account of being president of the Mothers' Club, and have been fairly overwhelmed with literature of all kinds, none of which I could read without rushing over to Grace and Quentin. George Shepherd told me a few of the choicest reforms advocated — not throwing refuse into the streets, not spitting in public, keeping your clothes all neatly buttoned about your person, saying 'Excuse me' when you bumped into anyone. You better come quick and visit us before we lose our local color entirely!

"Tuesday Mr. Wright appeared on our doorstep again — the business man I took in last fall. He always appears when Lloyd is away, and as he is very young and very beautiful it is rather a joke. He proved a most welcome guest, however, for he got us excellent seats on the roof of one of the stores where one of his agents holds forth, and from which we viewed the marvelous lantern parade. [This lantern parade came two weeks after the Chinese New Year and signified its end.] I realize now that I had never really seen one before. Since the Republic this particular festival, which is always celebrated by carrying dragon lanterns through the streets, has been discouraged,

175

partly because it was tied up to the moon calendar which the government wanted to do away with, and partly because the dragon is the symbol of imperialism. But this year for some reason the ban was not only off but the people were encouraged to put on the best kind of a show possible, and believe me, they went to it with avidity. They say there has been nothing like it since the days of the Empire, and I can well believe it. The procession began to go past the store we were in just at five, and to our amazement it lasted without a break for two hours and a half. There was every type of lantern imaginable, for every locality and guild in the city was represented, and the lanterns were largely symbolical of their professions. Mingled through them all were the most marvelous and wonderful dragons, lions, dogs, horses, people on stilts, floats symbolizing old folk tales, girls on boats, automobiles with dragon lanterns wound around them — everything you can imagine. And everywhere were the slogans telling the world to buy native goods, and nowhere were there any signs of superstition. It was the government, utilizing this old festival for its own purposes of developing an interest in the new. There were lanterns made to represent Chinese-made flashlights, native-made cotton goods, huge boxes of cigarettes. As darkenss fell the lanterns began to glow with a lovely soft light which made the whole scene a kind of fairy land, especially when we began to saunter home and saw the dancing chain of lights encircling and reflected in the lake. The people entered into it all with an abandonment of joy. Every now and then the procession would halt a few minutes while the dragon was made to coil on itself most marvelously, or the jugglers would perform, or there would be some kind of pantomime. All the time there was the rhythmic beating of drums and clapping of bamboo instruments. The most remarkable part of it all from one point of view was the perfect order. There wasn't a hitch in proceedings from beginning to end and there was no crowding. The whole city was out to see but they stood where they were meant to and walked where they were told. It was of course a never-to-be-forgotten occasion for the children, beginning from

176

the moment that Peyton discovered the roof on which we were seated to be 'flat like the shoe woman's,' and I was gifted enough to understand that he meant the Shunamite who entertained Elisha.

"I have a picture in my mind from our New Year calls. We were walking along the street when a little boy suddenly let out a cry of joy, flung his arms around Miss Chang, and said 'Miss Chang' in the most joyful way. He was so cunning, and literally dragged us into the home of one of our recent church members, and looked radiant when he presented us to his mother, who has seemed to me a particularly nice person. There were pictures of Christ on the walls, the Ten Commandments for Parents had been pasted up, and the daughter was studying her books and planning to take a nurse's course next year. They in that house are all refugees from the Reds and nice kindly folk. We are having a great opportunity to reach these people who have been torn up from their old environment, are lonely and eager to receive what we can give them."

A wedding took place in March in our Parish Hall for two young people who were not Christians but wished to be married in the modern fashion but not, of course, a prayer book service. It shows some of the difficulties of adjusting the old to the new: "We had a funny time yesterday with this marriage a la mode. The invitations put the time at 1:00, and as one of the New Life rules is to be on time for things, I was horrified to discover that it was one o'clock while I was at the table crunching a crust or two in lieu of dinner, since the wedding was to be followed by a feast. I rushed off without waiting for my leisurely husband, largely to give him a lesson in promptness, and arrived at the church all breathless and panting, only to discover no signs whatever of a wedding. I pushed on up to Miss Chang's room, and was cheered to see the bridal robe and a crown lying out on her bed, but when I asked what was the probable time of the wedding, she had no idea. She was horrified to find me without a dinner, and cooked two eggs with a bit of grease and sugar. [That's the only thing the Chinese cook which I don't care for.] I managed to swallow one; then I bummed around observing and feeling a bit sheepish as to the lesson I was teaching Lloyd. At long last Kimber arrived, having had his hair cut in the meantime, and said there was a mistake in the hour: it should have said three o'clock. He had met Lloyd and told him. I then sauntered back to Miss Chang's room, where I found the bride and groom, both adorning themselves in different corners of the room — truly an up-to-date proceeding for China [where the bride and groom aren't supposed to see each other until after they're married]. The bride was revealing the fact that she had paid $9 for the rent of her crown, a pink voile braid, and was being upbraided therefore, for if she had only gone to the photographers she could have gotten one free, for nothing but the promise to have her picture taken there. Finally the stage was set and Miss Chang began to play the wedding march — *Onward Christian Soldiers, Marching as to War.* At that point arrives Lloyd, all pink and self-satisfied, and wondering if I had been on time. The bride came up to the platform to that martial refrain, and had to wait at least ten minutes for the groom, who was reported to be cramming himself into new shoes. At long last he arrived, and the proper seals were affixed and vows given. Just two schoolchildren in their teens they were. Finally when all was over the band boomed forth rather gently: *God be with you till we meet again,* and as the bride and groom still stood uncertainly at the platform, Mrs. Den came up, turned them around, and pushed them a bit, and they came down the aisle to the tune of *Tramp, tramp, tramp the boys are marching.* Then they had to take a little ride in the auto, so it was quite a time before we got at that feast, about four-thirty I believe, so it turned out to be a supper instead of a dinner party, just a discrepancy of a few hours."

I was invited to dinner by Mme. Chiang together with some

of the teachers at Baldwin School and tell of it in this letter of April 2, 1934. "There were ten of us there at the dinner altogether. At first we sat around an open fire in the living room and the Madame showed us some of the toys which the children had made in the school in Nanking in which she is so much interested. The children do part time vocational work, and by keeping at it all summer they can cover the courses prescribed by the government and learn a trade in the meantime. The little wooden toys they made were very cute, and she had some gorgeous pots of hyacinths in full bloom which they are learning how to raise in the gardening department. Mme. Chiang is much interested in these youngsters. She didn't go to Shanghai at all on the week she was away a short time ago, for she found so much to do for her school.

"She looked perfectly beautiful that night with a long dark red velvet gown and a stylish little black velvet jacket atop. And it was quite a moment when the door opened and the General came in. She seized upon him with 'Darling, I want to introduce you to these ladies,' and we found ourselves being presented most informally to by far the most influential man in China! We none of us had the nerve to speak Chinese to him so our conversation was naturally limited, as he speaks very little English, but he beamed upon us with the gentlest and nicest of expressions and was far from terrifying. We had most delightful food, of course, a Chinese feast, but everything passed, so the table looked dainty throughout — a rare treat. We had 'crackers' [the kind you pull and they pop, like our birthday party favors] with which to make merry and as I sat next to the General I pulled his with him, and he, being a good sport, donned the pink cap which was contained therein.

"The Mud Era is still upon us. I went to church yesterday in rubbers instead of zippers, most unfortunately, and before I had reached the bridge, two minutes walk away, that horrible black ooze had pulled off one rubber five times. Picture me, holding

179

up Mary Kate on the bicycle with one hand while with the other I fished up that rubber and somehow put it on. By the fifth time I was as near to tears as I ever am in a public thoroughfare. Mary Kate saved the day by hopping off and carrying the rubber herself till we landed on firmer soil. 'How I love good ordinary clean mud,' I said to Lloyd today, and he understood what I meant. I begin to wish we weren't so progressive.

"George Shepherd was enthusiastic about the Lichuan work when he came in last week. [They had decided to take Lichuan, which was near George's old area of work, as a center for this rural reconstruction.] That group of about twenty young people, college-educated or more, are living there among the country people doing most of their own work and beginning right on the ground floor. The finest thing about it is the spirit of Christian service and group loyalty there. They really feel they are a group, and apparently any possible source of friction is overcome in the fine Christian atmosphere. They are none of them getting over $30 Mex. a month [about $10 in our currency]."

Rarely did we sit down to the table with less than ten, during these days when our house was an unofficial "guest house." Businessmen, Y Secretaries, a Dane from the League of Nations, our two men working on the rural project — all came and went in steady succession. I wish I had been able to keep our guest book of this era. One of our visitors was Sherwood Eddy, a much traveled and well-known evangelistic speaker of those days, who presented the Christian message for the most part to students under the auspices of the Y.M.C.A.

Nov. 22, 1934. "It was most interesting to have Sherwood Eddy right here in the house with us, and get to know him a bit in those four or five days. He arrived in an airplane which General Chiang had lent him on Friday, and that afternoon

180

there was a long round table discussion at Baldwin, taking up some of the problems of youth as the various workers here in Nanchang had found them. Mr. Eddy was receiving official bulletins most of the time so couldn't pay much attention, which gave the whole thing a somewhat farcical air to me. However he had told us at noon that he had some things to say to General Chiang which would have warranted his whole trip to Nanchang in itself, and I knew these bulletins were arranging his dinner with the General that night. Dr. Eddy had just come down from Szechuan, and was simply appalled by the terrible plight of that whole province, the largest and potentially the richest in all China. He said he had never seen such fertile country any other place in the whole world, and yet it has been reduced to the most awful straits by the four war lords or old-style generals who are fighting there among each other and are letting the Communists slip in without lifting a finger. They exult as each of their enemies are defeated in turn by the Communists. The result is that all the remnants of the Reds from Southern Kiangsi are marching there as fast as they can make it, will join up with the forces already there, and there is every likelihood that Szechuan will turn entirely Red in the next few months if nothing is done. He feels that it isn't too late to stop this menace if there is a complete change of government there, and that Chiang is the one to bring this about. So no wonder he was eager to see General Chiang. Now the rest of us are eager to know what General Chiang will do about it. The Szechuan Governor is in Nanking now with the General probably trying to negotiate a loan, which if it is given to that particular man will go into opium and 'squeeze.' Dr. Eddy says the opium trade in that province simply beggars description — and he has powers in the way of description if anyone has!

"You can imagine that we sat around open-mouthed as this dynamic person imparted information. He has been everywhere, knows everyone worth knowing, and is really very much of a dear. We hated to lose him for as many meals as we had to, for he would entirely forget to eat as he told of his latest visit to Ghandhi, or of wonderful Amy Carmichael's work, rescuing slave girls in India, or of the differences between Communism in Russia and China, or of his opinion of modern Germany. He doesn't see a great deal in common between the two brands of Communism, by the way. He has a much higher opinion of the Russian variety than of what he has seen in China.

"He held two meetings daily for three days, one for students in the afternoon, and for a prepared group in the evening. That prepared group was to have consisted mainly of interested non-Christians, but as a matter of fact there were many Christians there. Too many, for it meant that most of those who should have distributed tickets were content to give them to their Christian friends rather than give them to the non-Christians whom he was particularly trying to reach. The three topics he took were first, 'China's Need,' giving some of the encouraging things he had found and then some of the things as shown by Szechuan, for example. It was a pretty black picture at times. Then he spoke the second day on 'God as the source of All Power,' with something of the philosophy of religion and a reconciling of it with science. The third lecture was 'Christ the Way Out.' He was very fine and forceful and made a strong appeal. Over a hundred signed cards that they either had decided to make a decision for Christ that last night, or were willing to study for three months. A lot more students took cards, too. Now we are eager to see how many will come to the Y on Saturday and get organized into classes.

"Brewer Eddy was here with Sherwood, and was just a dear. In fact his sermon to us in English Sunday afternoon was quite the high point of the whole campaign as far as we were concerned personally. He spoke of St. Paul's words to the sailors who were planning to selfishly leave the shipwreck in a boat by themselves, 'Except ye stay, all these others will perish' or something of that wording. Then he went on to give a splendid talk of the need of the world for co-operation, for fellowship and understanding sympathy. I'm sure we will all remember it."

Dec. 9, 1934. "George Shepherd is most happy with the way the Lichuan work is spreading out not only through the one district that was allotted them but through the whole hsien as well. One of the men was here on his arrival, and his report fairly set George prancing. It is splendid from every point of view, not only for what they are accomplishing but for the spirit with which it is being done. The Government has started many such centers, but the head of the work is a non-Christian with very little vision, and the amount of red tape and the overloading of the office staff is all rather typical of the way the government does things, and the way they can make any such service most irksome."

Mr. Clausen, a representative of the League of Nations from Denmark, and an agricultural expert, boarded with us for all those months, with a room elsewhere.

"Sunday afternoon nice Mr. Clausen, who left for good this morning, took Gene, Lloyd and myself out to see one of the rural centers run by the government. [Gene Turner of the Y.M.C.A. who was another one of our boarders.] It was great fun for me to ride out into the country again in a car to see what they were actually doing in rural work under this government grant which Mr. Chang and Mr. Clausen had been working with. It's really heartening. They're using old temples as buildings, fixing them up to look spotlessly clean with whitewash and paper and mats to lower ceilings. One building is to be used as a primary school, another as an adult school, and a third as a hospital. They have a group of six or seven college graduates and some of the country girls are in training as nurses. It certainly is a new day in China when people begin to take the rural problems seriously."

V

The next year, 1935, was one of increasing responsibility in the diocese for Lloyd, and of lessening responsibility for the routine matters in Nanchang. It could hardly be otherwise, as each trip up and down the river required hours of time in travel. My letters of this year are constantly referring to Lloyd's departure or arrival home again. One of his increasing responsibilities was for the Kuling School for English-speaking children of whatever nationality, located in that beautiful summer resort which gave opportunity for much outdoor life as well as a good preparation for college. Students were also accepted for the lower grades of school, almost a necessity for parents living in isolated communities. Our son Lloyd entered this school in the fall of 1935, when it became evident that he needed competition in school and companionship of his own age.

Feb. 25. "Lloyd has gone to Kuling now for the school board meeting of which he is treasurer, a Council meeting, and the ordination of Mr. Underwood. Then the Bishop wants his help in getting trouble in Kiukiang straightened out. Moreover he'll only be home three days before he'll have to set out again to help with a difficult situation in Anking, and then a Standing Committee meeting in Wuhu. The fact is that nothing much can or does happen in this diocese without my Buddy — so many times they need his wise head and his willingness to be a scapegoat when the other clergy are afraid to do anything; but I consider it's my contribution as well, especially now, when his being here would be such a help and comfort."

Early in January 1935 our son Lloyd came down with a case of scarlet fever, which of course dominated our lives to a great extent from then on. It was a light case, and we followed the doctor's prescription carefully, but a kidney complication followed which kept our active son in bed for five months. Those were anxious days, but the saving grace was Lloyd's fine spirit of cooperation. He accepted what was required without complaint. He wasn't allowed to sit up in bed, but lay on his stomach with his head propped on his hands and read every book we could find which suited his years. However, he couldn't write or work his arithmetic problems in that position, which hampered his future progress in school.

April, 1935. "It's cold and miserable, and the earth is just sozzling. The roses are all beaten until they look fairly black and blue, and worst of all I hear the river has risen over its banks and the countryside is flooded. That, after the perfectly unprecedented drought of last year must be too dreadful. My own personal reaction to this flood time is mainly with my nose. You may remember my various letters on the subject of cleaning out the lakes last spring, and our own fear that it was money spent in vain, since all the drains of the city continue to pour into our beloved lakes. Now my nose would tell me that it was worse than in vain. For the first time in all our years in China the lakes smell like open sewers, and we get the whole benefit of it. As all this deluge washes out the drains and the lakes fill up with the rich black water, the smell gets — well, I'd rather live by a paddy field. We think that in the digging out of the lakes all the vegetation, that lovely green scum around the edges, and the lotus was destroyed and in doing so they also destroyed the one thing which has successfully destroyed this smell, and somehow made a chemical balance which kept the air pure. Isn't it worse than pitiful? Hundreds of thousands of dollars, and the last state far worse than the first. Of course in time they will have sewers and things will be better, but in the meantime I may get me a lodge in a garden of cucumbers, or wear a continuous clothespin on my nose. I rose at 2 a.m. last night and doused myself with cologne. When Lloyd comes back I'm going to make him help me plant more scum on the lake. There's a wonderful lot in that dispirited little puddle right back of us."

May. "This afternoon Quentin came in to ask about just what formula one used when throwing a bottle out of a boat in its christening. I was all interest. Was it possible they were going to christen the five rowboats which have kept us in a twitter all spring? That, it seems, was the case. A member of the press had heard that the rowboats were to be launched that afternoon, and he had immediately decided he would like to have his fiancee do the christening, even offering to provide all the beer necessary. But how could she christen all the rowboats at once? Would she be nimble enough to leap lightly from one to the other, and would it be necessary to smash a separate bottle on each, or could one give merely a mighty all-inclusive smash, uttering at the same time the whole list of names? I left him to struggle with the problem, and never did know just how it was done. But it was done, and each of my imps have had a ride over the noisome waters, which fortunately do not smell as bad as they did."

June 8. "Mother, you were grieving about the lakes when you wrote. Those horrid smells kept up, when the wind blew, for about two months, and then thank heaven the green scum began to grow and the green stuff filled the water, so instead of the horrid sewage smell we get the well-known odor of that, quite agreeable with a suggestion of lotus. So there's a specter laid. Let's hope they don't decide to clean the lakes again!"

June 5. "Lloyd had a most interesting two-day trip this week, to a village where one of our catechists, trained in rural work, has been working for a year. He went back to his own home town, and in this short time has accomplished all kinds of things. He got the farmers to cooperate in building up the dikes high enough so they couldn't be flooded out each year as they have been formerly. Then he has started a system of cooperatives which are keeping down prices, has fixed up the big temple as a lecture hall by the simple expedient of putting the idols up on a high shelf and covering them with a curtain. Lloyd said he

186

pulled back the curtain and showed them off and the crowd roared with laughter. He is hoping to get all the individually owned cows, which now reside in the front yards and probably sleep in the houses, to be kept in a common pasture.

"Lloyd and Kimber were so very rare and precious that they were treated like princes. They were fed bread and bananas and canned pineapple and milk; I was expecting to hear they had marmalade and oatmeal for breakfast! It was an altogether encouraging experience and shows how much good a little such training can do. The catechist has been going slow on the preaching, preferring to win confidence and following first, but when he does preach he does it earnestly and well."

The old and new continued to jostle each other in Nanchang during this period, sometimes quite amusingly.

"Something right here made me think of my attempt to buy a large-eyed carpet or wool needle the other day. I went along a main shopping street and stopped in the stores where I saw thread for sale and asked for needles. With one accord they repudiated the notion of having such a thing for sale, and one and all told me to try my fortune on Fiddle Street. I've always loved its name but didn't know just where it was, nor that that was the only spot in the city selling needles. Finally I came to the street, or alley, in question, and sure enough, the first shop did have needles. The salesman proudly produced a battered little cardboard box, carefully pulled out a paper of needles, which had evidently been opened, picked up a pair of tweezers, and held out a needle to me temptingly. 'Two coppers,' said he. No wonder I have to keep my Montgomery Ward package under lock and key, and that Sister Constance saw only bankruptcy ahead of her when she supplied needles to her sewing women. Now they bring their own and none are ever lost. They had no carpet needles, I might add."

"Just here I must stop to tell you about getting our new puppy's license the other day. I went to Police Headquarters, and after awhile the English-speaking official arrived. He tried to make me write my name in Chinese with a brush, which was not very easy. Then the questionnaire began. He wanted to know the dog's name in English and in Chinese. His nationality. His birthday. His sex. While we sipped the tea he began to write. Five documents had to be properly filled in and stamped with a red seal, and half an hour passed before I finally achieved the coveted tag. At this time last year every mangy cur had roamed at will. When we do a thing we do it well nowadays."

Another important visitor from the point of view of the Lichuan project had come to Nanchang. I tell of this as follows:

May 28, 1935. "Sometime early in the week Lloyd was asked to take Mr. Fairfield, the American Board secretary visiting here, up to Lichuan, and it finally turned out that the government was willing to let them have a private bus in view of the importance of Mr. Fairfield and George Shepherd, whom he bosses, to the project. And of course that meant just one thing to me — that at last the time had come when I could go too! For months and months I have seen people depart for that project, and never have I had a chance to leave with them, but here I could get a free ride, the children were well, Gene was here to carry on and open the store room, and I was responsible for no meetings.

"When the bus came Friday and Mr. Johnson saw me all equipped to go he said Ina must join us, so over we went and got her into the bus too, at last, pretty flustered by such a hasty summons. And off we started for the country. It was a little overcast and there were occasional spurts of rain, but that just brought out the marvelous green of the rice fields, which at this time of year are so lovely. We went through a most beautiful fertile plain all the way to Foochow, which we reached about twelve. The little narrow dikes between the rice paddies were covered with close cut green grass, and looked like the paths in some well kept garden. All along these paths the trees were scattered. It made me think a little of a home orchard when the grass is green and high. Miles and miles of beautiful cultivation which hadn't been ravaged by war, for the Communists had never gotten in there. From Foochow on we were in territory which had been in Communist hands time and again, and the difference was apparent. It began to be hilly here, and wilder. The paddies were fewer and the groves thicker. Finally we came to Nanchen, a city situated right on the river, which we crossed on a stone bridge built a thousand years ago. It was thrilling to me to see a city of such interest and beauty way off here miles from the beaten track of port life. All around were forts and pill boxes and breastworks, signs of the terrific struggle through which this country had been. As we got nearer Lichuan it was still more apparent. At one place I gasped and said, 'Lloyd, from the top of this hill I can count eleven forts.' There was a monument on one of the hills too, and we found later that a general had been killed there and five thousand men in a big battle for the river, which flowed through a wide valley below.

"We climbed up and up over really mountainous roads before we reached Lichuan, about five-thirty. A lot of people were there on a grassy open stretch inside the old pre-Taiping city, to welcome us. Bessie Meeker, the Methodist women's worker who lives there, and whom mother and the girls know, was most happy to see us. She took us right to her house — the old Chinese pastor's nouse with the barest of furnishings but clean and airy. We climbed into our camp cots very thankfully after a good supper, and how I slept! Busses in China are not streamlined and air cushioned! We had joggled and rolled along till we felt fairly battered.

"The next morning we started on our walk to Kao Tsai Chow where the project is located in a huge old house which holds all

189

the group and about six families as well. It was one of the prettiest parts of the whole trip, that three mile walk through the fields of rice and tobacco with the blue, blue mountains rising all around us.

"I just wondered, when I got inside the building, how anyone could bear not to spend their entire time in the open, beside the stream which flows right along it. The building has all the dampness and gloom of a typical Chinese house, and I did truly admire and marvel at the spirit of those fine young people who stay there cheerfully and give themselves splendidly to the job. I felt as though I'd grow mold and warp if I were left there long. Fortunately it was pleasant enough so that we could have the long two hour meeting that afternoon, when one of the men who had been off having two months research travel among the various other rural reconstruction projects gave his report, out under a circle of lovely camphor trees which grew near the building. That is where they have the Morning Watch, too, which Lloyd led Sunday morning before we came into church in the city.

"Hugh Hubbard, who is a remarkably fine person, has written such a good report of what they are doing in the project and what their successes and difficulties are so far that I think I'll wait and swipe one of those for you rather than try to write much more of that here. Their greatest difficulty is the lack of good human material to work with since the young men are gone, and this whole area has been isolated for years. But they certainly have come to a tremendous need and I believe with the kind of intelligent service they are giving they will see that human material change. The whole visit gave one a most hopeful feeling of the value of such applied Christianity both for those who give and those who receive."

VI

During the Kuling summer, usually so carefree, family letters began to bring news that my mother was far from well. As the summer progressed our anxiety for her increased and we were not unprepared for the cable which reached us in October asking that I advance my furlough and return to Englewood as soon as possible. By early November I was on my way with the two younger children. Lloyd, Jr. and Lloyd went in January 1936 soon after the Kuling School closed for a long winter holiday, but they arrived just a week after Mother Gardner had quietly slipped away. It was a sad loss for the devoted family. Among the many letters which came at that time I shall quote only one, a sentence written by one of her nieces. "I think Aunt Ettie knew more about loving than anyone I ever knew" — It was in that Englewood home that we had spent all our furloughs, as Mother and my sisters opened up their home to us with such a welcome that we knew we were really wanted. It made our months in the United States immeasurably easier and happier than was the lot of most missionaries on furlough, and gave Lloyd an opportunity to know better the beautiful spirit of unselfishness and thoughtfulness which was his "Mother Gardner."

We began our visits to the South as soon as school was over in June, including a trip to Williamsburg, which held our children spellbound. On a visit to brother Peyton in Leesburg I wrote, "Here we are all established in Leesburg with three Lloyds and two Peytons under one roof in a delightful mix-up which so far hasn't led to any catastrophes."

At five, seven, and nine the children were able to enter into all the joys of camp life at Rockbridge Baths, learning to swim and having wonderfully gay times with their cousins. They rode the horses to Mrs. Chesterman's camp, picked blackberries, jumped the rocks and were carefree and happy. When a Gardner

cousin came from New Jersey to join the fun Peyton explained
that she came from North America. "But where are you now
Peyton?" I asked. "I think I'm in South America," was the
answer.

On August 1st 1936 we started out in our secondhand
Chevrolet to cross the continent on our way back to China. We
were still in the Depression and we had been assured that we
could afford a long slow trip, stopping for nights at motor
camps where the charge was never more than $2.00 a night for a
double room since we supplied our own linen. We usually found
we could cook our own breakfasts and suppers on hot plates,
but stopped at noon for a good nourishing meal at a restaurant.
We took the Northern route crossing Iowa into South Dakota,
seeing the Bad Lands and the Black Hills, through the wonders
of Yellowstone and Glacier Parks, along the Hood River Valley
and then down the Pacific Coast, through the redwoods to San
Francisco. It took us a month for we "rested on the Sabbath
Day" — as much as parents of those ages can carry out this
Commandment. We looked like tramps as we arrived at the
Y.M.C.A. hotel, but fortunately no one worried about that and
washing machines were available even in 1936. I wrote my
sisters: "We are at the Y.M.C.A. Coffee House and such good
meals as we got — four course luncheons for 25¢ and you could
hardly pay more than 35¢ a meal!"

VII

After the long ocean voyage on the Hoover and the two or three day trip upriver it was a wonderful joy to be in Nanchang again, with our church members and staff greeting us at the train and our staff of servants awaiting us at home, making the process of settling in after furlough much more speedy than anyone could have imagined who had seen our masses of luggage. We had no intimation that this would be our last return as a family to that beloved home of ours. We had feared Japan's intentions in China for so long that perhaps by now we were immune. From my letters we get no hint of a situation of fear and instability. In a letter of Nov. 4, 1936 I wrote: "I'm glad Japan seems to be less in evidence, just now — on the front pages, at least. She's had something to think about in the outpouring of patriotic demonstrations here, on Chiang Kai Shek's birthday. For the first time since I've been in China the people seem to be solidly behind their head. Chiang had discouraged any plans for this celebration of his fifty years, but the people would have it. It was very spontaneous. Here they planned a lantern procession of about 600 students, and 6000 turned up. It was about like that everywhere. The Roman Catholics gave General Chiang two airplanes, and nearly all the provinces gave him two or more. I believe Shanghai alone gave five. But you may have read all this in the papers. The General, the Statue of Liberty, and Lloyd have all achieved fifty years, this year."

On Nov. 13th I wrote of a visit to the Leper Hospital and how that had developed in the years since it was started: "The Friday of that week we all of us except the children went out one morning to the Leper Hospital to attend a confirmation service. I hadn't been out in a long time, and was most interested to see all that had happened in the meantime. The government has gone in on the organization, and has just completed enough buildings to enlarge the numbers from the original sixty to 250. Private funds are still supporting the original sixty, and for a while they had better food than the government cared-for lepers, which precipitated a near riot. The poor things have so little to think about, and food means so much. Incidentally, the privately supported were having the equivalent of a dollar and twenty cents U.S. currency, per month for food, and the others had less than a dollar. So now they all have less than a dollar a month spent on their food, but a brick kiln has been built which some of them are well enough to operate and the money they can earn from that will go into food.

"What I really started to tell about the lepers was that the service was most impressive, and Christ's outgoing love and ministration to these forlorn people became most real to me as I looked at that group. A China Inland Mission pastor who has the leprosy has been training these men — the twenty-four who were confirmed — and he had such a fine face and such a nice way with the men that I could see what it must be meaning to them to have him there. One of the two resident doctors is a leper, too. You never heard anything more wonderful than the way those men sang the hymns — perhaps remarkable is a better expression. We none of us knew what the tune was until they had nearly finished the first verse, but it made up in heartiness for what it lacked in tunefulness. Evidently leprosy does nothing to the vocal chords. The ones who were confirmed were in all stages of the disease, from one poor cripple who could hardly get to the rail, to a nice youngster of about fourteen who didn't show a trace of the trouble to the outward eye. I never go to that place without a deep feeling of thankfulness for the Christian spirit of service which first started Kimber and Dr. Wu at the enterprise of founding a leper hospital, and now that they are having a chance for Christian knowledge and the kind of loving ministry which I could see that pastor was giving them."

A news item which shook all China happened at this time,

written in my letter of Dec. 18th 1936: "Sunday morning I thought Quentin was preaching with unusual earnestness, and I heard him speak about 'When we saw the papers this morning' — but it wasn't till I came home that I heard from the cook that General Chiang had been captured by Chang Hsueh Liang. Everyone is simply outdone — it was so utterly unexpected, and so dastardly. Chiang has always been so good to Hsueh Liang and given him power and position — and now to have him turn on him is just too much. At first everyone feared he had been killed, but we now know he is alive, for Mr. Donald, his foreign adviser, has been there to see him. He's a friend of Chang Hsueh Liang's, as well, and we're *hoping* something may be negotiated which will free Chiang. Of course you know much more about it by the time this reaches you, than I do now. But you can imagine the reaction of rage and horror on the part of everyone. George [Shepherd] wrote us last night, and he seemed to think they would be able to find some way out of the impasse. To have the king [of England] abdicate and Chiang be captured all in one week is certainly enough!"

Dec. 27, 1936. "I sent apples and candy and toys around, hither and yon, for Christmas and had flower holders for the grown-ups. One afternoon we all went on the street and bought toys for the servants' children, and then Mary Kate helped me make and fill red stockings. We had lots of fun in the process, of course, and Christmas Eve it was even more when the sets of little padded youngsters gathered around the tree, which was lighted this year for the first time, and simply gloated over their presents. We had the creche up in the bay window and talked to them a little about that and played some of the Christmas records. There was a fire in the fireplace, and the red candles were lighted, and while the musty atmosphere was distinctly that which is created by Chinese padded clothes in winter, it was even more that of Christmas. I wish you could have all been there.

"The climax of that very full and gay day came that evening when we were at supper. Suddenly the siren began to blow, the signal for an air practice raid, but none seemed to be happening. Then we had the exciting thought — could it mean that Gen. Chiang was free? There had been two false reports so I was wary about believing anything without pretty good reason, but in just the fewest possible minutes we began to hear a great popping all over the city, and through the cook we found that it really was so this time, sure enough. Such excitement! We felt we all had to do something, and firecrackers seemed the only adequate expression. Lloydie volunteered the dime he got for his tooth, Peyton offered his allowance, and we all chipped in for a most wonderful string of crackers with occasional enormous ones scattered through it. It was hung to a tree on the back porch, and our bang was the biggest and best in the city, we were sure. And to make our joy all the more, the evening we found was the first clear one in nearly two weeks, with a big moon shining down on the city till it was almost as light as day, and the loveliest balmy air. Over our porch hung a star which was so much bigger than any ordinary star that we could only think of the star of Bethlehem — or was it the star of General Chiang. Anyway the whole scene was dramatic, and the wave of joy which was filling the city simply permeated the air. The complete stock of firecrackers was exhausted, in Nanking, and I feel sure there were none left in Nanchang. The next day there was another explosion of joy — the whole city went out parading, and that night they had a torchlight procession."

And so ended another year, on the note of joy and thanksgiving. The Generalissimo had been rescued — all was right with the world!

Social Welfare Association, Nanchang, Ki., 1935.

SECTION IV

WAR WITH JAPAN: REFUGEES AGAIN

1937-1939

I

There was nothing in the early months of 1937 to indicate that this would be the beginning of China's eight years of agony, starting with a war with Japan which became in 1939, the Second World War into which the United States was drawn after Pearl Harbor. Letters written during those first months remind us that, for the most part, life continued to be rewarding and interesting. The church work was expanding and developing under the leadership of the Rev. Kimber Den, the Youth Church connected with the Student Welfare Center next door had become an important aspect of our work, and Lloyd had been asked for the second time to be the Bishop's Commissary when Bishop Huntington went on furlough.

This required his traveling about in the diocese to the port cities of Wuhu, Anking and Kiukiang as well as to small out stations, trying to help in any way he was needed. My letter of January 10, 1937 shows just what could be involved in such a visitation in those unsettled times:

Jan. 10, 1937. "I came home from a party to find Lloyd, returned from his three day trip to Chin Teh Chen. 'You certainly were lucky to have such grand weather for the trip,' said I. 'I was lucky for more than that,' said he, in a significant tone of voice. And then he proceeded to tell me that after the bus had been going from Chin Teh Chen for about an hour they suddenly heard a popping and found they were running right into a lot of bandits, standing by the side of the road and peppering the bus with shot as fast as possible. Everyone ducked of course, and the blessed chauffeur kept his nerve, stepped on the gas, and dashed right into and through the band. If he had been hit this tale would have been a very different one. Or if, which was even more miraculous, a bullet had gone two inches lower, it would have pierced the tire, and they would have been completely at the mercy of the bandits. Thank God this was an inexperienced group which hadn't done anything except cut the telephone wires by way of preparation. They might so easily have put a barrier across the road or planned their attack by a bridge which they had burned. And then I would have been like some of the other most pitiful people in this country — a woman whose husband is in the hands of bandits. When I think of the agony these days could have held for Lloyd and me — well I just can't think of it, that's all. The bullets did pierce the mud guard and license plate, and one or two other shots hit the car, but most of the twenty or so rounds which were fired went pretty wide of the mark. You don't wonder that I have been having a constant and continual thanksgiving all this week. To me the thing which Lloyd so narrowly escaped is much worse than an outright death. These bandits are so unbelievably cruel and death usually comes as a merciful release to their captives after terrible suffering. This is the first time there has ever been a bandit attack on this road, so you never can tell when it is going to befall. We did know there were bandits in the hills beyond, but had no idea they were between us and Chin Teh Chen. Live and learn. "

Our Kuling summer started out as most of our summers had, with joyous meeting with old friends, hikes over the mountains up and down unbelievably steep trails to clear mountain pools or old temples with marvelous views of water-falls dropping down the cliffs to the valley shimmering in the summer heat. The children were old enough now to join us on these hikes. Lloyd, Jr. was a Scout and Peyton a Pioneer. We hiked and swam and enjoyed contacts with our mission family and many other friends — until the blow fell. Fighting began at the Marco

Polo Bridge outside of Peking between Japanese and Chinese forces in early August, and before long we realized we were involved in that full-scale war which we had been dreading for many years. Japanese nationals were being evacuated from places as far up river as Hankow, so we knew there was a good chance that the war would come far into the interior. Lloyd felt his responsibilities for the diocese and hoped he could leave the family in Kuling for some months anyway, while he traveled about helping our staff plan for the future, as much as any of us could plan.

On August 13 Shanghai was bombed. A little later we heard that Nanchang had also been bombed. Thousands of civilians streamed out of the city in all directions, seeking their old homes or some village so small that it might escape notice. Planes flew over Kuling, dropping bombs on Kiukiang at the foot of the mountain. Lloyd decided that he should get to Nanchang at once. Among other matters he needed to get winter clothing for the family who by this time [Aug. 20] were planning to stay on in Kuling. The first time he took over responsibility for the diocese he had a flood to cope with — the second time, a full-scale war!

After a visit to Nanchang he decided to go to Anking and consult with the staff there, which included Dr. Harry Taylor, who would keep the hospital open as long as possible.

In early September a member of the Hankow Consulate arrived advising all women and children to leave China at once, but with their husbands all staying on, the wives were very loathe to obey that advice. It was about this time that my cousin Beth Shaw who had been vacationing in their summer home west of Peking, arrived with her two teenage children, hoping to put her children in the school. The family had been unable to get through the lines to Peking and so had come south to Hankow. Her husband had been able by this time to return

203

to Peking and the embassies had agreed that their nationals might stay on in Kuling, at least for the present, so Beth had come up the mountain. It was quite wonderful for me to see this cousin again, who had been in China for many years with her husband, who was principal of a large boys' school under the Congregational Board, but these weren't the circumstances I would have chosen for the reunion.

By October 1st our children were in school and I had decided to move there, where the building would be heated and food provided.

I did return to Nanchang, most unexpectedly, for a two days visit, the last time I would see my home for ten years, as it happened. I collected some pictures, china and books of snap-shots, also bedding. The few things we still have from our 19 years in Nanchang were rescued during this trip.

Lloyd continued his travels, returning to Kuling to look after the family there, then visiting Anking. His visit to Nanchang had shown the devastation which the bombing had brought the city. The ladies house at Baldwin School had been completely demolished, and the Women's Hospital in the center of the city, quite near our home, so shattered that repairs were impossible. We were thankful that Dr. Kahn hadn't lived to see that happen.

After a final farewell to the family, Lloyd went to Wuhu to take up his residence there for an extended period, during which time he met the Japanese army on its arrival in early December. This proved to be a dress rehearsal for their later arrival in Nanking, which received great publicity and made the world realize to just what depths this army would descend.

II

From now on Lloyd and I will frequently have different stories, for during the next six years until his release from an internment camp at the end of 1943, and return to join me and the children in the United States, we were separated for much of the time.

This article was written by Lloyd for the "Anking Newsletter" of January-February 1938.

"Refugee work at Wuhu during the past five months has given one a new understanding of the moated castle during the middle ages. Just as the castle walls furnished a place of refuge for the villagers and peasants when war raged without, so our mission compounds have become a place of refuge for all sorts and conditions of men during these days when the terrors of war have been ravaging the city and countryside around us. Our puny eight foot compound walls would have furnished no protection from the destruction that rained from the sky if they had been situated in the midst of the devastated city, but the fact that our St. Lioba's and St. James' School compounds are well out in the suburbs of Wuhu have made it possible to keep a foothold, whereas many mission compounds within the city were entirely untenable. In the first rush of the conquering army, fresh from the slaughter of battle, these walls seemed a most inadequate defense, too, but there was a strange conviction beyond reason among us that they were overtopped by spiritual bulwarks that in God's mysterious way may have been built by the prayers of many intercessors in distant places as well as of the faith of those within.

The first refugees to arrive were mostly of our Christian families and staff members from Nanking, Soochow, and other cities in the war zone to the east of us. Many of these sought only a temporary refuge and then pushed on up river.

205

"Not until Sunday morning, Dec. 5th, when during the morning service the church was racked by the explosion of bombs on the foreshore nearby did we realize that the flame of battle had spread to Wuhu. The mangled and maimed soon were brought into the True Light Dispensary where they received attention at the hands of Dr. Janet Anderson, Sister Constance and others. Stretcher bearers were sent out to gather up other wounded refugees who had crowded the foreshore waiting to get on board the doomed Jardine steamer, the 'Tuck Wo.' The work rooms of the True Light Industrial Building were hastily converted into emergency wards, and furnished with beds and mattresses from St. James' School across the way. Mr. Lamphear and Mr. David Lee, with their knowledge of the inner workings of the two compounds, kept things moving in a most efficient manner.

"The next wave of refugees were mostly church members from St. James' Church over in the city. Fortunately, after the first morning's bombing, most of the population fled to the country, so that when the droning flocks of bombers appeared over the city time after time during the succeeding days their destruction was mostly of homes and shops and not so much of human life as on the first day. But every day the heavens were black with the smoke of the burning city and every night the sky line was lighted with flames of a dozen fires. The deserted shops and homes were being looted by the retreating soldiers, and the destitute who had nothing to lose were helping themselves to the goods that had been left behind.

"From then on for several weeks in Wuhu there were no electric lights, no telephone or telegraph, no post office, no shops where anything could be bought, no banks, no police, and except for a few thousand refugees in three mission compounds, almost no inhabitants.

"On Dec. 10th, just five days after the bombing of the

206

railroad station and the foreshore, the first contingent of Japanese soldiers arrived and almost immediately our gates were besieged by another flood of refugees, mostly simple country folk from our neighboring villages. I will not dwell on the horror of those days — the shocking condition of some of the women and girls who were brought in, nor the terrible tales related by old men and old women of sons bayoneted or beheaded, and of village homes burned. I would rather dwell on the constructive work going on within the compounds in caring for the refugees.

"Here again the simile of the castle close holds good. We soon found ourselves jostled down into a self-contained community of about two thousand souls. Many of the families had come bringing such of their possessions as they could move with carrying poles — bedding, 'flower pot' stoves, kettles and pans, bags of rice and even fire wood. School rooms with school mattresses spread on floors accommodated from twenty-five to forty in a room. With remarkable little fuss many of these families set up housekeeping and looked after themselves in a manner incomprehensible to the Western mind. Some were even able to bring in their indispensable water buffalo, their pigs and goats, to save them from being slaughtered, so that soon our compound resembled a country village in more ways than one.

"Many arrived with only the clothes on their backs but these, too, were soon cared for. Sister Constance and Mr. Lamphear seemed equal to any demand on their resources and energies. Bedding and warm clothing appeared from cupboards well stored in advance for just this refugee relief. The kitchen facilities were miraculously expanded until at one time nearly four hundred people were being fed daily. Whole fields of vegetables on adjoining farms were bought as they stood from refugees within our walls, and parties of old women, with Sister Constance's white veil often in the thick of them, were sent out in the early morning hours before the soldiers appeared, to

207

gather in the nourishing Chinese cabbage. Pigs were killed, rice and salt were procured by various and devious means. Meal tickets were sold to those who could pay, and others were given their meals. Gangs of water carriers were organized to carry water on their shoulder poles from a nearby canal. Latrines were dug and old women undertook the daily task of carrying the night soil to fertilizer pits in nearby fields. Coal and wood had to be brought in for the kitchen and the hot water stove. Soon the cobblers and the tailors and the barbers among the refugees were plying their trades for the benefit of our little community.

"There were many expectant mothers among the refugees and these were all taken care of as occasion arose. There were broken legs and apoplexy and pneumonia and sundry ills that needed medical attention. And, to add to the medical cares, a number of babies were left on our door step by mothers who in these desperate times could not care for them, so that Sister Constance's family of such children has been increased to nineteen.

"All expeditions from the compound whether for water or fuel or to take patients to the hospital or to bury the dead, had to be convoyed by one or more of the American staff to assure that the coolies would not be molested by the soldiers. Regular hours were fixed for opening the compound gates, and at these times a foreigner had to be on duty to check on who and what came in and went out, and to deal with any Japanese soldiers who might appear. In dealing with the latter Father Morse [a member of an Anglican order who had formerly been stationed in Japan, but who had come to China at the outbreak of war to see how he could help] with his knowledge of Japanese, has proved an invaluable help. Contact had to be made with Japanese consular and military officials to secure notices to put on our gates for the protection of property, permits of various kinds, and in the adjustment of problems as they arose. The

208

higher Japanese officials have without exception been helpful to us in their attitude when we have brought our difficulties to them.

Sister Constance and one of the church families.

"Undergirding all this effort was the religious life of the community and the regular services of worship that were maintained even when the bombers were overhead, by the faithful and fearless leadership of the Rev. Irving Wang. How many souls were comforted in their distress and strengthened in their faith by the hours of quiet spent in the presence of God in the beautiful St. Lioba's Chapel. Opportunities for the non-Christians to hear the word of God were afforded by the special services for them organized by the Rev. Hunter Yen and many were moved to enter more deeply into the knowledge of Christ through classes arranged especially for them. Even the high festival of Christmas and Epiphany were celebrated with almost their accustomed splendor, and in spite of the surrounding darkness, brought to us the comfort and assurance of Emmanuel, God-with-us."

Sister Constance, referred to in the preceding article, was a most unusual character, known widely throughout our part of China not only because of the beautiful embroidery and cross-stitch articles which were made in her work room, which I have mentioned earlier, but because of her energy, resourcefulness and charm.

Lloyd has told something of what she accomplished during

the terrible days of the looting of Wuhu. At this time a good many new-born infants, all of them girls, were left in the fields outside the Sister's compound, with the hope that Sister would rescue them since the families had no way of providing for them. She finally had nearly fifty babies. It meant that a house had to be built for them, so, after the emergency was over, she left on a short trip to the U.S. and returned with the funds to build the baby house. Many of these babies died, but many survived the exposure and lived. I tell later how they were cared for when the time came for Sister Constance to leave China.

III

While Lloyd was experiencing these dreadful days the children and I were preparing as best we could for Christmas at the Kuling school. There was very little left for sale at the Gap, the business area, since the shopkeepers had fled to the country, but we knew this Christmas without our Daddy would be so different that there wasn't any pretence that we must follow our old traditions. We mothers decided that we would have our family celebrations in our rooms with our children, and that there would be an opportunity for a school celebration later in the day. Lloyd and Peyton went out to break off a large branch of a pine tree in the wood below our house, and we managed to decorate it with a few bits of tinfoil, a real refugee Christmas setup. It was just a few days before Christmas that Mr. Allgood, the principal, called all the parents together and told them that he had decided he could no longer be responsible for keeping the school open since it was evident by now that the Japanese army was advancing up river, slowly but surely. When they reached Kiukiang, our source of supply would be cut off. Provisions were inadequate to keep the school open for any length of time, and the only prudent course was to get down from the mountain top while we could. "When?" we asked. "The day after Christmas," was the answer.

The Japanese authorities had promised that an international train would set out at the end of December from Hankow on the Yangtze to Canton in the extreme south near Hong Kong, which would be free from bombing. We would have to leave as he had planned, taking with us only necessary baggage, to catch a boat which would be awaiting us at Kiukiang, and after a few days in Hankow travel south through territory completely new to us, to end up in Hong Kong. My memories of the days after this shattering talk are confused, and letters of this period have been lost. I remember looking at our lovely Kuling house, the pantry shelves loaded with the deep blue Canton china so prized in this country which we used every meal in both Nanchang and Kuling. I reflected for a moment that I wouldn't have a piece of it in the future which is, alas, the case.

I shut the door and came away, and it epitomized the farewell I was making to the glorious, friendly, carefree summers which Kuling had given us for over 20 years. My memories of Christmas are rather vague, I was too involved in packing up and wondering about the future; but I do remember that the children were delightedly celebrating with their friends, having a boar's head brought to the table all resplendent and properly Old English, and after a day filled with all kinds of excitement, with practically no presents, one of them said to me, comfortingly, "Except not having Daddy, this has been our nicest Christmas." From then on everything moved on the same hilarious and adventurous note for them. I was trying to conceal my anxieties and heartache.

The 26th of December saw a long procession of school-children, mothers, teachers, baggage-coolies, and even pets start out from the school to take the trip along the winding paths through the estate and the Gap, and down the 3500 feet to the bus, which would carry us from the foothills to the river-steamer in Kiukiang. I usually traveled in a chair carried on the backs of four coolies, but the chairs were so limited and transportation so disrupted that most of us preferred to walk. Somehow we all came through it, and the trip on the unbelievably crowded steamer up the river to Hankow, where we arrived early in the morning. Usually the children's gaiety was infectious and I responded, but this time I couldn't; I was too preoccupied with wondering what we should do. Should we go to the Philippines, or back to America, which we had left just a year and a half ago, or could we perhaps go to Shanghai, now occupied by Japanese troops in the kind of order developing under a military dictatorship. The loving kindness of the mission family was evident even before we landed, as we

212

picked out familiar faces among the throng lined up on the dock to meet us. Fred and Meg Brown of our mission took us in tow, and carried us off to their house, their warmth and concern helping me any amount. From then on we had a few days to prepare for our long journey south. We were told that the train was unheated and offered no food or water, just transportation.

I filled a basket with water bottles, and another with food of various kinds, topping it with a wash basin and a small stove of German make which ran on alcohol, which, with the proper techniques, could produce a hot flame. Not in vain had I lived upcountry for 19 years. Among the following days I went to the consulate, to attend to various legal matters, and while there discussed with the consul about what I should do in the future. I remember, that as usual he advised return to the States, but the thought of leaving Lloyd behind whom I hadn't heard from in weeks seemed impossible to me. I knew Wuhu had fallen, and feared he might be in a dreadful situation. "If only I could ask my husband's advice!" I burst out. "Where is he?" asked the consul. "In Wuhu," I returned, and thought that closed the matter. I was to learn later that it hadn't, and I've had a warm regard for consulates ever since.

Our train left from Wuchang across the river from Hankow, and the morning of our departure we assembled not only our group of American schoolchildren and their mothers and teachers, but a large group of all nationalities except Chinese, seizing this opportunity to escape from China on a train which wouldn't be bombed.

A few harrowing memories of that departure still linger. I hurried to see if our baggage was there, and getting properly checked. In the process of hunting, I set down my basket of water bottles, and when I remembered them, they had disappeared. It was a nightmare, but of blessedly short duration.

213

Walking along the platform appeared Clara Shepherd, swinging my basket in her hand and asking loudly, "Anyone lost their water?" This was the first intervention of Providence on my behalf on this trip, but not the last.

The train had compartments, and in one of these we established ourselves, and there with the help of the stove, placed in the wash basin for safety, I managed to feed five of us — I had another mission child in tow — for the two days and nights of the seemingly endless journey. The first night, I was completely exhausted, and rolled up early in my bedding, hoping that I'd brought enough to keep us all from freezing. We stopped at a station. I heard many voices, and farewells, and then — my name. I was being paged. I jumped up and rushed out to find Mr. Tyng of our mission waving a telegram for me. "Who from?" "Your husband," said he. Tears of joy came flooding to my eyes. Lloyd, alive, and able to get word to me! Past all the Japanese lines, and all the impediments of every kind. It was unbelievable, but there he was speaking to me, my beloved, saying "Thankful you have left Kuling. Advise Shanghai. Telegraph Bishop Roberts." He was telling me what to do when I needed him so much. The consulate had sent a message to him via the British gunboat and this was his reply. At last I could lay my burdens down and sleep.

I needed one more act of Providence on my behalf to set the record straight, and I had it. I was conversing with one of the many dear friends on this unbelievable train when someone appeared, stopped in front of me, and said, "We think you ought to know." "Know what?" I asked, a bit frantically. "About Peyton," she answered. "What about Peyton?" I gasped. "About his falling off the train. He's very muddy and scratched and crying and I think he wants you."

The story was this. Whenever the train slowed up for a station, the older boys jumped off before it quite stopped,

214

knowing of course that they shouldn't. Peyton, only seven, followed suit. One time the train didn't stop, but after slowing, picked up momentum. The big boys managed to jump aboard. Peyton couldn't, and after several tries saw the train pulling past him about to leave him stranded in the midst of this unknown area. Someone, who it was I never knew, pulled the cord, and the train slowed up. Peyton was pulled aboard. Once again I gave thanks and took courage.

The prestigious Peninsula Hotel in Kaoloon, across from Hong Kong, would take us in at a nominal sum, so we were told. I had visions of a comfortable bed, climbing out of clothes I had worn for two days and nights, of relaxing. What I found was a children's nursery, filled to the brim with camp cots for all the women and girls, with our bathrooms the ones reserved for servants, several flights down. But we had food and shelter, and barring the fact that the little boys went sliding down the bannisters into the magnificent lobby, rode up and down on the elevators and even shot a water pistol from the balcony at an elegantly attired Englishman arriving for dinner, all was well. In due time we got tickets on an Italian line and after about ten days in Kaoloon, off we set for Shanghai, destined to be our refugee home for the next year and a half.

In a letter from St. John's University of January 25, 1938, I wrote: "Here I sit in the lofty old Victorian parlor of #19 St. John's University just where I was ten years ago writing letters to you, no doubt. What a strange turn of fate it is which lands me not only at St. John's but in the very self-same house where Mary Kate was born and where I spent those refugee days long ago." After descriptions of the Italian boat we had traveled on, I wrote: "I'm never very happy on ship board, as you know, so it was a great joy to get into the muddy waters of the Yangtze Thursday morning January the 13th and feel that the last lap of the trip was behind us. We had been on the road eighteen days from Kuling to Shanghai, and we were more than ready to stop.

215

But I assure you that a real refugee never does stop. She just goes from one situation to another, but as I look back I believe the curve has been on the upward slant, for the most part. But getting those twenty-four pieces of baggage off the boat and onto a lighter was a Herculean labor, all right, particularly as I was assured that the boat took no responsibility and yet I couldn't seem to get anyone else to do so. All my worldly possessions were probably contained in those horrible looking baskets and boxes which were therefore highly prized, but in all my twenty-three years in China I never saw anything harder to find than they were. I fairly groaned for Lloyd, and vowed I would never travel again without him. His stock has risen sky high on this trip, I assure you.

"I had been most interested to see what the waterfront of Shanghai would look like as I set my foot for the first time in enemy territory. I had kept wondering what the Chinese were feeling, too, for there were numbers on our boat. I had felt their state of mind most when I went out the first thing in the morning as we were slipping in among some islands, and anchored among them, gray and half-obscured by the mist, lay a sinister looking warship which they and I knew was Japanese. Usually those early appearances on deck are filled with friendly chatter, but these groups were saying nothing, just looking. What must they be feeling when I felt so much. It was a shock, too, to see Japanese flags flying everywhere, and the sight of the burned and ruined buildings on all sides was sickening. The harbor was empty of boats, too. It was indeed a different Shanghai from the one I had left."

Dorothy Roberts, the wife of the Bishop of Shanghai and a dear friend, was there on the dock to meet me, and bring me two all-important letters from Lloyd, my first in many weeks. I had heard by now from letters which had come through from American friends of the atrocities which had happened in Nanking, and its fall to the Japanese. "John Magee wrote that

216

the only parallel he can think of is Jerusalem in 70 A.D. George Fitch calls it 'the rape of Nanking' and tells how he has had to stand by and see men and women, peaceful citizens, used as bayonet practice; seen numberless cases of women and even little girls raped; seen the most poverty stricken robbed of every last copper and all their bedding, with absolutely nothing ahead of them but freezing and starvation; seen ricksha coolies with even their rickshas stolen from them. There isn't a house in the city, Chinese or foreign, which hasn't been broken into and looted, and most of the stores have been set fire to, as well. In two weeks a quiet orderly beautiful city had been turned into a shambles. I have heard some people say that the Junior officers are completely out of hand and that the Senior officers have no way of stopping such things. The spirit which the Japanese army is showing here leads me to feel that the only hope for this country is in the collapse of Japan. God hasten the day when that comes. I am so thankful that I was able to get some mail off to Lloyd on the British gunboat which sailed yesterday." It was the first time I had been able to write him in six weeks. Alma Taylor — the wife of Dr. Harry Taylor, who was remaining at the hospital in Anking, and her three children, who were at the Kuling School with us, had decided to follow Lloyd's advice and come to Shanghai. From then on we cast our lots together; since we were devoted friends Alma decided she would like to live with us and unite our two families under one roof.

We got our children enrolled in the Shanghai American School, to which they traveled daily by taxi, which in good Shanghai fashion collected up to eight or ten children. The compound of St. John's University was beautiful and spacious with a great park-like lawn in front surrounded by huge trees. It was an oasis in an area of misery. Every time we crossed the beautiful park we stepped out into a crowd of refugees coming in to the concession and to the village next to the park, who were the most pitiful human beings I had ever seen. They had in their arms bits of dried bamboo or pieces of charred timbers or roots of just anything they'd managed to get from the villages round about, bringing it in to sell. "The other day it was pouring rain and they were trudging along in their sodden cotton garments, soaked to the skin. Even my ricksha coolie had no rain coat. My heart aches and I feel so helpless in the face of such enormous suffering — worse than the flood, for this is man made."

IV

Lloyd was at last able to get to us in April after weeks of separation. He had been asked by Bishop Huntington to go to Anking to prepare the people there for the arrival of the Japanese army.

Lloyd takes up the story again. "I had ten precious days with my family on that beautiful compound, saw the children well established in the Shanghai American School — and had a chance to see some of our many friends congregated in that city before I started out to carry out the Bishop's orders. It involved a thousand mile trip by every means of transportation available and it meant leaving my family for an indefinite period as I set out for the interior of China not yet fallen to the Japanese and under heavy bombing attacks. It was a difficult parting but I was going on an important mission to try to prepare our huge group of Chinese and foreigners at Anking for what lay in store for them if they stayed on. The direct route up river from Shanghai to Anking, of about two hundred miles, was impassible as the Japanese army was established there and no boats were allowed to pass them.

"My route took me via a small Italian liner, south along the coast to Ningpo, still in Free China — I met two of the English Church Mission ladies on the boat who introduced me to Mr. Chang who proved to be a Ministering Angel in that he was that very morning going by private car in my direction. In a few hours I reached Iwu on the railroad. I spent the night in a mission compound and caught a train next day which arrived in Nanchang by early afternoon — less than four days from the time I left Shanghai, incredibly swift for that time in history." A letter he wrote me describes his trip as follows: "My auto ride through Chekiang was the loveliest trip imaginable. Masses of pink, lavender and yellow azalea everywhere, great clusters of rhododendron, 'wu tung' trees in bloom [a kind of tree from which oil is processed] with its exquisite white flowers, shad bush and a kind of wild rose as big as our Silver Moon. Mountains and sparkling streams everywhere."

Lloyd was met in Nanchang by our faithful coolie, and later the Rev. Quentin Hwang. Our home looked very lovely with the garden well cared for. There were American friends on the Methodist Compound who entertained him, and he had a chance to discuss the situation with our Chinese staff before leaving for Hankow, where he discussed plans with Bishop Huntington, recently returned from furlough. It was a hasty trip, as was one which followed it to Kuling to get his summer clothes. After a wait of a few days in Kiukiang at the foot of the mountain he got a launch to carry him across the the river to the North bank. It took him over three days to get to Anking: a trip which takes only six hours by river steamer. He took a bus for part of the route, then a wheelbarrow, and of course walked part of the way.

"The refugees from the east were already lining the road in almost continuous procession. Some were riding in rickshas, some on wheelbarrows, a few rode donkeys, but the great majority were trudging along patiently and resignedly, carrying a few possessions on a shoulder pole, or perhaps a whole family would be tugging or pushing at a rude home-made cart with a few family possessions piled on top. And they were only a small fraction of the millions who have been streaming west along every pathway and river for months on end. Finally I reached Anking, where I had a most heart warming welcome from my friends assembled there."

The compound there is inside the city and would undoubtedly be bombed when the Japanese army arrived. They couldn't offer those inside protection as they had at Wuhu, and certainly couldn't be responsible for large groups of refugees who would be much better off in small villages.

It was finally decided that they would gather together the Chinese staff and their families [it meant about 450 people, as "family" in China is an expansive term] and move them to Kuling and there they would set up a training institute in buildings which they had rented from the Kuling Council. They started out the last of May and before long had set up an active program. In a letter of July 11 he wrote: "The institute is well under way. On July 7 and 8 we had a retreat for the Evangelistic staff led by Robin [Mr. Chen]. It was about the finest thing of its kind I ever heard from anybody. Nine Bible classes and a period of class work and discussion groups will begin on Monday. Periods for morning devotions and regular services are already under way. All the Bible-women are working as an altar guild under instruction. It's a full project in learning by doing—"

Back in Shanghai I paid a visit to an old resident of Lexington, Virginia who still has relatives in that area who remember her, the extraordinary personality, Deaconess Henderson.

May 27, 1938. "Last Sunday afternoon Alma and I made an interesting call on Deaconess Henderson. Have I ever written you of her? She was brought up in Lexington, one of the real F.F.V.s, with her grandfather one of the founders of V.M.I., and she herself living on the campus always. Thirty-five years ago she came to China, and has never been home since then! She says she couldn't leave without chartering a steamer which would take all her family as well. At first she was in our mission, then she transferred to the Children's Refuge, but being a bit too liberal in her theology for them, in 1922 she started a St. Faith's Settlement, over on Jessfield Road, and there she was when we called. I had heard a lot of how she lived absolutely like the Chinese around her and how she shared her bedroom with the babies and how she did everything for the orphans who came to her—your only credential seemed to be

221

that of need. I went as far as the door with Pearl Buck in 1927, to see if she would take in her amah's unborn child if it turned out to be a girl—and she had the only place that would, Pearl said. I believe the child was a boy, however. With this introduction you can see my real curiosity as we pounded on the wooden gate in a narrow crowded alley off from Jessfield Road. At first we thought we would pound in vain, but finally we heard a voice and through the chinks we saw Miss Henderson, rattling with keys. As she opened the gate she asked us if we thought we could get in, for the courtyard was flooded, and we had to crawl along benches. Right in front of us was the main room of the Chinese house she lives in, simply full of recumbent figures of young girls, taking their afternoon rest. They were covering every inch of space, and the wooden affairs they were lying on proved later to be their desks and benches, and still later their dining tables when they brought in a kind of orange peel tea, as we were leaving.

"We went first into Miss Henderson's room—study, office, dining room, what you will, dark and dingy and covered with every kind of litter imaginable. Every square inch of wall space was covered with faded photos of every description, as well as cuttings from newspapers and Bible verses. One of the chief treasures of the wall were several photos of General Lee which had been given Miss Henderson by the General himself, as well as pictures of the Lee family and a picture of Mrs. Lee which she had taken down from her wall for her. There was a picture of 'Traveler' and she told of how the General had lifted her up to ride on his back, but the pictures were hardly discernible they were so faded. Above it all presided Miss Henderson, 71 years old, dressed in an ancient Chinese type garment, with the charm of manner and the lovely voice of a cultured gentlewoman of Virginia, and you really forgot her appearance entirely when you saw what she was doing. She led us through the two or three rows of rooms she had, and we saw how she stacked in her 180 inmates. They were all of them her old children, who had returned to her when the Japanese drove them out, or they were her original nucleus of children, most of them her 'grandchildren' for she had raised their mothers. Five of those girls had seen their fathers murdered by the Japanese before their own eyes. I was so impressed by the sweet clean attractive girls, and the fact that nearly all the house, excepting Miss Henderson's own rooms, was as clean as it could possibly be under such circumstances. Many of the girls, she told us, were in mid-career in boarding school, sent there by her, when the war broke out and all the schools were closed. So they had come back to her, and there they were, literally prisoners with nothing to do. For the thing which struck horror to my soul was that they are next door to Japanese headquarters, and she doesn't dare let the Japanese know of the existence of these girls, so they literally never go out. She can't even let them go into the little plot of ground which they formerly had to play in. They were playing hymns on the baby organ, and they do all the sewing—but what a life! I immediately offered to go there next fall and teach the girls. It would give them less of a feeling of frustration if they could keep up their English. But what will they do this summer? The amazing thing about it all is that the whole project is run on faith, with no visible means of support—and former Chinese contributions are all gone now. Isn't it a tale!" I went to teach them the following year, as other friends did. By then the children had been locked into those cramped quarters for over a year, and I never did succeed in bringing even one girl out to have a meal with me. [Deaconess Henderson managed to stay in Shanghai for some time after Pearl Harbor but was eventually repatriated and spent her last days in a retirement home in Richmond.]

V

Lloyd wrote to his sister Mrs. Marshall in October, 1938 telling of his decision to leave Kuling in late September, and the reasons. "You will see I am once more back in Nanchang. When last I wrote home we were in the midst of our training institute in Kuling. Our nucleus of about 300 staff members and their families from the occupied areas around Anking and Kiukiang was increased to 500 after the capture of Kiukiang. With the battle still raging after two months of fighting on the plains below us it became evident that even the reserve supplies of food we had laid up might not be sufficient and that our people might face starvation if we stayed on in Kuling.

"There was only one road open down the mountain and that lay within a few miles of the firing line on either side, on a very narrow steep path constantly subject to bombing from the airplanes, but there was nothing to do but to take this only way out. You can imagine how difficult it was to move our crowd of 420 [some had already left] including old men and women, expectant mothers, little babies and many small children down a precipitous mountain trail and along a road close to the front lines. We managed to get a few sedan chairs and baggage coolies, but nearly everybody had to walk and carry what possessions they could the thirty miles to Tehan. We divided the crowd into three groups, to go down on 3 days, with a day between each party. One party was bombed and machine gunned by a plane on the way. Many people were splattered with mud from bursting bombs, bedding rolls and boxes were pierced with shell fragments, and one old clergyman was scratched in two places by flying splinters, but thank God no one was killed. In the second of our parties a baby was born on the way. A thatched hut by the roadside furnished the only shelter and within two hours mother and son were on their way again in a chair. Three days later they arrived at Nanchang by boat and have been getting along well ever since. Simple, isn't it!

224

"Our group was the last to leave as I wanted to tie up all the loose ends before departing. The trip down the mountain was beautiful for me, but hard on the mothers with bound feet carrying small babies. The first night we spent at a farm house in the foothills. By 2:30 a.m. we were stirring again so as to get by the most dangerous part of the road before daylight. By 6:30 when the planes began to come over we were already past the worst part, but still we were so near the firing line just on the other side of the ridge we were almost deafened by the cannonfire, the incessant bark of the machine guns and the detonation of bombs. There was a big battle on. Fortunately the planes were so busy with the battle field that day they didn't pay much attention to us. All the same we made ourselves as invisible as possible whenever they came over.

"Our struggling band reached Tehan about 9:30 that night, the women and children pretty thoroughly worn out. There the government had provided trucks for the refugees which took us about 20 miles down the road to a place of greater safety from bombing. We were most fortunate to get another truck about midnight which brought us into Nanchang by 4:30 a.m. It was a wonderful chance to study stars on the way.

"In Nanchang we put up the crowd in St. Matthew's School as best we could, housing 15 or 20 in a room with no beds to offer. All were so glad to get to a resting place that didn't matter. A good friend of ours, Mr. Chang Fu Liang, was living in our house and I went to keep him company and share the excellent Chinese food his cook prepared. It was rather tantalizing to be in a place of so many joyous memories without Marian and the children there. Lao Den had kept the garden in good shape and had flowers in the house all the time.

"Nanchang was no place for a permanent retreat with air alarms sometimes five a day and half as many at night. The planes came several times in the three weeks I was there and dropped a number of bombs throughout the city. One dropped within 30 yards of Mr. Johnson's house where the Bishop and Miss Clark, his secretary, were working. Fortunately no one was struck though the place was pretty badly smashed up. With the thoughts of what a bomb might do if it dropped in the midst of our several hundred refugees, our precious church staff and their families, at St. Matthew's, you can imagine how anxious I was to get them farther up country. Some were able to make arrangements on their own. For the remaining 250 we sent out scouts to see what places could be found for them in small towns farther inland.

"This inland city of Kian, about 125 miles up the Kan River from Nanchang, was finally decided upon as the new center. I am here to set up an office for financial and administrative contacts, but most of the staff will be scattered in smaller places nearby. Those who are able will help in refugee camps, in rural welfare centers, and in doing evangelistic work in the villages where they take up their residence. It's quite an opportunity not only to do much needed service, but to extend the church's work in this area. We have had a church and primary school in Kian for some years.

"Mr. and Mrs. Tyler of the China Inland Mission have been here for years, and there are two younger missionaries with them now too. They have very kindly taken me into their home for the time being. This is a great help for our church here is in rented quarters and the place is already full. Moreover so many refugees have crowded into this section it's almost impossible to rent a room, much less a house. As it is I am very comfortably settled in this well ordered home with its green strip of garden, its orange and pomelo trees to the south. The Tylers, like all C. I. M. folk, are decidedly fundamentalist, but they are good sincere Christians and I like to be with them.

"All my winter underwear and my overcoat are in Shanghai,

but I've had prepared a long Chinese gown padded with raw silk, and some padded trousers that wrap around the ankles quite snugly so I guess I'll manage to keep warm. We are quite far south here and the winters are not long or severe.

"Bishop Huntington and Laura Clark started for Shanghai just before I came to Kian. The Bishop is 72 years old now and it was not for him to retreat farther and farther into the interior, though he would have been sport enough to do it if it had been his duty. Rather this seemed the job for me and so here I am. I confess I don't like the idea of being separated from Marian and the children indefinitely, but on the other hand I don't see how I can get away from this particular job while this phase of the war lasts. How long that will be no man can tell, but certainly no end is apparent even around the corner. It's a great world we live in. All the same I'm glad to have a hand in something I believe to be truly constructive in a time like this. There are some fine spirits among the clergy I am working with and I'm proud to be one of them."

My last letter of 1938 in the file, written on Dec. 10, says: "Yesterday and the day before brought letters from Lloyd which for the first time suggested that he might be able to get out from Kian for Christmas. The Japanese appear to be digging in and not advancing on Nanchang as was expected, so it looks as though there was time for him to come. Yesterday he even said that if all went well he would start on the 10th, which is today!" Lloyd was indeed able to start as planned and reached his family in time to have a most memorable Christmas with us. We had had to leave the house on the St. John's Compound in the fall and move to the American School as a family. Arrangements had been made there to take in refugees like ourselves. The school was closed but we were guests of the Sullivans, dear friends of ours, on the St. John's Compound. After those long and eventful eight months of separation we were once again a united family, and knew more than ever before just how blessed we were in having each other.

It was the middle of January 1939 when Bishop Huntington asked Lloyd to stay on in Shanghai for some months as the mission treasurer. We were to be given a house to live in at the St. John's campus. After months in an interior station we would be able to enjoy together some of the many pleasures which Shanghai had to offer. My letters speak of the Russian Ballet, of numerous moving pictures and of concerts; Lloyd realized how hungry he had been for some of these amenities of life when he was able to have them again.

We continued to live in the American School until a house at St. John's was ready for us. Lloyd began working long hours in the office, and found that his service was badly needed. The Chinese who had been engaged to help previously knew little about bookkeeping, so he had to go back and check every item, working each night until six. Fortunately his early training and natural interest in bookkeeping served him in good stead.

During this time I wrote on several occasions about the pathetic condition of Austrian and German Jews arriving in Shanghai, the one place where they could enter without either money or a passport. Soon boat loads filled with refugees from Hitler began to dock at the port of that great city. On January 3rd I wrote: "At this dinner party we discussed the problem of the German Jews, which is becoming more acute all the time as they pour in here on every boat. Alice tells me that Shanghai is the only place open to them, and this is no real solution, for this town is full to the brim of White Russians who are making a most precarious living. The rich Jews here are helping out for the time being, but surely they can't be counted on to support four thousand, and the numbers will soon reach that. The awful thing is that even though they were well-to-do in Germany they arrive here absolutely penniless. They can use their money to buy passage, and many of them come first class, but when they arrive they have nothing. The doctor and his wife who are headed for Anking were here this morning. The wife looks more rested, and I tried to use a bit of my German on her. She seems very pleasant and looks so unJewish that I think she must be Aryan. Her husband has had six years in the medical school in Vienna, and seven years of practice. Without any warning he was thrown into a concentration camp with 146 others in one room, unable to sit down for six days, and with one meal a day. Then he was allowed to come to China. Mrs. Tucher was so shaken by it all that she has been unable to sleep, or has had horrible nightmares, but she certainly does look better than she did. How I hope Anking will prove to be a haven for them. Certainly he seems to be the one hope of letting Harry Taylor get away from Anking. We're planning to have them go on the next gunboat — probably in February."

We called this interval in Shanghai our "peaceful interlude," knowing it would last but a few months, but all set to enjoy it to the full while it lasted, even though outside our compound walls murder and rapine were still rampant. We heard the sound of guns every night, caused either by guerrillas across the creek, or gunmen from the Chinese village. The gambling dens of Macao had moved to Shanghai, we heard, and were in full swing outside our gates.

All through this year my letters reflect the horror and fear with which we were receiving the news coming through from Europe. We seemed involved in an endless sequence of miseries of war and disaster, and we knew our own state of peace and well-being was most unstable. The steam roller of Germany had begun its inexorable drive. But in spite of this in March I wrote, "In the meantime one of the loveliest times of the whole year is upon us and one's faith in the love of God and the goodness of man is renewed in the light of the spring time. The daffodils are radiant again in the park, and every bush on the compound is either covered with bloom or just ready to burst."

229

VI

By September 1939 the two older children were settled in the Shanghai American School as boarders and it was evident that conditions had been stabilized enough under the rule of the Japanese Army for Lloyd, Peyton and myself to return to Wuhu. We lived for a year with Bishop Huntington, and I kept house for the family. Each time the Japanese army reached a new city there was a repetition of the atrocities which I have described earlier. Then, after some weeks of such horror, it was possible for the populace to carry on their lives unmolested but with great restrictions.

I describe our trip up to Wuhu from Shanghai in the following letter. "As soon as you cross over into the Hongkew district in Shanghai you feel the weight of the horrible destruction which has visited the country, from the blocks and blocks of gray ruins still standing or the even more eloquent stretches of open country covered with weeds in what was the thickest part of the former Shanghai.

"The old station which was a good brick building and rather new is completely gone, and the meanest kind of wooden shack has taken its place here. If you are traveling third class it is almost impossible to get a seat on the first train, for there is no adequate way to handle the crowds and they have to stand in line until they get on any train which happens to come along. Fortunately we were plutocrats with second class tickets so made our train.

"The country as a whole looks little changed. The crops are being planted and harvested as of yore, but those who are in the know tell us of the stranglehold which Japan has on all transportation, and what terrible taxes the poor people have to pay. There is a high percentage on all goods transported. All the stations are heavily guarded from guerrilla attacks and we hear

230

that the guards are always lined up with their faces toward the hinterland, watching for what may befall. The fact that the railroad line between Shanghai and Nanking has been cut twice in the two and a half weeks we have been here in Wuhu speaks for itself. The guerrillas are right on the job. Of course I was glad it wasn't our goods and chattels which were wrecked. Thirty of our thirty-five pieces of freight have just arrived more or less intact. There was a lot of breakage in my few pieces of china, but that was because we had expected boat transportation and all the things came by train, traveling very hard indeed.

"A lot of Nanking is left, so you might be deceived into thinking things were better than they are, but many of the fronts have been hastily constructed anew, and here and there are masses of utter destruction. Some of it made me think of the Tartar city we saw in 1915, when I had my first idea of the ravages of any war. But I loved to see Nanking again in any guise, for it has such a place in my heart.

"From Nanking on we took on Japanese soldiers at every station. Lloyd thinks that the train is run at the time it is, causing a wait of nearly three hours in Nanking, because the guards are afraid to stay at night in any isolated places, and the train acts like a kindly amah and collects its charges before dark. Anyway our train was full of soldiers by the time we reached Wuhu."

Sept. 1939. 'And now for a few impressions of Wuhu under war conditions. You know, don't you, that we can't go anywhere in the city without having somewhere on our person a pass, which is a wispy piece of paper upon which is pasted a photo of oneself with some remarks in Japanese. This must be produced whenever asked for, and it is never certain when that will be. I have been to the town several times without being challenged but as Lloyd and I were coming home the other

231

night we heard a sharp call from the sentry sitting 'way inside one of the sandbag shelters, and he came out to demand our passes not at all pleasantly. It was at that place that Winston Haskell and Miss Cassidy were slapped for not hearing the sentry — an incident which got in all the papers this summer, so I keep my ear to the ground there, I assure you. The people in Japan this summer were telling us how amazed they are at the slapping incidents, for they say that whipping a child or striking one at home is almost unknown, and practically never do grownups strike each other. To which the only reply is, 'What doesn't war do to human nature!'

"I am so afraid I'll forget my pass sometime, for I never carry a handbag as a rule in China, and I have no infallible inside pocket, like a man. I have been playing with all sorts of ideas — an addition to my wrist watch, or a silver amulet to be worn around my neck on a chain, large enough to contain the paper. But Lloyd has thought of sewing a pocket onto a garter. That, I consider, quite practical and after all the practice I have had with a safety pocket I should be able to slip it in and out with ease and propriety.

"I'm not familiar enough with the city of Wuhu to notice great differences, but Lloyd and B. W. [Lamphear] tell me that all the glory has departed. Certainly it seems like a shabby little city compared with Nanchang as I knew it. But we can get the essentials here. We can buy fruit and meat and vegetables, and live much as we always have. For us with our affluent rate of exchange there is no hardship from that point of view. Our life will be very quiet, never going out in the evenings and with almost no social doings, but after the years in Shanghai we will be glad of a quiet spell in which to have a chance to think. For the Chinese the high cost of living now is stupendous, and the cause of it is partly the Japanese tax, but far more the guerrilla activity which is preventing the farmers from bringing in goods to occupied cities. They brand as a traitor all those who are

232

found bringing food in to sell, and if any Chinese are suspected of having dealings with the Japanese they have a sorry time of it if caught by the Chinese army which hovers just across the river, and back not far south of us. We have just had word that the Bishop's former coolie who went to intercede for a relative who was in trouble with the Japs, was shot by the Chinese army when he returned, on suspicion of having dealings with the enemy. The fact which B. W. notices is that such occurrences are growing more frequent rather than less so.

"To go back to the problems of the Chinese — in one day charcoal jumped from $6 a load to $18. Firewood which formerly sold for 200 lb. to the dollar is now 30 lb. to the dollar, and so on. We are so thankful to B. W. for buying our coal before we arrived, for since then the Japanese have sealed up all the coal yards and are keeping it all for themselves. It will probably be $100 a ton if it can be bought at all, while our coal was $75. The result of fuel being so high is that you see all the children of the neighborhood out pulling up the rice stubble to burn, all the grass on the compound is being cut gratis, while I feel cruel to even suggest to the coolie that I would like the leaves saved in a pile to fertilize the garden next spring."

I wrote to my family about the Wuhu setting and our colleagues there as follows: "We always used to approach Wuhu from the river, and it was quite an imposing sight. First you pass the oil installations about a mile below us, and then at a curve in the river and high above it is the big up-to-date Methodist hospital built of red brick with white columns. All around it lie the various houses connected with it, each one of which gets a magnificent view of the river, for they are much closer to it than we are here. From some of those houses you get exactly the sensation of being on a river boat. Foreigners stayed there all during the occupation, and the property wasn't injured. There are delightful grounds there with flower-bordered brick walks and a drive winding back and forth to the hospital which crowns everything.

"The hill next in line from the hospital is the one topped by St. James' School, Episcopal, the ugliest building along the length of the Yangtze, alas. Mr. Lund did many fine things, but as an architect he was of the old school. Our house is on a knoll some distance back of the school, and usually we are only a five or ten minute walk from the river reached from the front gate of the compound, but that gate has been closed since the war. Now we use only the gate at the rear, across from the Sisters. I asked Lloyd how many acres there were in this compound and he says eight or nine. There certainly is an estate, and so much land around this house that I can't get used to it after our small holding in Nanchang. The glory of the house is its view, which is lovely at any time. Now that the leaves are off we see miles in every direction along the river and over such a typically Chinese landscape of little ponds sparkling in the sunshine, of paddy fields and hills, each one topped by some edifice and most of them foreign residences. It makes a curious impression of the dominating foreigner. The Asiatic Petroleum house, where lives a pleasant young English couple is on one hill; the Christian mission house and school where lives Joe Wharton, the delightful Irish bachelor who is such a friend of Lloyd's, in another; the mansion of the Commissioner of Customs, where now resides the Japanese General, on another, and about a twenty minute walk away from us is the Long Street and the Horse Street, where are the shops. Those have lost much of their glory, but they are all functioning, and you can get most of the necessities of life there. Everything costs so much that people can talk of little else, but thanks to the produce of this place nearly everyone has a job of some kind. Wuhu has always been a great rice center as well as having every kind of fowl. The queer thing is that we can't get geese to eat although they are numerous, but it seems to pay better to sell the feathers than to sell them as meat. Ducks are everywhere, and one of the continually diverting sights on a walk is to see the duck herds

234

going after their flock in wobbly wooden tubs. I counted eight such tubs on a little pond the other day, the men in them catching fish and standing in the most precarious of positions. The women work in the fields a lot here, and in a very picturesque costume of bright and dark blue, with touches of red. Lloyd and I go out somewhere nearly every afternoon, and the beauty of the sunset sky over the golden Yangtze, or the big old moon rising up over Chieh Shan, the pointed hill to the east, is unforgettable."

In addition to Bishop Huntington and the Craighills I write of some of the other Americans in our mission. "The two Sisters who are here now are Sister Louise, the head, beautiful, quiet and efficient, with a grand sense of humour. The other, Sister Lucy, formerly a trained nurse in Anking, is new to the Sisterhood and great fun.

"St. James' Church, where Elda Smith works, is in the city and a half hour's ride from here by ricksha. There was a big school there, too, but nothing now. Elda must begin from scratch to build up a new work. She is going at it in fine spirit and will go far, I know. B. W. Lamphear, the widower whose daughter Marion is Mary Kate's age and dear friend, lives in this compound. He has always done the business management for the Sisters, and been in charge of the property, as well as doing some teaching. He is most capable in many ways. He has done splendid work among some of the boys who were formerly his students at St. James. Next door to him, in a little house like his own, lives Laura Clark, the Bishop's secretary and diocesan treasurer, a remarkably fine and able person."

I also wrote of someone not in our mission. "Hyla Watters, an old friend of mine from Smith days, is the surgeon in this Methodist hospital. Hyla is such a grand and interesting person. She is one of the busiest people imaginable and one with the widest interests. She touches life at any number of points —

stars and flowers and animals and music as well as surgery. She can tie more intricate knots than most sailors, and taught herself the Morse code so she could signal with flashlights to the men on the gunboats in the harbor in case of emergency. She has had a marvelous influence all through her years here, on both Chinese and foreigners."

SECTION V

BISHOP OF ANKING;

PEARL HARBOR; WITH INTERNMENT AND REPATRIATION;

FAREWELL TO CHINA

1940-1949

I

We decided to go to Shanghai that December in 1939, taking Peyton with us, to do some Christmas shopping, and bring the two older children home for the holidays from the American School where they had been since September. Lloyd knew that the House of Bishops was meeting in Shanghai at this time, but even then he wasn't fully prepared to have Bishop Huntington come up to him one evening with the greeting, "You have just been nominated as the next Bishop of the Anking Diocese." It was an awesome responsibility to undertake at this time in China, but he realized that his various terms as Bishop's Commissary and Treasurer of the Diocese had prepared him as well as anything could to cope with the problems which would lie ahead if this nomination was confirmed. That occurred at the meeting of the General Convention in Kansas City the following October. Since by that time Bishop Huntington had retired in June and gone to America it was decided to have the consecration on St. Andrew's Day in 1940.

It was gratifying to him to receive the congratulations and good wishes of his many friends in Shanghai when the nomination was announced. One little unexpected angle came from our son Lloyd who was enjoying some of the special table delicacies which Shanghai alone could offer at this time. He leaned toward me during the service in the Cathedral next morning and whispered, "This will mean a great deal of entertaining with real butter, won't it?"

We returned as a united family to Wuhu to have our usual

239

happy Christmas, made meaningful by the beautiful services in the Sisters' Chapel. It was the custom in the mission for the students in the school to go around to the various residences and sing Christmas carols at almost any time after twelve midnight. We were aroused in this fashion before daylight that Christmas morning and, for the first time in our experience the serenaders had with them our blind organist, specially trained in a school in Hankow and knowing every tune and number by heart, who played their accompaniment on a baby organ. Above the ominous sounds of shooting and bayonet practice rang out the strains of *Joy to the World, The Lord is Come* — the hope of the world above the black despair of total warfare.

The first half of the year 1940 moved along with surprising lack of adventure or even unusual episode. Bishop Huntington was still living with us, but gradually getting ready to pack up his household goods that he wished to take with him, and leave for the United States to rejoin his family there. I know it was a time when he was torn by conflicting emotions. China had been his home for very many years, and the break with his past would be exceedingly difficult, but his family were eagerly awaiting him in Wellesley, Massachusetts and he had much to look forward to.

Lloyd was very aware of the great contribution Bishop Huntington had made to the diocese in finding young men eager to study for the priesthood, and helping them with their education. Occasionally an outstanding member of the clergy was sent by him to the U.S. for postgraduate work. All this meant that the leadership of the diocese was in the hands of men highly educated and of intelligence and dedication. Lloyd would have that one essential to count on in his future work. Later it was Robin and Dan and Graham and Ralph and Kimber and others on whom the burden was to rest, and all too often who would have to face persecution, as well.

On June 4th there was a Diocesan Farewell, with a few of the clergy getting there from other cities, and crowds of church members from the mission as well as representatives from other churches. As usual, the more important the occasion the longer the program, which was held outside. After two and a half hours it began to rain, which brought things to a conclusion. Bishop Huntington had grown dear to us through the years, and especially so after our months of living together. One of his very endearing qualities to us was his enjoyment of Peyton and his quaint ways. I can still remember the hearty laughs with which he would explode when Peyton produced some new plan for his [Peyton's] future life, especially when he decided on being a Captain in the Salvation Army.

We had decided earlier in the spring that this would be the summer for us to take our long-hoped-for trip to Peking, which we had never visited. We knew the imperial city was far different from any other in China. My cousin, Beth Shaw, was urging us to come, and the yen required for the trip would cost less in U.S. currency than ever before. We went to Shanghai at the close of school in June, got the children, and by the middle of June were on the steamer sailing from Shanghai to Tientsin, and thence by rail to Peking.

Our relatives met us at the station and we were soon settled in the Language School, which became a boarding house in the summer months. We were seeing Peking under Japanese occupation, but because of this there were very few tourists and often we would find ourselves quite alone in some huge building. It made it easier to imagine the pomp and circumstance of other days, and the ghosts which peopled it now.

I wrote of our arrival in Peking and the days thereafter in a letter of July 2: "It was eleven o'clock at night, and as we drove through the dark streets, along such high solid walls as I had never seen before in China, and under huge mysterious gateways

241

and arches, lit up dimly by the street lights, I had almost as many thrills as the night I arrived in China for the first time. I was eager to see it by daylight but I realized that it might be even more romantic by night than by day. What a place this is! The first morning after Beth's arrival we decided to go up to Coal Hill to get the view of the whole city from there. It was exactly the thing to do, for there from those pavilions on the great hill built from earth dug out from moats and lakes, we got that breath-taking view of the golden roofs of the Forbidden City stretching away as far as we could see. It gave us our best idea of the grandeur which lay about us. The distance from North gates to South gates was amazing to us. Far into the south rose the Temple of Heaven. On the west, the blue outline of the Western Hills, with the Yenching Pagoda to be seen in the foreground. Rising through the trees, tantalizing glimpses of splendid roofs and bell towers which we knew we would never see. From my window I see a mass of temple roofs, beautiful in shape and outline, which aren't even mentioned anywhere.

"We've taken rickshas everywhere so we would have more of a chance to let the street sights penetrate. It's still old China with vendors and funeral processions and handicrafts of every kind in bewildering profusion. We've been impressed by the easy-going ways of the place, too. Our ricksha men are well-paid and helpful. You don't hear the wild reviling when something unforeseen happens on the street. Our shopkeepers always have time to accompany us to the door of the shop and bow a farewell. The doorways show glimpses of such delightful-looking roomy paved courtyards. The difference in house planning is very real between this city and any other I have visited. Never have I seen red gates with gilded beam ends above, before. Peyton has at last learned that the pictures he has seen of China, and scoffed at as being unreal, have come to life up here.

"We've 'done' nearly all the important trips. Friday we spent

242

Above.
The Summer Palace at Peking.

Right.
At the Western Hill, Peking, 1940.

243

the morning at the throne room in the Museum of the Forbidden City, again speechless at the vastness of the great plaza in front of it, and the magnificence of the carved marble balustrades, as well as the gorgeous roofs. We had an hour in a museum full of priceless works of art, where Lloyd and I clutched each other over the porcelain and the children went mad over the clocks, collected, I believe, by the Empress Dowager. They *were* pretty exciting, particularly when the hour struck and every little creature came to life and performed in some manner. It was a relief to us to know that so much is still here, although the treasures have been taken pretty generally from the rooms in the Palace. No one knows just where they are now. [We learned later they had reached Taiwan safely before the Communist take-over.]

"Another morning we spent visiting the more intimate living apartments of the Forbidden City. We saw the palace rooms where the Empress Dowager lived, the library of Chien Lung, an Emperor of the Ching Dynasty, and his favorite pavilion for writing poetry, and how we have come to marvel at the genius of that man, and of Yung Lo, the Ming Emperor of Columbus' day, who laid out the plan of the city! The most joyous whole day was the one we spent at the Western Hills with the Shaws and some other friends. We chartered a bus of our own and went in comfort. A trip to the temples was most interesting, going for ten miles or so through country which sprouted historic relics. It was a poor wheat field which didn't have a marble turtle or arch decorating it.

"We left the bus at a hotel and began climbing up through temple after temple, all immaculate and so beautiful, combining ancient building of Ming days — even Mongol — with beauty of distant view and nearby trees and pools. We rode donkeys through the Imperial Hunting Park. We drank from an ice cold spring which bubbles out of the rocks. We ate our lunch beside a goldfish pool."

244

One of the paradoxes of this period is that we could buy yen so cheaply with our U.S. currency that we were able to have another summer in Japan. We had been eager to have our children see the difference between the pleasant friendly ways of the Japanese farmers in contrast to the Japanese militarists, so were glad for two reasons for these three summers at Nojiri.

That summer in Nojiri was overhung by the clouds of war so that my letters have a noticeably different tone from those of the other two summers, even though the children's happiness in their achievements in swimming and sailing was unabated. Lloyd stayed with the family for a very short time, since most of his vacation had been spent in our wonderful Peking visit.

II

One most important event for the diocese of Anking was the election by the Standing Committee of the Diocese of the Rev. Robin Chen, who had been lent to work for six months with the National Christian Council, to be the Assistant Bishop. There was nothing which would mean more to Lloyd, for he was one of the most able and consecrated Christians we have ever known, and Lloyd honored and loved him, as did the other members of the diocese. We were more than thankful when he accepted the nomination, realizing that he might be the one to go into unoccupied China to be a shepherd to the large group of clergy and teachers who had settled there, while Lloyd would stay behind in Wuhu to do what he could for the remnants of our diocese in the occupied area.

It was in November that my letters show how seriously the United States was regarding the political situation. We had already been urged by our consul to send "all unnecessary personnel" to America. Now we heard that the American School would not reopen after Christmas. There was nothing for it but for me to take the children to the United States and put them in school there. Apparently our consular officials were more aware that the U.S. might become involved in this war than were the commanders of the fleet at Pearl Harbor.

So, in the midst of preparing for the double consecration of Bishop Chen and Lloyd, with the date set for St. Andrew's Day, Nov. 30th, and the locality Wuhu, we were shipping out a few of our household possessions and preparing ourselves as best we could for a separation which might well be the ultimate one.

Only three bishops were able to get to Wuhu for the wartime consecration. The first to arrive was the Presiding Bishop, the Most Rev. Arnold Scott, who had managed to get through from Peking and arrive in plenty of time, no small feat for those days.

When Peyton first saw him in his gaiters, for Bishop Scott was Church of England, he requested him with some urgency to stay where he was on our lawn until he could get his camera and take his picture. The amused and obliging bishop did just that, and we cherish the picture which resulted.

The Rt. Rev. Lindel Tsen, Bishop of Honan, arrived from his diocese in the West, and Bishop Roberts from Shanghai. On the 29th, we all went to the station in the evening to meet the Shanghai train which would bring our oldest friends in China, Arthur and Netta Allen, who as luck would have it, were then also stationed in Shanghai where Arthur was assistant treasurer of the mission; quite a number of former students from Nanchang now studying or teaching in Shanghai; Miss Alice Gregg of our diocese now in the National Christian Council; and last but not least, our own two children, using their Thanksgiving vacation to see their father consecrated bishop.

The train arrived and we welcomed the group, thankful as always these days that they had been able to obtain their passes and get to us as we had hoped. It wasn't until after the consecration next day that we learned that their safe arrival was a miracle. It happened that some high Chinese officials who were collaborating with the Japanese and so were hated by the Chinese guerrillas, were on that same train on their way to Nanking for a conference. The guerrillas were informed of this and massed high explosives on the tracks — mercifully for us, just a few minutes *after* the train had passed. The tragedy was that a train which followed 50 minutes later, filled with country people on their way to market, was blown to bits. What was our miracle of salvation was their destruction. I'm glad I didn't know this at the time of the consecration.

The following account of the consecration is quoted in part from a Shanghai newspaper: "By ten o'clock the ten lay delegates and twelve of the thirty clergy of the diocese, together

Rt. Rev. Robin Chen and Rt. Rev. Lloyd R. Craighill at the time of their consecration, Nov. 1940.

with the guest pastors of local Wuhu churches, guest clergy from the Hankow and Shanghai dioceses and the three bishops, made an impressive procession. The body of the church was filled to capacity with Chinese members of the two local parishes, St. James' and St. Lioba's, together with most of the foreign community in Wuhu, missionary and business folk, and guests from Shanghai and elsewhere.

"Following the processional and ante-communion service, the Consecration Sermon was preached by Bishop Tsen. He took as his text, using it throughout as a refrain, those stirring words spoken of Paul and Barnabas: 'These two did not care for their lives, but only for the name of the Lord Jesus Christ' (Acts 15:26)."

There follows an account of the actual consecration itself. Bishop Roberts, representing the Presiding Bishop of the Protestant Episcopal Church in the United States, was Lloyd's consecrator, with the Most Rev. Arnold Scott, representing the English Church, and the Rt. Rev. Lindel Tsen, representing the Chinese Church, as co-consecrators — all, of course, part of the Sheng Kung Hui. After his consecration he was able to take part in the laying on of hands on his Assistant Bishop, Robin Chen, a very unusual procedure. "The Communion Service, celebrated by Bishop Scott, assisted by Bishop Roberts, closed the impressive ceremony, and the two new Bishops went out to meet the joyful and hearty congratulations of their people."

So the account ends, and so ended our day — one of the greatest significance to my husband as he faced the new responsibilities which devolved upon him in this era of history, realizing how much he would need the help and guidance of the Holy Spirit.

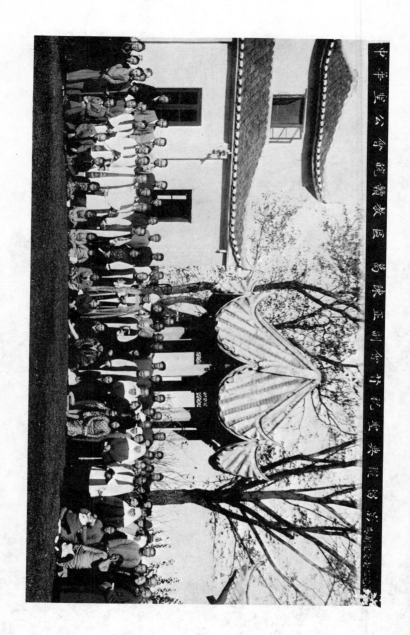

中華聖公會總教區為陳主教及卜主教祝聖紀念攝影

The consecration of Bishop Craighill and Bishop Chen, St. Andrew's Day, 1940.

III

Soon after Christmas we started off for Shanghai and on January 7th, on a cold rainy night, Lloyd saw his family set sail on the President Pierce for the United States, for a separation which we *hoped* might end in June when his furlough was due, but which we both realized might last much longer.

He returned to Wuhu, mercifully numbed by the sorrow which such a separation posed for us. A group of friends, Chinese and Western, met him at the railroad station on his return, helping him through with his arrival at that lonely hilltop house.

From then on his letters to me told of the happy relationship which existed between him and Bishop Robin Chen as they worked together to face the problems which beset the diocese at this time. Just a short quotation here from a letter of January 14th: "Robin and I have been getting things accomplished in the office. It's such a help to have his advice on so many questions that come up. He was today preparing a fine circular letter to all the clergy catechists and Bible women to go with a copy of *Victorious Living* and urging the importance of personal devotions as the basis of any spiritual work. He is beginning on the fundamental needs at once. What a joy to have such a co-worker."

One of the difficult tasks which confronted him was to tell the women workers in Anking — Miss Bowne, in charge of nurses training in the hospital, and Miss Montiero, the evangelistic worker and teacher, that the time had come for them to go into unoccupied China to Maolin, some distance south of Wuhu, where the Japanese army had not penetrated and where our schools and many members of the staff were located. In fact the Japanese army was mainly concentrated along the Yangtze, occupying the important ports there. The cities and towns of the vast interior were not occupied but were being systematically bombed, with the hope of causing such widespread disaster as to bring the nation into a state of submission. As I trust we are learning now in Indochina, that policy doesn't work, and in the meantime it is the helpless noncombatants, the old people, the women and children, who are suffering the most, as they have no foxholes to hide in. Fortunately for us, the area in which our schools had settled in southern Anhwei and southern Kiangsi had been comparatively free of bombing so far, and we could entrust our precious staff to these localities without too much anxiety. Of course any locality in China during that period was risky, but these fine courageous women were determined to stay and cast in their lot with their Chinese friends.

They arrived in due time from Anking and with Sister Louise and a Chinese nurse started out from Wuhu dressed in Chinese garb to make them less conspicuous, with coolie hats to protect them from the sun, leaving literally at the crack of dawn to get through the lines before the Japanese guards were alerted.

The story of their life and work in the city of Maolin, where they bought a handsome old Chinese house, named it St. Boniface, and carried on active evangelistic, medical and educational work for some years, is a tale in itself, but too long to be included here. As I think of Miss Bowne, who at times treated up to seventy patients a day, assisted only occasionally by a refugee doctor, of Elda Smith, who combined her church activities with raising pigs, chickens, and growing bean sprouts to eke out the few canned goods which would occasionally be brought them by faithful friends who risked taking a trip through the lines to do so, and of all the others who were there, I can only say humbly, "Of such is the Kingdom of Heaven."

As I looked over Lloyd's letters of this period which I had saved, I saw that all of the Westerners were well aware of how short this time of comparative calm might be. Lloyd kept referring to the fact that they had no idea whether the war would involve the Pacific area or not — but of course they were well aware of the possibilities. After office hours they found it was very important to relax tensions by getting together with the rest of the Western group as much as possible, for tea or tennis at Joe Wharton's, or trips to the gun boats when they were in port, where they had occasional meals, and frequently moving pictures, with the screen on the deck. The shores would be lined by attentive Chinese villagers who couldn't understand a word of the script, but who were delighted by the novelty of the performance.

The group at the Methodist hospital became almost like family — Lloyd dined with them each Sunday, they lent each other books, discussed politics occasionally, and felt the close bond which tied together all members of the Christian family. When Paul and Stella Sommerfreund, the Jewish doctors from Vienna, very much needed a change after Paul's operation, they became Lloyd's guests for two weeks. It was a pleasure to him to have their company and to learn more of their past life, and to have them leave looking well and rested.

My letters he said were his real blessing during these days — he read of the family's safe arrival in San Francisco, of our visit to the Grand Canyon, of our arrival at Englewood, New Jersey, of how we walked into an apartment which my family had completely furnished for us with furniture lent by them or their friends. I even had an Oriental rug on the floor and a davenport in front of the fireplace. A day or so later a kitchen shower, engineered by my sister, filled my kitchen with all the necessary utensils. I got the two younger children into public schools, and Lloyd, Jr. into Episcopal High School in Alexandria, Virginia, and began a busy career of speaking to Auxiliaries or Foreign Policy groups or whoever invited me. One evening it was a college group of young women, the next afternoon an Old

253

Ladies Home. I felt it was something I could do for China at this time, and there was great interest in that country and its heroic resistance to the might of the Japanese army. Perhaps "strategic retreat" would be a better description of this period than "resistance."

In the summer I took the children to camp at Rockbridge Baths, with all the family there doing their best to make up to me for the one essential to my happiness, which was having Lloyd there to share these carefree days with me.

IV

It was on the morning of December 8th, by the Chinese calendar, when it happened — the event which they had been dreading but could never have foreseen would occur in such a devastating fashion. For some reason Lloyd didn't learn of Pearl Harbor over his own radio, but a coolie came racing over from the hospital to bring him a note telling him of it. At first he didn't believe it. How could our fleet have possibly been there like "sitting ducks," with no radar warning of what was about to happen. In a few moments, however, the Japanese consul, Mr. Okabe, with whom he had had consistently pleasant relations, arrived to tell him that it was indeed so. He took away Lloyd's radio, wrapped and sealed it, and then returned it to him, showing unusual trust by doing this. He was told that he was under house arrest and couldn't leave the compound. This was true, of course, of all the other Americans in Wuhu. His cook was free to go out to get supplies as he was able to find them.

Money became a problem, but they managed to get the yen they needed by selling off household articles to the Japanese civilians who had followed in the wake of the army. They also had some money on hand in the office to help out.

In a short time all the Americans in the city were moved into the Sisters' Convent, the men staying in the Industrial Building and the women in the Convent proper. At this time I saw a news item in the Herald Tribune headed, "American Bishop confined in a Convent" which was probably quite an eye-catcher.

Their days in the Convent moved along with nothing noteworthy to mark one from another. They read a good deal, walked around the compound, and found pleasure in each other's company. He said he couldn't even remember distinctly when they were ordered to leave for Shanghai. He thought it was early in the fall of 1942. He stayed on the St. John's campus for several months at the home of Donald Roberts, a member of the faculty whose daughter, twenty years later, would marry our Peyton.

There were four of them who ate together there, a kind of "grass widower's mess." It was rather well described by that word, for the rice was so full of weevil that they decided to go over it carefully each day and purify it as much as possible. One of their number would read aloud, a rather scholarly work, while the other three busily concentrated on getting rice minus worms. Their other food was poor in quality. They were allowed to go around Shanghai but their status as enemy alien was designated by a red armband with the letter "A" — not like a Red Letter of Hawthorne's tale, I should explain, but signifying their nationality.

In February word came that they were to move into an old tobacco factory in Pootung across the Hwangpoo River from Shanghai, which would be their concentration camp. They were each allowed to take with them a bed and chair (lent to Lloyd by Donald Roberts), bedding, a steamer trunk and what baggage they could carry. A group of the younger men were sent in ahead of them to try to make some preparations for the thousand men, who would follow.

I have often been told of their life in this camp. The outstanding fact is that this great group of men from every walk of life, from bank president to missionary to beachcomber and drug addict, were in there together to somehow work out a possible way of life. The Japanese guarded the place but made no attempt to contact them except for a daily roll call. Of course the first thing was to form committees, and that they did in good American fashion. These ranged over every aspect of this abnormal life of theirs. There was a public health committee, of course; a strong arm squad to enforce some kind of discipline, for there were plenty of thieves in their group; a recreation committee; a religious worship committee [of which Lloyd was chairman] ; a library committee which had them pool the books they had brought in and made them available by using library cards made from cigarette boxes; and among many others a group which concentrated on getting the teachers among them organized to form the Pootung University. In due time a good number of courses were offered and met in all sorts of odd nooks. There were courses in history, mathematics, navigation, science of various kinds, and more languages than I can remember. The courses which Lloyd took and the singing group to which he belonged, organized by a Welshman, gave real interest to his days.

The most difficult thing for him was never having any privacy. There were a hundred men sleeping in the room with him, and his only means of getting away from it all was to sit in his chair beside his bed and shut his eyes. He thought that the moron who roamed around saying he wished there was a door to shut had real intelligence. They were all divided up into squads of 25. Most of his squad were old friends of the St. John's faculty, though there was one old black man who had been brought up in Buchanan, Virginia, had become a Fiske Jubilee Singer, and in course of time had gone to Russia to sing. When the revolution broke out, "Uncle Ted" as they called him, took off his collar, called himself a Black Bolshevik, and had no trouble — until his wanderings brought him to Shanghai and into this war.

The plan worked out by the committee for worship services, which had to be held in the dining room before and after meals, was to have the Episcopal form of Holy Communion three Sundays in the month, with one Sunday non-liturgical. The eleven o'clock service was non-liturgical for three Sundays and on the fourth they had the service of Morning Prayer. Everyone was welcome at all services. With their large group of mission-aries there they were always sure of a congregation, and they found there the spiritual resources they needed so desperately.

They were all beginning to lose weight due to the very poor diet of food which was of such bad quality that it had been rejected by the Japanese army. No effort to sift the worms out of the rice now; they ate what they could get and decided they needed the protein they got from the weevil! They knew that on this diet of rice and stew they would have a difficult time to recover from any illness, but none of our mission had anything serious happen to them.

The men had an opportunity for exercise in cleaning off the rubble from a former village which had been destroyed by bombs and which was next to the camp. It was enclosed by barbed wire and they were allowed to use this as a recreation field. In time they had a football field there, while some individuals worked at small plots and achieved gardens of flowers and vegetables. Once a month the church members of the Shanghai mission, under the leadership of Bishop Yu, used the facilities of the Red Cross, and sent in packages of food. What a Red Letter Day it was when those arrived! The quantity was divided into lots according to the number of mission members, and they drew numbers to see who got first choice and so on. Number one usually got a can of stew, while the lowest number just might get nothing but a can of shoe polish.

There were too many aspects of this Pootung Camp for me to enlarge on it further. Some group in their midst had a forbidden radio. If it had been detected the punishment might have been death. As it was, they all profited from the news which filtered through. They learned that the constant Japanese victories seemed to be getting closer and closer to Japan, which could mean only one thing. And in August, 1943, they learned that a notice was on the bulletin board with a list of names of those who were to be repatriated in exchange for Japanese personnel who had been interned in the United States. Those of them who were no longer young and who had sent their families home were given first choice. Young men of military age were not included. Many of our friends' names were there, and Lloyd's name was one of those on the list! He had had no letters from me in these nearly two years since he was under house arrest and internment.

V

The old French vessel, renamed the Taia Maru, was a hopelessly overloaded ship by the time all those who were to be repatriated had crowded aboard. Lloyd couldn't remember the numbers but recalled they had at least three times as many passengers as they were supposed to accommodate. He was quite elated when he was assigned to A Deck for his sleeping quarters, but that elation was rapidly dispelled when he found that the alphabet began at the lowest part of the ship and worked up to the decks above water. He was to sleep in the cargo hold. Encircling the walls of this black cavern two wide shelves had been constructed, one above the other, on which were placed mattresses about two feet wide and six feet long, stuffed with straw, and each pressed against the one adjoining. There a great crowd of men were to be accommodated lying like sardines. There was no light or air from outside. The only ventilation came through the hatch.

He knew he could sleep on a mattress two feet wide if he lay on his side. His greatest anxiety was that these flimsy straw-filled mattresses might catch fire from the cigarette-smokers, who continued that habit in spite of the obvious danger. It didn't help to know that some of the sailors among the repatriates had examined the life boats and termed them "a bunch of junk." They probably were in greater danger during that month of travel from Shanghai to Goa, a Portuguese city on the west coast of India, than at any time during their internment. But in spite of the hazards his heart was filled with thanksgiving that every turn of the screw was bringing him closer to that eventual reunion.

There was no mirror on that ship, but Lloyd knew that he must be quite an odd-looking specimen, and quite different from the one I had last seen, nearly three years ago. His suit sagged around his waist, his collar dropped down under his chin, and he was sure his face had changed. But if only they could make it during this last month before they reached Goa and the Gripsholm, to which they would be transferred, that was all that really mattered. As a matter of fact, they were hungrier on that trip than they had been at any time before this. Some of the men on the ship had money and were utterly unscrupulous in bribing the dining room stewards to sell them food which should have gone to the passengers.

The water was severely limited. Each day they were given one thermos bottle of the precious liquid; with this quart Lloyd first brushed his teeth, then shaved, and then took as thorough a bath as was possible. Rarely was so much achieved from so little.

It was good, after those seven months of a completely masculine existence, to find many ladies aboard, among them Dr. Watters of Wuhu, who had, of course, been very active in keeping up the health and morale in the camp to which she had been assigned.

The day which will never fade from his memory was the one in which they found they were approaching the shore line, and heard with good authority that the buildings which they saw faintly in the distance were those of Goa, where they were to transship to the Gripsholm. From then on they began to feel that wonderful sense of being free again. Even though they reached Goa three days before the arrival of the Gripsholm, they were forbidden to do more than take very short strolls on the pier. He would have liked to visit the tomb of St. Francis Xavier in the town of Old Goa, nearby, but of course that was impossible.

And then came the never-to-be-forgotten moment when far on the horizon they saw the smoke from the Gripsholm, the miracle ship, the hope of joy and freedom, "coming for to carry

261

us home." — From then on life was a thrilling experience. As in time they saw that Swedish ship pull into harbor, saw the Japanese with their handsome clothing and well-appointed baggage debark, and thought of what a contrast awaited them not only on the ship they were leaving but on their arrival in Japan, Lloyd found he was pitying them.

When the repatriates actually boarded the Gripsholm, the ship's crew was then in the process of cleaning the cabins after the departure of the Japanese, so a feast had been spread for them on a long table on deck, a real Smorgasbord that had in it all they had ever dreamed of in those hungry days of the past years. Here was orange juice and sliced meat and bread in abundance and salads and cheese and milk and so on and on. They had been warned to eat warily at first as they might easily become ill from this abundance after days of near famine. They tried but it was difficult.

Before long the mail was distributed and Lloyd found not only letters from me and all the family but packages of magazines I had collected for him that summer when I heard of his repatriation and had also found a nurse who would be on board and would take these directly to him. So Lloyd was the first one to have this food for the mind which meant almost as much as food for the body. He found from my letters that I had received none of the messages he had sent from time to time through the Red Cross, and of course Lloyd had received none from me. We had been parted for nearly two years without any communication. No wonder those long letters were like manna in the wilderness or streams of water in the desert. At last we had made connection and he knew that all was well.

They stopped at two ports only, Port Elizabeth in South Africa, and Rio de Janeiro. I find his first letter to me, mailed in Brazil, reports the thrill of that first landing. ". . . At Port Elizabeth we went ashore the first time as free American citizens with no restrictions on our movements. In fact the whole town gave us a royal welcome, invited us to their attractive homes for meals or to spend the night and made us feel very much at home. It is an attractive, clean city of about 120,000, not unlike a California coast town in coloring and vegetation. I was the guest overnight of the Vicar of St. Mary's Church, an English clergyman and missionary of the finest type, whose easy hospitality quite won my heart. In spite of gas rationing he drove some of us out along the shore for miles, then we got out and walked along the windswept moors and watched the surf breaking on the cliffs. It was the first walk I had had in the country for two years or more, and nothing has given me such a thrill of renewed freedom. The next day Ellis [Tucker] and Donald [Roberts] and Randal [Norton] and I had a swim at a fine beach with green rollers to ride. I was thrilled to find the old boy had so much kick left in him. You know how I love it. Mr. Alderson asked me to take the early celebration at St. Mary's after my night at the Rectory, and that was a rare privilege to be holding service in a real church once more, and such a lovely one too. We used the Collect, Epistle and Gospel for All Saints since it was within the Octave.

"Our stop for two days at Rio was a great experience too. We were landing at one of the most beautiful harbors in the world on a fine clear day. I was met, unexpectedly, by the Rev. Franklin T. Osborne, who had been in Virginia Seminary with me and was now a missionary in Brazil. He gave me a most warm-hearted welcome and took me on a sightseeing tour of the city. A friend of my cousin Margaret Kinnear lived in Rio, and had studied at Randolph Macon. I had a letter of introduction to her from Margaret, and she responded by inviting me to her home for the night. The next morning I had a swim from the beach right in front of their house in the blue water of the bay, surrounded by beautiful homes nestled against the mountains. Later that day on our way out heading for New York, I first saw high on a mountain peak the colossal statue of Christ with

263

arms uplifted, which dominates the harbor."

The news came to me that summer when I was at a Companions Conference at Adelynrood. Our son Lloyd phoned it to me from Mountain Rest, with the laconic phrase, "Mother, Dad's on!" When I got him to elucidate over the none-too-clear long distance line I remember I burst into tears of joy, ran out of the booth and embraced the first person I saw — an elderly spinster who looked at me as though I had lost my wits, until she knew what had caused this unusual behavior, and patted me gently on the back. Back at home my impatience mounted. I cut out a picture of the Gripsholm and pinned it on a map of the world, moving it from place to place as the news items in the paper reported its progress around the Cape of Good Hope, up the coast of South America, and finally the wonderful day when our ship of Hope was due to arrive in Jersey City. We received word from the Department of Missions that none of us relatives could go to meet the arrival at the pier but that we were to gather in the lobby of the Prince George Hotel in lower New York. Buses would bring the arrivals to the door.

Needless to say I could sleep but little that night and rose at an early hour, so distressed that Kate's cold made it impossible for her to go with Peyton and myself as we took our way to New York and this long-awaited rendezvous. The hours we waited at that hotel will never fade from my mind. Here were many of my closest friends, gathered from all over the country, all assembled with but one aim, and our attention riveted on but one place — the revolving door through which our beloveds would eventually return. I remember vaguely greeting these friends but in a most distracted fashion. I also remember one friend gently insisting that he bring us something to eat, as lunch time arrived. I couldn't leave the neighborhood of that door, so he brought us our lunch in a paper bag.

Finally the first repatriate arrived, a doctor whose wife was being rushed to the hospital to beat the stork if possible, while he looked after their five small children. The next arrival was Phil Sullivan, looking so dear that we all rushed to embrace him, though his straggling hair and clothing which had been handed him by the Red Cross made him seem quite unfamiliar. From then on the door kept revolving and the husbands kept arriving. With each appearance there would be a new outburst of joy and embraces by all and sundry. It was well into the evening when one of my very special friends told me, her voice so joyous that I've never forgotten the sound of it: "Marian, Lloyd is just getting out of the car." I rushed through the revolving door and the streets of New York were much more private for that first wonderful greeting than was the lobby of the Prince George Hotel.

But where was Peyton, who had kept this watch beside me? I looked around in vain. He had been sent to take a note to someone, we heard. Suddenly a cry rang out, "Daddy, Daddy" — and a small boy slid all the way across the lobby and into the arms of his father, almost knocking him down in the process. That dramatic meeting was too much for most of us and we wept for joy. On the way home I said to Lloyd, "Now I know what the Pearly Gates look like — they are revolving doors!"

From then on nothing seemed to stand out in my memory except that we were once again together. I know there was a service of thanksgiving at Calvary Church in which Lloyd took part, for all those of our mission who had come safely through these years of peril, there were trips to the South to visit Lloyd's brother and sister and Nancy Bell the widow of Dr. Cosby Bell at the Seminary. It all seemed a wonderful dream come true, and everyone tried to conceal their concern at seeing Lloyd actually thin, for a change, with a scrawny neck above his too-large clerical collar, knowing that good food and vitamins were all he needed.

The summer vacation in 1944 was all we could have ever hoped. All the Virginia family made a point of getting to camp at Rockbridge Baths for a month of the best of family reunions. Dr. Bethea, the rector of R. E. Lee Memorial Church, gave a reception for us in Lexington, and Lloyd preached there one Sunday. He felt the important thing to tell was how the Chinese staff and their American co-workers were carrying on in the remote country regions, bringing a knowledge of Christ and His love, demonstrated through our clinic and in many other ways, to those who had never known of Him. He also wanted to tell how our schools and colleges were continuing to carry on their work in the far West of China, and needed all the support they could get. He would have stopped with that until he found that everyone without exception wanted to know what life was like for him in the internment camp. "What did the Japs do to you" was the universal question — and he had to answer it.

Then began a round of speaking in the fall of 1944, and since I could talk to the auxiliaries we were sent on these trips together. My sister in Englewood looked after the two children, which made this possible. In these trips we got an intimate view of our country which we very much enjoyed. We went to West Virginia and then took a thorough tour through two of the three dioceses of Texas. In the spring of 1945 we were sent to the far West, where few overseas missionaries had journeyed. We went to Idaho and Oregon and California and Arizona. It was a busy and interesting time; but tiring, and we were glad that July at camp could revive us, with August in New Hampshire, where a cottage had been lent us by a friend.

We were at a conference at Adelynrood in Massachusetts when we heard the news of the Hiroshima bomb. I remember talking with that great seer and gifted philosopher Vida Scudder about what this portended for the future of mankind. The news of V.J. Day came when we were back in New Hampshire and was marked not only by the firecrackers we heard exploding in the distant village, but by an invitation from our hostess next door to take a drive to see some lovely villages in that Monadnock region. At last she could buy all the gas she wanted.

We went to Cornell that fall to take a short course offered there for missionaries about to return to the Orient. While we were there came word that a sailing had been secured for Bishop Roberts, the Rev. Claude Pickens and Lloyd on a freighter sailing to Shanghai. They would be off in November, "hull down on the old trail" — to try to pull together and rebuild the pieces of our scattered and broken Mission during the post-war period.

VI

It is rather dreary to arrive in China with its unheated houses in the depths of winter, and their arrival in Shanghai in the last of December, 1945 was no exception, though they were thankful to be able to return and help with the work of reconstruction which they knew lay ahead of them. Large areas of Shanghai were piles of rubble, but the business section was much as it had always been. However, Lloyd began to notice even then a factor, always present, but more evident then than ever before. The rich were richer, and the poor poorer. The avenues were filled with shiny black limousines, driven by chauffeurs and occupied by well-dressed businessmen or officials, who, they knew, had collaborated with the Japanese regime and had made incredible amounts of money which they had stashed away in Switzerland or America for safe-keeping. The streets were filled with men, women and children showing signs of great poverty. The middle-class had begun to return from their years in Free China to find their homes and shops destroyed. Those who were always poor were now beggars, and they heard that every morning cart-loads of frozen corpses were being driven away to the pauper burying grounds, as the streets were cleaned.

Bishop Roberts' home had been occupied by an Englishman who moved out at their arrival, so Lloyd had a place to stay for those first days while he prepared to return to Wuhu. As soon as he could make arrangements he was on his way to that city, where he was met by old friends who were already there. Sister Constance and Laura Clark had returned as soon as they were released from Ash Camp, where they had been interned for two years, since the doctor had decided that Sister Constance was physically unfit to attempt repatriation on the Gripsholm, and Miss Clark had made what must have been a terribly difficult decision to stay with her to the end of this war — which at that time couldn't be foreseen. Now they were both back, and with them Sister Louise, back from Maolin to join them.

It was in 1944 that the four American women of our diocese in Maolin with two other women of another mission who had been working with them there were warned by our government that the Japanese were advancing and they must escape as rapidly as possible to Kweilin. They eventually ended up in Kunming at the Chinese end of the Burma Road. That trip with its terrible difficulties of travel by foot, by army truck, and by hired car which broke down for days in succession was one of the first stories Lloyd heard on his return. It was a saga of heroism in the midst of appalling difficulties which may never be fully told, but is worthy of being listed high in the annals of the American Church Mission.

He found that the Bishop's House had been completely looted and was practically falling to pieces. The Japanese soldiers who had been quartered there plus the termites had had their way. He realized we could never live in that house again, but the other houses on that compound were in much better condition. He had been invited to have his quarters with B. W. Lamphear, who had returned from Shanghai on his release from the camp there.

There was a great deal to be decided about the repair of buildings all over the diocese. The Church in the United States had raised a million dollars for this purpose, and the Diocese of Anking had its proportion. It was at this time that Lloyd evolved a policy which he stuck to throughout the post-war years, and which has proved its justification. He would supply money only for the repair of those buildings for which there was a present need. For example in Anking it meant the repair of the schools, some of the dwellings, one church, and the restoration of the extensive wall around the compound. The inflation of the currency, which was to be such a continuing problem throughout his post-war years in China, had already

269

made any building a most expensive item.

It was here that Miss Bowne, the nurse who was head of the Nurses Training School, showed her remarkable ability as a business executive and financier. She would get estimates on each aspect of the work as it developed, send them to the Bishop for approval, and then supervise to see that everything was properly executed. Miss Bowne has just sent us the 44 letters Lloyd wrote her that year, covering every aspect of these repairs. She and Miss Montiero worked together to rebuild the walls of Anking as Nehemiah worked at the walls of old, and how I wish I could do justice here to what they accomplished. The wall around the compound must be rebuilt to keep out thieves, who were a constant problem. The hospital must be made ready for the return of Dr. and Mrs. Taylor; a few dwellings must be put in order to receive the return of the refugees, the compound itself, full of foxholes from the days of the war, must be leveled off and a place of worship must be restored to become the center of the spiritual life for all those who would be returning. To say that this was all accomplished before Dr. and Mrs. Taylor's return on Jan. 1, 1947 is probably as much as this narrative can undertake, but I will leave it to my readers to supply in their imaginations what was involved in the process. It was an outstanding achievement.

The Roman Catholic Sisters in Wuhu were Spanish and so neutral. It was a wonderful blessing to us that they were so friendly long before Pope John had made this a policy. Before Sister Constance left for internment she had managed to get most of the altar brasses and hangings to them and I'm sure other things which I don't recall now. Most important of all, the Roman Catholic Sisters were willing to take the orphans who had not already been adopted and who were absolutely dependent for their care on money from abroad. Lloyd had been afraid of this complication from the very beginning, but who could turn away these helpless bundles found on the grave mounds near our compound. The Spanish Sisters took over this responsibility with the understanding that the orphans would not be returned to us, but we rejoiced in the return of our church equipment. The friendly Roman Catholic Fathers had harbored some of our household furniture, and I look now at one of our two Coromandel cabinets, our nest of carved tables, and other bits and pieces as a direct gift from them.

VII

By the fall of 1946 a former American troop ship, the Marine Lynx, was due to arrive in Shanghai bringing many American missionaries returning to their work, and I was among them. Lloyd went to Shanghai in November of that year to greet me and bring me back to Wuhu with him. I had great tales to tell of what it was like to travel on a troop ship, to sleep in a huge hold on a so-called hammock, a kind of cot hung from the ceiling on chains, surrounded by hundreds of other ladies; of standing in line for cafeteria meals which were ladled out rather unappetizingly; of the lack of bathing facilities, of the lack of deck space, and how fortunate I was to have brought a folding chair and a slack suit as essentials in my equipment. It was a joyous reunion after a year of separation, and Lloyd could promise me that before long I would have a small house on the school compound ready for us to live in. In the meantime the hospitable Sisters would take both of us in.

It had been decided by this time that the Bishop's House would be pulled down, the termite riddled wood burned, and that most of the rest of the material could be used to build us a new house. It was wonderfully satisfactory to see every bit of material being used in this way, and knocking cement off the bricks provided a job for many of the poverty-stricken.

How I had hoped that we would have years on our hill-top, to see this work, so dear to our hearts, grow and develop after the years of warfare. But this was not to be.

By the spring of 1947 Lloyd had found an able and responsible man to supervise the repairs and building on the compound and decided to set out with me for his first visitation to the West and South of the diocese since his return. In several places there were groups waiting to be confirmed, and he wanted to see the situation for himself. We knew that transportation had begun again after the war but was in a most primitive stage and we had to be prepared for almost anything in the way of a conveyance. Our first visit would be to Anking, up river from Wuhu, but since no large river boats were running as yet we would go by steam launch. A bitter wind was blowing that March morning as Lloyd and I, together with several members of the staff at Wuhu, boarded the little launch. We decided to pay extra and get into the one so-called cabin, which was available and would give us shelter if not warmth. For some reason we found the deck hand was not leading us to the door but to the other side of the boat, and the whole proceeding seemed to be conducted in a somewhat stealthy fashion. He then motioned to us that we were to climb in through the window! We were so wrapped up in sweaters and overcoats that we didn't see how this could be managed, but the least bulky of our number tried it first and found he could squirm through. Then he stood inside and pulled mightily while the other members one by one were pushed from outside. When the last one finally squeezed through we were told that a soldier was sitting outside to hold the door for an officer who would arrive shortly — only to find the unwelcome foreigners already in possession. The officer would pay nothing and we had paid well, so we were much to be preferred.

After what seemed like an endless trip in the little launch, so close to the angry waters of the great river, whipped up by the March wind, it seemed a special miracle to arrive at Anking, to be received with a wonderful welcome and get into a house full of warmth and comfort. Our hostesses were Miss Bowne and Miss Montiero. Dr. and Mrs. Harry Taylor had arrived, the work in hospital and schools was progressing well and our fine Rev. Graham Kwei and his wife were building up the church activities.

It was hard to leave these dear friends but we had a lot of territory to cover so off we started again, to stop next at

273

Kiukiang, which we had visited so often in our past on our way to Kuling. Ten years had passed since we had last been there. One of the heart-warming touches we especially remember there was that the Rev. and Mrs. Irving Wang had decided not to have us sleep in the Rectory since they feared their baby would disturb us, so they had moved all their bedroom furniture to a room off the parish hall so we could rest peacefully. Such memories remain when I have entirely forgotten the number confirmed and the situation in the school, which had recently been re-opened. I do know Irving was having a fine group of young men for Bible study and discussion.

Then on by train to Nanchang. We found ourselves rather dreading that return. We knew the Japanese had burned much of the city, but that St. Matthew's Church and parish hall were still standing. When we reached the station and had been lovingly welcomed by the Dens and such of the old church members as were still there, we had a chance to hear of a remarkable dream Kimber had had when he was desperately ill with typhus in Lichuan where he had kept a center for some of the church members and where they had had a chance to earn a living with handicrafts of various kinds all during the war. He dreamt that he had returned to Nanchang and found the streets a mass of rubble, but there he saw, to his astonishment, our church and school rising untouched in the midst of the surroundings.

He told himself, on awaking, that this was impossible and he had steeled himself for a return to complete devastation. But what was his amazement when he turned into our street, to find that his dream was prophetic. The fire had spared our buildings, and he soon discovered that sand bags, piled later in front of the gate by some Japanese officer who, we think, might have been a Christian, had kept the contents from being looted. He found the whole plant almost as he had left it nine years before. Nanchang was the only city in the diocese where this had

Rev. and Mrs. Kimber Den and their family, 1948.

happened.

No wonder that our Sunday service in that beautiful church building, its carved camphorwood chancel quite unharmed, the black and gold lacquered medallions all in place beside the pillars, is one which will live always in my memory. Moreover the church was full to capacity with a group intelligent and well-educated, eager to find in the worship and fellowship there the courage they needed to face the difficulties of today and the fears for tomorrow.

We even made one trip to our old home, but we found it standing stark and bare, all the trees cut down, the garden and summer house gone, looking more unkempt and hopeless than when we first saw it nearly thirty years before. We would try to erase this memory from our minds.

We were to leave Nanchang on Monday, taking a bus to Kian.

We knew the buses were not what they used to be, but nothing could prepare us for what we found. The oblong wooden box on wheels which was the bus body had been filled with straight-backed wooden benches reaching across the entire width, so that to reach your reserved seat you had to step over one back after the other until you reached your proper number. I was already seated in the 12 inches reserved for me when Lloyd tried to crowd down beside me. He found this was utterly impossible. The space was too narrow, his legs were too long. He could merely perch on the back of the bench, his head bent over under the low ceiling, like Atlas holding up the world, and reiterate firmly, "This is impossible." Fortunately Mr. Den was going with us as guide and friend. He saw Lloyd's situation and went to the bus driver. Lloyd heard him say he was too stout for his seat. "Too tall," Lloyd shouted after him. Whichever it was, we won the driver's heart, and he managed to get Lloyd in beside him on the driver's seat, and off we started.

From Kian we were to continue to Kanchow in the far south of the province, a place we had never visited. We thought we could go there by bus, but for some reason they weren't running just then. Finally, after we had stayed a day longer than we had planned and were wondering if we would have to turn back, Mr. Chang, the priest-in-charge, came in beaming with joy. "You are to go as passengers in one of the army trucks," he said, as if he were bringing news of a great honor which had been given us. We replied in the same vein, and off we started to find our new conveyance, a worn old Japanese truck which had most evidently been through the wars. Lloyd was to sit in the rear, surrounded by soldiers and bags of rice, but I was given a seat of honor beside the driver and his two assistants. I found that the engine was perfectly visible as the body part which separates it from the front seat had long ago been destroyed. I had a very vivid demonstration of what made a car go when you turned the ignition switch. In this case the driver held the wheel and steered and his assistant held a wire in each hand which he put together when he wanted the car to move and pulled apart when he wanted it to stop. As simple as that. The boy on my left held a bucket and whenever the car approached a pond the wires would be pulled apart, the car would stop, the water boy would get out, dip up a bucket of water and fill the radiator, and on we would go, steaming our way along. "Is this the way you travel in America?" I was asked. "Not often. We were without much gas in the war," I tactfully replied.

To report all the break-downs would be tedious. Suffice it to say that we did get to Kanchow late in the evening, where we found our dear friends the Dan Lius, who had been in Nanchang with us years ago, waiting for us with a delicious meal and most comfortable bed. I remember that the next morning we found a real American breakfast — toast and eggs and even ginger cookies. We showed our wonder, and Dan explained. The Maryknoll Fathers had heard we were to come and had sent over a supply of baked food to add to our delicious Chinese meals. All the work in Kanchow was flourishing — a kindergarten as well as a grade school, and a fine and hopeful congregation. We hated to say goodbye to these dear friends but of course we would see them again — next year, perhaps? [We never did.]

And off we went on the most hazardous lap of our trip, for the road had been thoroughly destroyed by the Chinese troops to prevent the Japanese army from using it. As we sat in that bus we began to lurch and stagger from one hole or rut to another. I tried to cling to Lloyd but he told me to keep my arms free, we might turn over at any moment. We sat there thinking each breath would be our last — but finally we realized the worst was over, and we had survived. Several of our fellow passengers had been rocked to sleep.

It was on our way home from Nanfeng, our next stop, that we woke up to find the rain pouring down. What would travel

277

be like with this added hazard, I wondered. Kimber, the ever optimistic, had the right remark. "We had to have this rain to get rid of the clouds," said he. I've thought of that a good many times since and it reminds me of the rewards and punishments, the humour and pathos of that first post-war visitation in the Diocese of Anking.

VIII

Already we had deep apprehension as to what lay ahead of us. We knew that the Communists were gathering strength in the North, and then we heard that they were reaching South with almost no resistance. I can't go into details of why the Kuo Min Tang had "lost the mandate of Heaven" as they used to say to describe the fall of a dynasty in the old days. We saw distressing signs everywhere of corruption and indifference to the needs of the common people who had lived through nine years of the bitterest kind of warfare, when Japanese planes flew without opposition over the country, bombing every target they thought worthy of the expenditure of a bomb, from small villages to hospitals and cities. The people were exhausted and longed for a return to normalcy — but what did they find? They came back from unoccupied China to find their homes in ruins, their means of livelihood gone, and the Communist armies approaching. Worst of all, inflation began to take on unheard of proportions. As soon as we paid our servants they would rush out to spend their wages for articles of certain inherent value, such as soap and cloth, knowing that by the next day their cost might have doubled. To quote from Dr. Taylor's book, *My Cup Runneth Over*: "In August 1944 we deposited a check for U.S. $30.00 and received Chinese $186,000,000, or 6.2 million for U.S. $1.00. Later on we received eleven million for U.S. $1.00." The usual rate of exchange was three Chinese dollars for one U.S. Our cook had to carry a basket full of bank notes to buy enough food for one day's supply. This regime had made it almost impossible for the ordinary citizen to exist.

Corruption among the official class at this time was so widespread that it hardly merited discussion. Ellis Tucker, who was acting head of St. John's University notes in his brochure, *Farewell to Teaching* that he found several of his faculty members taking classes in different universities with two scheduled at the same time, so of course, not attending to their

279

duties at one of them. He spoke of many cases where students bribed their teachers so they would pass their courses.

Never, even in the war years, had we seen China at such a low ebb, and it wasn't a surprise to us to know that the Communist armies were marching almost unimpeded, winning their objectives as they progressed. As we faced the fact that Communism would probably take over a country which was so ripe for any change whatever, Lloyd knew that he would ask the American missionaries to leave. He had had experience with Communism in Kiangsi, knew of their bitter anti-foreign attitude, and felt that the Chinese Christian Church had much more hope of existing as an entity without Americans in their personnel than with them. So in late 1948, he sent out word that he wished the withdrawal of the missionaries, and the turning over of the work to the Chinese.

It was a terrible blow to many of our fine group, and he knew that his attitude was not shared by many people, who hoped that Communism in China would be only an "Agrarian Revolution" and that it heralded the day when there would be land distribution to the farmers and equality of opportunity to all — a kind of co-operative movement. Lloyd's judgment was that we were faced by hardcore Communism, and that the Diocese of Anking would be much better off under Bishop Chen than under him. He would send as many of the women off as soon as possible, with the men to follow.

I had had such a short time in China. Our new house was delightful, I loved teaching English in the girls' boarding school which had opened with a fine woman principal. How could I pull up stakes again after only two years since my return? But I had heard from a missionary who had come to Wuhu from the West of the terrible torture inflicted on the Christians when the missionaries stayed, and I agreed with Lloyd that our presence might bring great suffering and couldn't be a help. In December

280

of 1948 I set out for the United States, realizing that this was in all probability my final farewell to China. I have one happy recollection in the midst of that sorrowful leave-taking. My English class had come to the train to see me off. They clung to me, some of them weeping. As the train started I leaned out of the window to wave my goodbye and what should I see but the whole class running pell-mell alongside the train, calling out goodbye and waving. As long as I could see, there they were, running and waving.

Lloyd followed a few months later, knowing that Bishop Chen would carry on much more adequately than he could do under these circumstances. Many friends came to see him off, and he felt, without words, that they approved of what he was doing. And so, without fanfare or firecrackers, ended his thirty-four years in China.

And what has happened to China since that time, twenty-two years ago now? At first we said we were separated from China by a "bamboo curtain" for a few letters did get through and members of our mission who had stayed longer than we did visited us in our home after their return and told us details which were not then for publication. At the take-over the communist army announced that there would be religious freedom, and our mission friends were much impressed with the way they went about in the cities, in a manner which is best described as Puritanical. Spitting on the streets was a misdemeanor; food for sale on the street must be covered by mosquito netting; there was to be no tipping, no drinking of liquor. Clothing was to be of the plainest cotton material. We even heard that the fly became practically eliminated from the country. The best of the rules from our point of view were the penalties exacted for any proof of corruption or bribery.

We wondered if we could have been mistaken and that, when they achieved power, the Communists had adopted new tactics which would include real religious freedom and would allow missionaries to continue at their posts. Any such idea was of very short duration. The terrible period of public accusations soon arrived, when some of our finest missionary friends were made to stand on platforms in front of crowds of jeering people and be accused of crimes of all descriptions. Outstanding Chinese Christian leaders were attacked if they didn't "cooperate" with the government, which often meant signing statements which had only a modicum of truth.

I remember several stories told me by intimate friends who had been under this regime for a year or so. A fine Chinese couple, earnest Christians, highly educated and teachers in a university, were publicly accused by their teenage daughter of being "running-dogs of imperialists" and pro-Western in their attitudes. We didn't wonder that the father some years later succumbed to melancholia and tried to commit suicide. Another friend told of passing someone on a narrow path as he was walking through the rice fields, whom he thought he had never seen before; but as he was passing he heard his named called after him. He walked back, looked closely, and to his horror saw that the stranger was none other than the former principal of his school, his face so changed by the agony through which he had passed that it was no longer recognizable. His friend began a sorry tale of the torture he had endured, with the object of getting him to sign documents of accusation and denunciation — and at last he had succumbed. But the fact that he had done this so haunted him that his days were misery and his nights sleepless. He threw himself on the ground before our friend and begged his forgiveness. "I am lower than the lowest animal," he said.

Our former colleague, neighbor and student chaplain, the Rev. Quentin Hwang, who during the war was consecrated Bishop of Yunkwei in the southwest of China, was arrested in December 1949 and put into a wooden cage, sixteen by eight feet, with 18 other persons, "with no place for lying down or sitting." After three days he was put in a slightly less crowded cell for some months until, in a miraculous fashion, he was able to escape from the country and rejoin his wife in Hong Kong and later went to the United States.

But in spite of all these glimpses into the cruelty and utter disregard for truth which we found in this regime, we knew that in the cities the churches were still functioning to some degree, and that Christmas was still observed. We prayed constantly that our dear friends might be able to endure whatever was in store for them. It was the advent of the Cultural Revolution in 1966, when hundreds of thousands of youths were told to leave their schools, which were closed for as much as 18 months, and go about through the country attacking anything which seemed to smack of "old thinking, old customs, old habits, old cultures" — that the last vestige of the outward forms of Christian worship were destroyed. The few churches which had remained open were looted and used for secular purposes. One elderly clergyman of our church, we learned from information which leaked out, was dragged out of his home and beaten up, a bonfire made of all the prayer books, hymnals, church furnishings and personal belongings, and he was driven away never to return. We know from various reports of newsmen that this type of treatment was happening wherever churches had managed to keep open. Finally, after two years of such excesses, the schools have opened again, and that particular stage of complete disruption and anarchy lessened; but irreparable harm has been done.

It has been of extreme interest to me to read, since the reopening of China to newsmen in recent months, that the period of anarchy involved in the "Cultural Revolution" is over, and that along with a drab conformity in appearance and thought, has come the elimination of starvation and destitution and a return of a sense of national destiny and dignity which was painfully lacking during our thirty-four years in China.

I trust it is apparent how immensely all the Craighills gained from their years in the China Mission. We had made deep and lasting friendships, we had an opportunity to share in the cultural changes of a nation in revolution, we had had a small part in trying to help reinforce Chinese plans to meet the needs of the vast rural areas in our particular province. Above all we had learned the great joy of living as one family in Christ with our Chinese brothers, receiving from them inestimable benefits as well as imparting in our own imperfect way the blessings which had come to us in our Christian heritage and experience.

And so what do we think now about the future of Christianity in China? It has been a great comfort and help to us to have read recently a book by William H. Clark called *The Church in China. Its Vitality. Its Future?* This former missionary to China whose years there from 1925 to 1949 gave him a opportunity to know the church not only in Central China but in the Far West in Free China during the dangerous war years, has great faith that the Chinese Church will survive, though underground and silent for the present. He goes into past history, showing how the earliest beginnings of Christianity in China, a thousand years ago, and in Japan in the 1600's, was never completely stamped out. He reminds us of the fact that after 1930 the positions of leadership in the Church were all in the hands of Chinese, mature and disciplined Christians. The Chinese Church had come of age. We, who had as close personal friends so many of these fine deeply committed Christians — can we think that they have allowed this atheistic regime to drive out the faith which was the center of their lives? We know they have suffered unspeakably, that many have become martyrs, but we feel sure that in God's good time, the Christian Church will again be a power in China. Just how that will come to pass we cannot know, but we are content to leave it in God's hands. I couldn't close this chapter better than by quoting from

284

the book I mentioned: "Prevailing prayer implies trust in the Lord's promises that the fruit shall last and His ongoing purpose for the Church shall endure. It implies the expectation He Himself will work for them. The unfolding and the timing of His ultimate purpose lie in His overruling hands. The Church in China, a future? Yes, of a certainty, for its future is in the hands of an undefeatable Lord, who will yet work out that purpose in the Chinese people, for whom He cares."

A family reunion taken at Mountain Rest in the summer of 1970, with all the immediate family gathered together.